Mastering Database Design

Macmillan Master Series

Accounting
Advanced English Language
Advanced Pure Mathematics
Arabic
Banking
Basic Management
Biology
British Politics
Business Administration
Business Communication
C Programming
C++ Programming
Chemistry
COBOL Programming
Communication
Counselling Skills
Database Design
Desktop Publishing
Economic and Social History
Economics
Electrical Engineering
Electronic and Electrical Calculations
Electronics
English Grammar
English Language
English Literature
Fashion Styling
French
French 2
Geography
German

Global Information Systems
Internet
Italian
Italian 2
Java
Marketing
Mathematics
Microsoft Office
Microsoft Windows, Novell
    NetWare and UNIX
Modern British History
Modern European History
Modern World History
Networks
Pascal and Delphi Programming
Philosophy
Photography
Physics
Psychology
Shakespeare
Social Welfare
Sociology
Spanish
Spanish 2
Statistics
Systems Analysis and Design
Visual Basic
World Religions

Macmillan Master Series
Series Standing Order ISBN 0–333–69343–4
(outside North America only)

You can receive future titles in this series as they are published by placing a standing order. Please contact your bookseller or, in case of difficulty, write to us at the address below with your name and address, the title of the series and the ISBN quoted above.

Customer Services Department, Macmillan Distribution Ltd
Houndmills, Basingstoke, Hampshire RG21 6XS, England

Mastering

Database Design

Helen Holding, BSc (Hons.)
Lecturer
Department of Computer Science
University of Buckingham
Buckingham
UK

Series Editor
William J. Buchanan, BSc (Hons.), CEng, PhD
Senior Lecturer
School of Computing
Napier University
Edinburgh
UK

MACMILLAN

To my ever-supportive husband David and my beautiful
daughters Katie and Emily

Microsoft® is a registered trademark. Windows™, Access™ and Excel™
are trademarks of Microsoft Corporation.

First published in 2000 by
MACMILLAN PRESS LTD
Houndmills, Basingstoke, Hampshire RG21 6XS
and London
Companies and representatives throughout the world

ISBN 0–333–76317–3

A catalogue record for this book is available from the British Library.

This book is printed on paper suitable for recycling and
made from fully managed and sustained forest sources.

10   9 8 7 6 5 4 3 2 1
09   08 07 06 05 04 03 02 01 00

Typeset by W.Buchanan and J.Buchanan in Great Britain

Printed and bound in Great Britain by Biddles Ltd, Guildford and King's Lynn

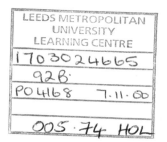

Contents

Preface

This book combines the theory of relational database design with a practical guide to the database management tool Microsoft Access. This book is ideal for undergraduates and business users, and provides step-by-step instructions to enable the reader to analyse tasks performed in a working environment and to design and build a simple relational database to support them.

The book takes the reader through the development process for the database, from the very start when the boundaries of the new database system are defined, through the analysis and design stages, and on to the creation of tables, relationships, queries, screens and reports. until the reader is left with a completed database system. The final chapters are devoted to practical guidance on important areas like testing, documentation, data set-up, backups, archiving and security. The four main design techniques covered are **data flow diagrams**, **entity-relationship diagrams**, **normalisation** and the **data dictionary**. Each of these techniques has been broken down into clear stages to enable the reader to understand and carry out some of the more intuitive tasks undertaken by analysts and designers.

Throughout the book, the same case study is referred to: a simple database system designed to carry out the functions required in a hotel reception area. In many chapters, instructions are provided on how to create the hotel reception database using Microsoft Access. These Access sections cover the basic and most useful features of the database management tool and enable the reader to see the database they have been studying and designing 'come to life' as an Access database – a feature not often offered in a database design book.

At the end of each chapter there are written and practical exercises for the reader to carry out in order to consolidate the material covered in that chapter. An additional and more complex case study, called Barnaby Electronics, has been provided in the Web Site http://www.macmillan-press.co.uk/study/masterseries/computing.

The book can be covered in one academic term, each chapter providing the basis for a database design lecture. The written exercises provide scope for tutorial and assignment work, and the Access sections and practical exercises provide invaluable material for computer laboratory sessions. It uses Microsoft Access 97 for the practical sessions, and most should work with Microsoft Access 2000.

Helen Holding

Note from Series Editor

Helen is one of the clearest writers of computer application books I have came across. Her style is easy to follow and does not contain the jargon and verbosity that is found in many books which seem to fill book shelves in ever increasing numbers.

This book is different from many database books in that it attempts to teach the fundamentals of database design and then illustrates these techniques with practical development applications. As an academic I appreciate this style, as it allows for the practical implementation of theory (the days of undergraduate courses containing just theory are, thankfully, long gone). It is also useful for professionals who are learning database development, as it covers the theoretical parts of database development – we have all seen cases of an excellent developer who has received no formal academic training in this specialist area.

I receive many requests from employers for good quality graduates. One of the most requested areas is in database development. It is an area which applies to virtually every area of business, and without databases many companies could not exist effectively. Praise must be given to Microsoft who, with Microsoft Access, have allowed database applications to be accessible to many users: Access allows excellent integration with other Microsoft packages.

The Macmillan Mastering IT and Computing series is expanding rapidly and this book is another key foundation book in the whole series. Others include:

- Mastering Microsoft Windows, Novell NetWare and UNIX.
- Mastering Networks.
- Mastering Java.
- Mastering Pascal and Delphi.
- Mastering Visual Basic.
- Mastering C++.
- Mastering Microsoft Office.
- Mastering Systems Analysis and Design.
- Mastering the Internet.
- Mastering Global Information Systems.

I would personally like to thank Suzannah Tipple, Isobel Munday and Christopher Glennie at Macmillan for their hard work and their continued support for the Mastering IT and Computing series. Thanks also to Helen for her commitment to quality and for her high standards.

William Buchanan

1 Introduction

1.1 Introduction

This book has been written with the strong belief that in order to develop an efficient and effective database system, however simple, the designer must understand the underlying principles of database analysis and design. These principles are demonstrated using the four techniques of **data flow diagrams**, **entity-relationship modelling**, **normalisation** and the **data dictionary**. The applicability of several well known design methodologies is examined and while no formal structured methodology is followed, each of the aforementioned techniques is well documented and used by many methodologies, including SSADM, and provides the reader with a sound basis for analysis and design.

Every effort is made to demonstrate the attributes that make the difference between a good design and a poor design. The book helps the reader to recognise the problems that result from duplicated data or incorrect relationships when the database is used over and over again to store and organise large quantities of data.

For example, in a well-designed database you should only have to enter a piece of data once: in a badly designed database you may have to enter the same piece of data many times. Imagine a situation where you had to type in the supplier's address for each product being ordered from that supplier. The database would be bigger than it needed to be, it would run slower than it should do, and when the supplier changed address there would be an increased chance of forgetting to update one of the addresses, or updating one of them incorrectly. The inexperienced "owner" of a badly designed database might just assume that Access is a poor tool and wish they could revert back to the fifteen spreadsheets they used quite happily before attempting an Access design. This book helps the new designer to avoid such traps.

This chapter, like many others in the book, is split into two parts – Part I: Database Design Theory, and Part II: Access Practical.

- *Part I: Database Design Theory* – This introduces relational databases, using the example of a University Administration office.

- *Part II: Access Practical* – This explains some of the terminology used throughout the Practical sections in the book and explains briefly what an Access table looks like and what an Access database can do.

Part I: Database Design Theory

1.2   What is a Database?

A **relational database**, in its simplest terms, can be defined as:

"A base on which data is stored, in which the base is made up of tables that organise the data, and relationships that link the tables together."

Imagine the main office in a science department in a university. There will be several wall charts, ring binders and index card files holding information:

- Wall charts – timetables showing the day, time, course code, location and staff name for each lecture and tutorial.
- Ring binders – containing details about each course, including subjects covered and duration.
- Index files – containing personal information about each member of staff such as address, salary grade and holiday entitlement.

It would clearly not be practical to store all this information on one enormous wall chart, listing the staff details underneath each member of staff's name on the timetable and listing the course details under each course code. One lecturer could, for example, appear ten or twenty times on the timetable, and a course code could also appear several times. This approach would waste a lot of space since any member of staff or course code appearing more than once would have their details duplicated with each subsequent appearance on the timetable.

Another drawback of holding such a large amount of different types of information mixed together is that it would take a long time to extract any information from the chart. For example, if you wanted to find the address of a certain member of staff, instead of simply looking through the alphabetically-ordered index file to find the staff member's surname, you would need to search through the whole timetable until you came across a lecture or tutorial taught by that member of staff.

It is important, therefore, that information is grouped correctly. This saves space and makes it faster to find information. The final database will be made up of tables representing each separate group of information, and diagrams to show how each table is related to other tables.

In the simple example of the **University Department** main office, there would be three tables: **Timetable**, **Staff Details** and **Course Details**. Each of these tables would be set up in the database, containing the appropriate information. Refer to Figure 1.1 to see the information stored in each table.

TIMETABLE	STAFF DETAILS	COURSE DETAILS
Day	Staff ID	Course Code
Time	Name	Course Title
Location	Address	Course Summary
Course Code	Salary Grade	
Session Type	Holiday Entitlement	
Staff ID	Holiday Remaining	

Figure 1.1 Initial tables for University Department main office system

Each item of information in a table is called a **field**. You can imagine each table looking like a spreadsheet, with the column headings describing each field and each row containing the data that is stored for one **entry** in the table. In the STAFF DETAILS table, for example, a table entry could be the details for Staff ID 4513.

To enable each entry in a table to be identified, a unique **key** can be defined for each table entry. In this way, there cannot be two lines of information in that table with the same key. For example, the key for the STAFF DETAILS table could be Staff ID, since each staff member would have a unique Staff ID. There might be two members of staff with the name Mary Brown, but they would have different Staff IDs.

The key to the COURSE DETAILS table could be Course Code, for the same reason. A key, however, can be made up of one or more separate items. For example, the key for the TIMETABLE would have to be Day, Time and Location. Day and Time would not be sufficient as a key, since there may be several lectures at the same time in a university department, but only one lecture at each location.

The keys must be shown on the tables. The format used in this book is to underline the key items that make up the key for each table. Refer to Figure 1.2.

To enable someone to see which areas of information link to other areas of information, it is useful to draw a diagram showing the relationships between tables. The links between the tables can be shown, by drawing each table in a box, and drawing a line between each linking piece of information. Refer to Figure 1.3.

The table descriptions and the diagram showing the links between the tables together provide the information needed to build the database. The example given was a very simple example, in which one table exists for each area of information. In practice it is rarely the case that a database is that simple. No matter how complicated the system, however, in order to build the database you still need to gather the information together into tables and show the relationships in some sort of diagram.

TIMETABLE	STAFF DETAILS	COURSE DETAILS
<u>Day</u>	<u>Staff ID</u>	<u>Course Code</u>
<u>Time</u>	Name	Course Title
<u>Location</u>	Address	Course Summary
Course Code	Salary Grade	
Session Type	Holiday Entitlement	
Staff ID	Holiday Remaining	

Figure 1.2 Completed tables for University Department main office system – with keys

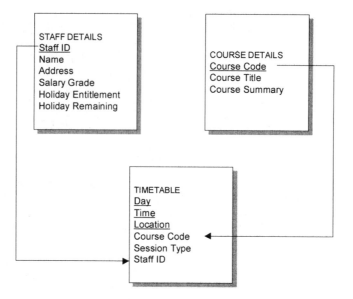

Figure 1.3 Relationship diagram for University Department main office system

The lines show how the same item of information is used in each table. The line is given an arrow to indicate which of the two tables can possibly contain more than one entry for that piece of information. For example, the line between the Staff ID in the STAFF DETAILS table and that in the TIMETABLE table links the two Staff IDs together. In practice, there will only be one entry in the STAFF DETAILS table for that member of staff, but there may be several entries in the TIMETABLE for that member of staff. The arrow is therefore at the TIMETABLE end of the arrow. The same applies to the Course Code.

Several methods can be used to group the information into tables. This book will explain two methods that can be used together successfully to design tables and relationship diagrams. These two methods are very different. The first method, **entity-relationship modelling**, is an iterative method. The data are examined and grouped, then the entity-relationship diagram is drawn and checked to ensure that it obeys various relationship rules. Any areas where it does not are re-examined and re-drawn until the diagram is correct.

The second method is a very structured method, called **normalisation**. This method uses a series of standard steps and rules to group the information, based upon actual samples of data.

Each of these methods builds up its own picture of the database. The entity-relationship model provides more of a draft version, showing how the items and events being described by the information relate to each other, whereas the normalisation method examines the actual information used in the system and provides a very detailed picture of the database. The advantage of using two methods to design the database is that the two results can be compared: any discrepancies can be examined and a definitive version then produced.

Part II: Access Practical

1.3 Terminology

In the Access sections used in this book, some terminology is used which you will need to be familiar with:

'Click the .... button' means that you should move the mouse so that the mouse pointer is over the requested position on the screen, then press the left-hand button on the mouse.

'Double-click...' means that you should press the left-hand button on the mouse twice *quickly* in succession.

'Select the ... option' means that when a list of options or menu is displayed on the screen, you should select the required one clicking the mouse pointer over the requested option.

'Icon' refers to a symbol or picture displayed on the screen, which, when clicked on by the mouse pointer, will activate a particular function.

'Click and drag' means that you should press the left mouse button down and keep it depressed whilst moving the cursor to the required position, and then release the mouse button.

'Folder' is the name of a location on disk where files are stored – it is similar to a folder in a filing cabinet, and may contain many documents, or even other folders which themselves contain documents.

1.4 Introduction to Access

Section 1.2 explains what a database is and how it is made up of tables containing information, linked together by common pieces of information. A **database management system** is a program that enables tables and relationships to be set up on the computer, and allows you to enter information into those tables. The database can be set up using your own specific designs, or using a tool called a **Wizard** that helps you to build the database using pre-designed tables for you to select and amend.

Refer to Figure 1.3, illustrating the three university department administration database entities defined earlier in this chapter. This diagram shows the three tables STAFF DETAILS, COURSE DETAILS and TIMETABLE, each having a key or unique item, and each linked to at least one other table.

In Access, these three tables would be set up as shown in Figures 1.4, 1.5 and 1.6.

Staff ID	Name	Address	Salary Grade	Holiday Entitlement	Holiday Remaining
F123B	Mr David Holding	15 Wood Close, Barton, Manchester	7	20	5
F126G	Mrs Amanda Davidson	Bootles Cottage, Hempton Lock, Bucks MK15 3DZ	8	22	18
G452S	Dr Phillip Goodson	45 Wells Drive, Great Hanslope, Hants. HT6 7GT	12	25	12

Figure 1.4 STAFF DETAILS table (unique key for each row is <u>Staff ID</u>)

Course Code	Course Title	Course Summary
WP1	Basic Word Processing	Basic features of word-processing: creating, saving, formatting and printing documents.
DBD1	Database Design	Principles of data analysis: Data Flow Diagrams, Entity-Relationship Modelling and Normalisation.
INT1	Introduction to the Internet	How to search for information, use e-mail and set up a web site.

Figure 1.5 COURSE DETAILS Table (unique key for each row is <u>Course Code</u>)

Day	Time	Location	Course Code	Session Type	Staff ID
Monday	09:00	Hall 3	INT1	Lecture	F123B
Monday	11:00	Hall 3	DBD1	Lecture	F126G
Tuesday	14:00	Comp 3	WP1	Practical	G452S
Tuesday	14:00	Comp 1	INT1	Practical	F123B
Tuesday	14:00	Room 25F	DBD1	Tutorial	F126G
Wednesday	09:00	Comp 1	INT1	Practical	F126G
Wednesday	11:00	Comp 1	WP1	Practical	G452S

Figure 1.6 TIMETABLE table (unique key for each row is a combination of <u>Day, Time</u> and <u>Location</u>)

Once the information is stored in the database tables, it can be amended and deleted if required. The information can be used in several different ways:

- The rows of information can be sorted into a specific order, for example the staff table could be sorted into alphabetical order of staff name.

- A selection can be made on the type of information shown in the table. These selections are called **filters**. For example, a selection could be made on the timetable to show just the rows of information containing a location of Comp 1.

- Specific selections of information linking tables together can also be made. These types of selections are called **queries**. A query is usually saved and can be used again. For example, a query may be set up to show the names of all the staff who teach in Computer Room 3 (Comp 3) on a Monday.

- Information from the tables can be printed out, directly from the tables, after sorting or using filters, or in response to a query.

The techniques above are useful ways of viewing and selecting information stored in the database. There are additional methods of entering and viewing information in a database, called **forms** and **reports**. A Form is a screen that has been set up to display or accept information either directly to or from a table. It can make the database much easier and quicker to use. Reports are pre-designed requests for information from the database that is laid out on the page in a specified order. This information, as with the Form, can come either directly from a table or as the result of a query.

In later chapters in the book, the features of Access most appropriate to the database analysis and design techniques being described will be explained.

1.5   Summary

This chapter has covered the following material:

- Introduction to the philosophy behind the book and the material covered in the book.

Part I: Database Design Theory

- A brief explanation of what a relational database is.

Part II: Access Practical

- An explanation of the terminology used throughout the book and a brief descriptive introduction to what Access can do.

2 Why Design?

2.1 Introduction

When you build any structure, it is vital to have some sort of plan. Not only does this provide you with guidelines to follow when carrying out the building of your structure, but it also enables you to think ahead and ensure that your structure will be as complete and functionally correct as possible.

Imagine building a fitted wardrobe in a bedroom. Without even the simplest of designs, you might well find that the framework you attach to the wall needs to be removed since the doors do not fit properly, or that upon completion the wardrobe is too narrow to contain a hanger. Or consider the example of carrying out a project to put up some shelf units without any design or planning. To start with, the 'shelf builder' had no trouble at all. The wood was the correct length, the screws fitted the Rawlplugs and the holes in the wall even lined up with those in the brackets. It was not until the shelves were used that it was discovered that they were too close together to fit a book upright, so the books had to be stacked up in piles!

When building a database, design is critical. Even when faced with the seemingly simple task of "putting the department's personnel details into a database", it would be very tempting to sit down at a PC, start up Access and create table after table, based directly upon the current personnel forms and index cards. You might well end up with a database reflecting your current paper-based system exactly, with a table for every piece of paper or card index in your current system. However, this new database would not necessarily help you carry out the tasks you require of it in an efficient or time – saving way.

For example, if you needed to correct or change a member of staff's surname, on your paper-based system you would have had to update maybe six or seven pieces of paper. If your database matched exactly your paper-based system, you would need to update each of the corresponding six or seven tables. One of the major advantages of using a database is eliminating this type of duplication of work. In a correctly designed database, the surname would only be held on one table, and updating would therefore require only the one change.

It has been recognised for a long time now that computer systems, including database-based systems, are best developed following what is known as the **Systems Development Life Cycle**. This chapter will briefly introduce the Systems Development Life Cycle and will explain which areas of the cycle will be covered in this book. This chapter will also describe some of the more recently developed alternative approaches to systems development used in the systems development industry, and will explain which approach will be followed in this book.

2.2 Systems Development Life Cycle

The Systems Development Life Cycle has been the traditional sequence of phases that are carried out when developing any computer system. Depending on the size of the system, some of the phases may merge and be carried virtually in parallel, but in the majority of cases, they occur in this order:

- *project selection*
- *feasibility study*
- *systems analysis*
- *systems design*
- *implementation*
- *changeover*
- *maintenance.*

2.2.1 Project Selection

This is the initial phase of the life cycle, in which the preliminary *aims* and overall *scope* of the new system are decided. Once the scope and aims of the new system are defined, it is then possible for further investigation into the feasibility of the system to be carried out. During this phase, the reasons for developing this new system are examined. These may be existing or predicted problems with the current system, such as the case where an existing computer system cannot cope with dates above 1999, or to satisfy new requirements. An example would be a personnel department using a paper-based system to record and calculate the monthly salaries for ten members of staff. If the company was going to expand, the personnel department might suddenly be required to calculate salaries for 250 members of staff instead of ten.

Such an increased volume of paperwork would indicate a requirement for a new computer system. It is important to determine the overall aim of the system. (In the personnel system example, the overall aim of the new system would be to allow large numbers of staff's salaries to be calculated accurately and quickly.) It is also important that the **scope** of the system is defined. The scope will set the boundaries for the system's development. It will state how much of the current working system is to be replaced by the new system. If this is not laid down 'in stone' at the start of the project, the development can go badly astray. It might be assumed in one phase of the development that a certain area of the current system should be included in the new system, and another later phase might assume that the same area should *not* be included.

2.2.2 Feasibility Study

This phase involves an examination of the possible ways in which the new system can be developed to satisfy the aims of the required system, within the defined scope. A preliminary investigation into the current working system is carried out, and several possible methods of accomplishing the desired new system are considered. The main output of this phase is a **feasibility report** which provides the project with **Terms of Reference**, upon which the rest of the project can be based.

The terms of reference define the scope and objectives of the new system, as well as information about available resources and limitations for the development and operation of the new system. A list of problems with the existing system and a list of requirements for the new system are also included. A draft project plan may be included, giving some idea of the time and resources required to carry out each phase of the systems development. The feasibility study, as well as suggesting a variety of possible solutions, with costs and benefits of each, will recommend one solution as the most feasible.

2.2.3 Systems Analysis

This phase requires detailed investigation into the current working system. When the current working system is described on paper, it is described initially as a **current physical system**. This description will include information about how data is physically passed around the working place. For example, "... An order may be received from the customer over the telephone or by post. The order is then written on an order form. A copy is taken of this form. The original is filed in the Orders file and the copy is sent to the Purchasing department ...".

After details about the current physical system have been obtained and recorded, they are converted into a logical model. This concentrates only on the data, the processes, the files and where the data comes from and goes to. The logical model does not refer to the method by which data is transferred, such as photocopy or telephone. This is called the **current logical system**. In our example, the order process previously described in current physical form would be written in current logical form as "... Order details are received from the Customer and stored in an Order file. Order details are then sent to the Purchasing department ..."

2.2.4 Systems Design

This phase is concerned with converting the current logical system defined in the systems analysis phase into a required physical system. This is achieved by initially comparing the current logical system with the problems and requirements described in the terms of reference. The current logical system model is then amended to include processes and data that correct any current system problems and incorporate the new required functionality. This updated model is referred to as the **required logical system**.

As with the current logical system model, this model does not include any reference to how the data will be transferred around the system. It will not say whether the data will be given to a department via a report or on a screen. This type of information will be provided in the final system model, the **required physical system**. This model will describe the physical details about how the information will be displayed and passed around the system. It will describe physical details about the new system such as which data will be displayed on which screen, which data will be included in each report, and what each file will look like. This phase will also include the creation of various levels of tests to check that the developed system works according to the original designs.

2.2.5 Implementation

This is the phase of the system when the programs, screens and database are actually built. They are also tested using the tests created in the previous phase. Documentation may also be written in this phase, which will provide information to the user about the system and how to use it.

2.2.6 Changeover

This phase will involve the introduction of the new system into the work place, thereby replacing the current system. This can be carried out in one go, often called the **Big Bang approach,** or gradually, using a parallel or phased method of implementation. This phase could also involve training staff to use the new system as well as transferring existing data from the current system into the new system.

2.2.7 Maintenance

This is the final and ongoing phase of systems development. This phase will include carrying out any corrections to the new system, as well as implementing any new requirements into the system. This phase also includes carrying out regular tasks such as archiving old data and copying the system and database onto a back-up to be kept for a defined period of time in case the system fails. These regular tasks are often referred to as **housekeeping**.

2.3 Traditional Systems Development Approaches

Although the Systems Development Life Cycle describes the tasks that have been traditionally carried out to develop a computer system, there are several methods of accomplishing this. These methods range from the rigid, model-based structured methodologies to the more flexible toolkit approach. These two development approaches are described next.

2.3.1 Structured methodology

This is a pre-defined sequence of tasks that use diagrams and tables to enable the development of a new computer system. Although a methodology may cover all of the Systems Development Life Cycle, the majority of methodologies span the systems analysis and systems design phases only. Most structured methodologies use several different types of diagram and table to represent two or more different views of the developing system. Some diagrams may provide an illustration of how data flows around the system; other diagrams may illustrate how the different objects in the system interact with each other.

These diagrams are then cross-checked to enable the resulting system to incorporate all these requirements and to iron out any inconsistencies between the views. An advantage of using a structured methodology is that the sequence of tasks helps project planning by describing which tasks are dependent on others and what the deliverables are from each phase of the development. The use of standard diagrams and tables, as well as cross-checking as part of the development, increases the quality of the final system.

However, a structured methodology can be viewed as rather rigid and inflexible. In some cases, it is not possible to continue to the next phase or task until the current one has been completed. If the task requiring completion is for a rarely used function in the new system and this is therefore holding up the rest of the systems development, it becomes easy to see why the structured approach can be viewed as inflexible. In some instances, where the system is relatively simple and contains few different functions and data flows, it can appear as if the documentation and procedure of the structured methodology are dominating the development rather than assisting it. It is possible to adapt the methodology to fit a small system development project. However, if too much of the structured methodology is removed, the remaining project development may resemble a toolkit approach rather than a structured methodology.

One of the leading structured methodologies is **SSADM** (Structured Systems Analysis and Design Method), developed for the United Kingdom government in 1982 by Learmont and Burchett, for the development of information systems in government departments.[1]

2.3.2 Toolkit approach

With this approach, a custom-made "structured methodology" is created for each project. The tasks required to carry out the development of the system will be carried out using the most appropriate tool or technique, depending on the size and complexity of the system. The most commonly used techniques are **data flow diagrams**, **entity-relationship modelling**, **normalisation** and the **data dictionary**. Although this approach can slim down some of the documentation-heavy developments, especially on smaller projects, it requires a certain level of skill to be able to select the appropriate tools in this approach. A commonly used approach to systems development these days is for a company to use the same series of tools and techniques to develop the majority of their systems.

2.4 More Recent Systems Development Approaches

Over recent years, the perception of systems development has suffered greatly under the reputation that projects are always completed late and over-budget and do not always do what the users want. Although this is not always the case, where these problems do occur, underlying reasons are often poor analysis of the original scope of the problem, lack of user involvement, and the desire to accomplish too much in an

---

[1] Learmont and Burchett later developed their own methodology called LBSDM (Learmont and Burchett Systems Design Methodology)

unrealistic time. Because of these continual problems, new techniques have been developed that attempt to reduce the effort required to develop a functioning quality system. These techniques do not follow the traditional Systems Development Life Cycle, but follow their own sequence of phases and tasks. Two of the most notable techniques are objected-oriented analysis and design, and Rapid Applications Development.

2.4.1 Object-Oriented Analysis and Design

The traditional Systems Development Life Cycle approaches to analysis and design generally creates a logical view of the system in terms of processes that are performed upon objects, about which data is stored. The **object-oriented approach** to analysis and design is based upon the principle that the *object* itself takes part in operations, rather than having operations performed upon it. The object-oriented approach would propose that a Booking in a hotel, for example, is not just a collection of data such as Booking Reference Number, Customer Name and Date, but that a Booking itself takes part in operations. For example, a Booking is placed by a Customer, generates a Confirmation Form and updates the Booking Log.

The object-oriented approach defines an ***object*** as anything about which data is stored. An **object type** defines the kind of object it is. For example, an object type of 'Booking' could have an object identified as Booking Reference '65130', and another as Booking Reference '71124'. So far, this sounds similar to several other techniques, where items such as *entities* are described in the same way. However, the object-oriented approach also includes descriptions of the way in which the object's data is used and updated as part of the object itself. This is called a **method**. Some appropriate methods for the Booking object could be 'Create Booking', 'Accept Confirmation', 'Change Date' and 'Calculate Total Bill'. Each of these methods would update the Booking object data, leaving them in a different state after each method is applied.

The triggers, or events, that lead to a change in state of an object are identified and object flow diagrams are used to illustrate the system. Those adopting the object-oriented philosophy feel that since we view the world in a way that combines both processes and data, a systems development approach based upon the same viewpoint, must produce more successful systems.

2.4.2 Rapid Applications Development (RAD)

The Rapid Applications Development approach to systems development is carried out with three main emphases: speed of development, user involvement and prioritisation of requirements. This third point refers to the need to develop the first working system containing the most important areas of the system only. Additional areas can be added in a later phase.

The main activities in RAD are carried out by groups of users and developers together in workshops. Each workshop will have a specified objective and an agreed time limit, often up to five days. The workshops, which should be documented, take place in independent locations where those attending must not be disturbed by routine work-related interruptions. Each workshop will have a facilitator, who will help the members to reach agreements and generally steer the workshop in a positive direction.

Although RAD is often regarded as a prototype-based iterative process, gradually refining a skeleton prototype until it becomes the working system, this approach does follows four distinct phases, each of which uses workshops as the main tool to complete its objectives. The first phase, **requirements planning**, will establish the strategic objectives for the company. Since the objectives in this phase are at a high level, senior management will be involved. The second phase, **applications development**, will produce a high-level design of the new system. The third phase is **systems construction** where the high-level design is developed to produce detailed designs and code is generated. The final phase is **cutover**, where the system is tested, the users are trained and the new system goes live. Throughout this approach, both traditional diagrammatic techniques are used, as well as Computer-Aided Software Engineering (CASE) tools, prototyping tools, database management development tools and fourth generation languages.

2.5 Systems Development Carried Out in this Book

The material in this book has been specifically written to enable anyone with an interest in database design to be able to analyse, design and build a small database using the analysis and design techniques provided as well as the database management tool, Access. Instructions on how to use Access to build the database are also provided. Although this is a database system only, in which there are no program specifications to design and build, it is still regarded as a computer system. As such, its development will be carried out following the traditional Systems Development Life Cycle, using a toolkit approach.

The main areas of the Systems Development Life Cycle covered in this book are feasibility study, systems analysis, systems design and implementation. The systems analysis and design phases use the four commonly used techniques: data flow diagrams, entity-relationship modelling, normalisation and the data dictionary. The book also discusses the main issues that should be addressed during the changeover and maintenance phases.

2.6 Summary

This chapter has covered the following material:

- reasons why design is necessary when building a database
- the Systems Development Life Cycle
- traditional systems development approaches such as structured methodologies and toolkit approaches
- more recent systems development approaches such as object-oriented and Rapid

Applications Development.

- the systems development carried out in this book (toolkit approach of techniques, covering feasibility study, systems analysis, systems design and implementation).

2.7　Written Exercises

2.7.1　Describe each of the main phases that make up the Systems Development Life Cycle.

2.7.2　Describe the advantages and disadvantages of the following systems development approaches:

(a)　structured methodology
(b)　toolkit approach
(c)　object-oriented approach
(d)　Rapid Applications Development

2.7.3　A greetings card manufacturer has its head office in Milton Keynes and four regional offices in Bath, Norwich, Reading and Birmingham. Head office receive weekly sales figures and future sales predictions from each region, and supply each region with cards based upon their own sales predictions for each week. Each region has its own paper-based index card system containing information about each individual card, such as its message, its illustration, its size and its price. The system also holds information about sales, customers and predicted sales. The sales and predicted sales information is posted to the head office once per week.

The managing director has decided to employ two new members of staff, familiar with systems development, to build a database system for his company. She wants there to be a central database containing information about each card, as well as information about each region's sales and predictions. Each regional office will have access to the database and will be able to enter its sales figures and predictions information directly into the system, removing the need to post it.

The systems development staff are arguing about which approach to adopt for this task. The managing director is concerned that since their company has not developed a system before, a proven and well-established method should be selected. Since the company will employ two extra members of staff to carry out this task, she does not see any immediate urgency that requires the system to be developed under unnecessary time pressure. A bias on quality rather than speed is emerging here. It has also been suggested that the senior managers in the company, as well as the regional managers, are rather sceptical about the system. Aware that some systems developments can take place with very little for the ultimate user to see for a long time, it would be useful to be able to provide these managers with some way of appreciating what the new database system will be able to do.

Which systems development method or combination of methods would you suggest for the new database system, and why?

3 Defining the Boundaries of the New System

3

3.1 Introduction

Before any design can be carried out, it is vital that the aims and limits of the new system are defined. It can be very tempting to start building tables and screens, since these tasks appear to be the productive ones, in which you are actually putting your system together. This can be especially difficult to resist when pressure is being exerted from a senior level to *"Show me some progress – stop talking about it"*. Sitting around a table discussing what your new system should be doing and how much of the current system should be incorporated into the new system doesn't *look* productive. It is in fact the most important part of designing your system. Without a clear target to work toward it is impossible to:

- estimate the amount of work to be done or the likely cost of doing it
- predict a completion date or know when you have truly finished all the tasks
- be sure that you are building no more and no less than others actually require and expect
- get agreement about the expected functionality and avoid needing to rework the system to satisfy different influences in the workplace
- be certain that no critical, technical or functional consideration has been overlooked, stopping the final system from working correctly.

Imagine a builder constructing a house with no written agreed plan. A quick discussion with the client for a "a grand family home, painted white, with a central front door, windows either side, a first floor and somewhere to park the car" could result in at least two very different interpretations. Refer to Figure 3.1.

Although the client may be delighted with the builder's idea, the neighbours may not, the planning office may not and the client's bank manager certainly would not!

In order to define the limits and objectives of the new system, an exercise is carried out to examine the current system, its needs and problems, and to identify a range of solutions. This exercise is called the **feasibility study** and the findings from this study are documented in the **feasibility report**. The starting point of this exercise is to list the basic requirements and limitations for the system. These are put together in a document called the **terms of reference**. This document will be referred back to repeatedly throughout the development to make sure that the system is being built within the original guidelines.

Figure 3.1 Conversation between builder and client

3.2   Terms of Reference

This document is the cornerstone of the system development. It is the main statement of requirements around which the system is designed and built. The terms of reference can be divided into six main areas:

- *Reasons for the study*
- *Aims and objectives of the new system*
- *Scope of the new system*
- *Resources and limitations*
- *Timescale*
- *Agreed approach*

3.2.1 Reasons for the Study

This section will outline any urgent or background reasons for the development of the new system being carried out. It is important to establish the core reasons for the development, since these reasons will be related to the major objectives of the new system. For example, the reason for the development of a new system could be because of a problem with the current working system. It will be essential that this problem is addressed and overcome in the new system, without the developer becoming too distracted with enhancing all other aspects of the system.

Another common reason for developing a system is to improve efficiency and productivity within the workplace. Again, if this is the reason behind the development, then efficiency and speed may well be the main objectives of the new system.

3.2.2 Aims and Objectives of the New System

This section will outline the main objectives for the new system. Even if these are to carry out the same functionality as the existing system, the main areas of functionality still need to be outlined. As mentioned previously, it is very easy for different people to have different interpretations of the functions of a working area. This section will enable discussion to take place and a definition of those functions to be agreed. Some of the aims and objectives will have been raised in the 'Reasons for the study' section of the terms of reference. Examples of some common aims and objectives are:

- improved productivity in the department by increasing the speed of information transfer
- increased customer satisfaction by delivering up-to-date product information over the telephone
- reduced errors in information on the system
- standardised product database for all departments
- weekly reports in various levels of detail and order
- the ability to produce ad-hoc reports quickly to satisfy customer enquiries.

3.2.3 Scope of the New System

This section defines how much of the current working system and new requirements are going to be included in the new system. It may be the case that a department's tasks will be included in the new system in more than one phase. If so, this section will outline which areas of functionality are to be included in which phase.

It is not always the case that a department carries out work totally independently from other areas of business. For example, a Quotations and Orders department may currently send a half-filled-in quotation form to the Purchasing department for them to complete and send back. One approach for the new system could be to computerise the Purchasing department and let them enter their information directly into the new system. However, the budget for the new system may not stretch to that, so the decision may need to be taken to print out the half-completed quotation form, send it to Purchasing who will fill it in as before, and then return it for the new information to be typed into the system.

3.2.4 Resources and Limitations

This section will define any restrictions there may be regarding staffing availability for the development and final usage of the new system. For example, it may be stated here that no development will take place during the two-week factory holiday over Christmas, or that the staff training will take place over the Christmas period. It will outline any business-imposed deadlines for the final completed system, such as the financial end of year.

This section may also define how much of the information being used in the current system is to be used in the new system. For example, the terms of reference may state that quotations with no matching orders over three months old will not be included in the new system database. This is important information since it gives the designer an idea of the size of the database, the amount of time it will take to set up the initial data on the new system, and how often the data can be archived from the database.

3.2.5 Timescale

This section will provide a very rough project plan for the development of the new system. It will illustrate when each part of the development will be completed and how many staff it will take to do this. It is very important to state on this plan how many staff will be required to carry out each phase. You may, for example, estimate that testing will take two weeks, using two people. If you do not write down how many people are required, when the testing phase starts and one of the two people you assumed would be available is being used elsewhere on another project, it will not be easy to explain why testing now takes four weeks, instead of the two. If you had written "two staff" on your plan, you could then explain the delay and at best shorten a later phase by introducing more staff where possible. The plan may be broken down into the following types of phases:

- *Analysis of the current system*
- *Design of the new system*
- *Building the new system*
- *Testing*
- *Implementation*
- *Training*
- *Setting up the database*
- *Documentation*

Figure 3.2 contains a project plan, showing the time and resources required to complete a small database system.

3.2.6 Agreed Approach

This section will ultimately contain details about the way in which the new system will be developed and implemented. The information will explain which proposal or combination of proposals from the Feasibility Study has been officially agreed upon.

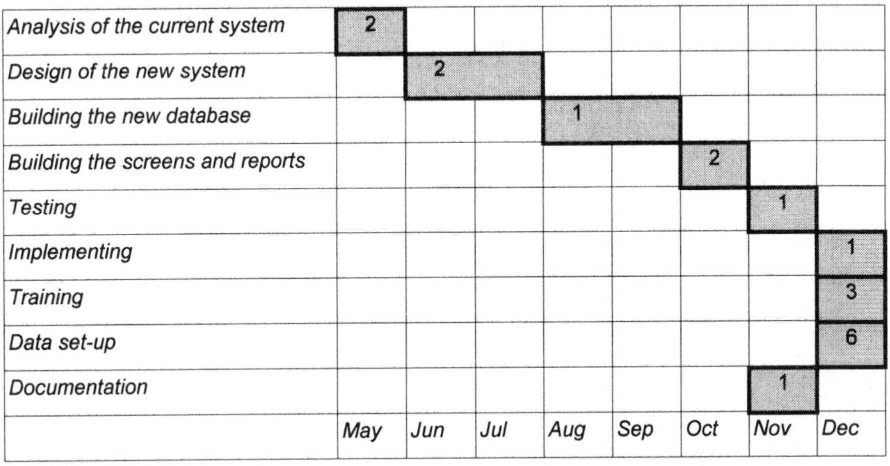

	May	Jun	Jul	Aug	Sep	Oct	Nov	Dec
Analysis of the current system	2							
Design of the new system		2						
Building the new database				1				
Building the screens and reports						2		
Testing							1	
Implementing								1
Training								3
Data set-up								6
Documentation							1	

Figure 3.2 Project plan

This section will provide the structural outline for the new system, upon which the detailed analysis and design can be based.

Initially, however, this section will be left empty. It will only be completed after the feasibility report has been examined and an approach agreed upon. The terms of reference will then be the main system document, referred to throughout systems development, containing both the requirements and the scope of the system, as well as the agreed design and implementation approach.

3.3 Feasibility Report

The feasibility report documents the findings of the feasibility study, referred to in the previous chapter, where an examination is carried out of all the possible ways in which the new system can be developed to satisfy the aims of the required system within the defined scope. The main areas addressed in the feasibility report are as follows:

- *Introduction*
- *Terms of reference*
- *Description of the present system*
- *Problems with the present system*
- *Requirements of the new system*
- *System proposals*
- *Comparison of proposals*
- *Conclusion and recommendations*

- *Appendices*
  - *Cost-benefit analysis for each proposal*
  - *Outline project plan for each proposal*
  - *Technical configurations for each proposal*
  - *Glossary*

3.3.1 Introduction

This will be a very brief introduction to the feasibility report itself, outlining the various areas to be covered in the report.

3.3.2 Terms of Reference

Refer to Section 3.2.

3.3.3 Description of the Present System

The current working system is analysed and its main objectives, inputs, outputs and data stores are described. In a Quotations and Orders department, for example, one of the main system objectives may be to match received orders from customers with previously issued quotes. System outputs relating to this objective are the quotation itself and an order acknowledgement, whereas a system input relating to this could be the order from the customer. A data store is a file of quotes.

3.3.4 Problems with the Present System

The problems arising from the current system will probably vary depending to whom you talk. There may be an overriding set of problems that have resulted in the need for a new system. There may also be other problems in the day-to-day running of the system that could be removed or minimised in the design of the new system.

It is not always the case that all problems can be removed by the installation of a new system. Some problems may be operational and will still occur regardless of how the new system is implemented. Some problems may be too costly to solve using the new system and may have to be suffered or put off until a second or third phase of the system. An example problem could be that when a customer telephones with a query, the operator finds it very time consuming to find the customer's order details in the files: the customer may often lose his/her patience, and the company may then lose the order.

3.3.5 Requirements of the New System

This section will outline the areas of the current system's functionality that will be carried out by the new system, as well as any additional functions to be carried out. For example, an additional requirement of an office system could be to hold the e-mail address of each customer, which is something the company does not do currently.

3.3.6 System Proposals

In this section, ideally two or more alternative system proposals should be outlined, describing the following for each proposal:

- *Description of the proposed system*
- *Technical requirements and feasibility*
- *Operational requirements and feasibility*
- *Economic requirements and feasibility*

In some environments, however, it is not possible to propose more than one solution. If this is the case, the reasons why no alternative solutions are being proposed should be made clear.

3.3.7 Comparison of Proposals

A comparison of the technical, operational and economic feasibility of each of the proposals is made. If there is just the one proposal, this section should discuss the suitability of that proposal in terms of its technical, operational and economic feasibility with regard to the requirements of the business.

3.3.8 Conclusion and Recommendations

Finally, a conclusion as to the suitability of each of the proposals is made, with a recommendation for the proposal that matches the needs and objectives of the new system as well as being the most suitable in terms of technical, operational and economic feasibility. Remember that it is not always the cheapest solution that is recommended. For example, a system for an air-traffic control system would not value price above reliability and accuracy, whereas a proposal for a small stock-control system in a new company might well prefer to select the cheapest system, happily trading bells and whistles for least cost!

3.4   Agreeing the Approach

Once the feasibility report has been drawn up, it is very important that it is approved formally before any further work is carried out. The recommended proposal may be agreed, or one of the other proposals may be agreed. It is also often the case that one of the proposals is agreed, but with some parts of one or more of the other proposals.

The important task here is to obtain formal agreement by the person or people who will take on ultimate ownership of the system. It is no good the computing department's manager agreeing the recommended proposal for an accounts system if the accounts manager, who will be using the system, does not agree the approach. It may not be what his/her department wants at all.

The following example illustrates the consequences of carrying out a systems development project where the initial feasibility report was never formally agreed. Whilst areas of the feasibility report were being negotiated with various levels of management, the developers were instructed to start working on the recommended proposal. Several months and thousands of man-hours into the project, the senior manager was replaced and the developers were told to 'shelve' the original version and start work on another approach. Again, a few months and a new senior manager later, the developers were told to go back to the previous version. It is very difficult to find accountability for such a sequence of events when the original feasibility report was never signed.

Once an approach has been agreed and formalised, details of the agreed approach for the new system must be written down in the 'Agreed Approach' section of the terms of reference, which itself is part of the feasibility report. (Refer to section 3.2.) The feasibility report should contain a section, perhaps after the terms of reference section, for the signatures of those formalising the approach.

A project inevitably changes during its development, since one of the first tasks is detailed systems analysis, in which any unforeseen problems and complications are identified. A signed feasibility report provides a valuable resource when negotiating extended timescales and increased resources for additional requirements and unforeseen problems. It is the same as if a decorator produced a quote for completing a job: once you have accepted that quote, if you want him/her to do any additional work, the cost and increased time to do it will be added to the original cost and timescale of the quote.

3.5 Summary

This chapter has covered the following material:

- Reasons why the boundaries of the new system need to be defined.
- The terms of reference.
- The feasibility report.

3.6 Written Exercises

3.6.1   Describe each of the five main parts of the terms of reference.

3.6.2   Ask several people to draw a picture to illustrate the bear trap they imagine the following text is describing:

"Two tall structures are located a short distance apart. Each has several overhanging poles. Several ropes are used to connect the two structures. A container hangs from the ropes, connected by chains. Inside the container is some bait and on the ground under the container is a trap."

Compare the drawings and work out how many different ways the descriptions can be interpreted.

3.6.3 Draw up a feasibility report to record the requirements of the following **Painting and Decorating Company** and to discuss the two system alternatives, and recommend one:

"A well-established painting and decorating company have recently decided, after a spate of lost quotations and double-bookings, to replace their paper-based system. Their current system uses three sets of folders. The first one is used to store the names, addresses, dates and quotes of future decorating jobs. The second folder is used to store the same details about those quotes that are agreed and are now jobs, including a price instead of the quote and a note on each to say whether the customer has paid or not. The third folder contains details about orders made with suppliers for materials.

The managing director wants to cut down on the amount of paper held in his offices and wants to be able to find out where his decorators are at any one time. Currently, it takes the administrator several hours each Friday afternoon to put together a plan for the next week's jobs, and it takes most of the Monday to put together a list of all unpaid work. The administrator also finds it takes a long time match up cheques and cash paid for completed jobs, since it is often paid in parts and one customer may have several jobs with outstanding payments at once.

The company is set to merge with another smaller company at the end of the year, and the managing director would like the new system to be up and running by then, so that the new business details can be added to the system. The company is currently during its busiest period and the managing director does not want any system development work to start until the beginning of September. The staff always have the last two weeks of December as holiday.

The managing director cannot decide whether he wants to have one PC for the administrator to use, producing a report each week listing the following week's schedule and other details. The staff could then refer to these reports. The other option he is considering is whether to have several PCs around the office. The administrator would still enter the information, but the staff would use the PCs when they needed to look up any information."

4 | Documenting the Transfer of Information – Data Flow Diagrams

4.1 Introduction

Before you can start to think about designing the database, screens and reports, it is important to look at the current system, since your new computer system will be based upon this. One of the main tasks that must be carried out at this stage is to describe on paper the activities that take place in the current workplace. It is important that this is done accurately, since this information will be used to design the screens and reports for the final system.

If you have ever tried to build a piece of 'flat-pack' furniture, I am sure you will agree that the hardest part of the whole exercise is trying to understand the instructions: "slot sides B5 and F3 into leg T1 ...". Are the people who write these instructions trying to make life difficult? Not necessarily! Describing a physical activity so that many different people can understand it, such as putting together a shelf or even tying a shoelace, is very difficult. One of the hardest parts of designing a computer system is trying to do exactly that: put onto paper the activities that take place in the workplace. One of the reasons why this is such a hard task is that there is often more than one way to correctly describe a task on paper.

Several tools and techniques have been devised to help you in this difficult task. The most commonly used of these techniques is the **data flow diagram** which, as its name implies, is a diagrammatic method of illustrating how data flows around a system. This technique represents physical activities on paper in terms of flows of information, data stores, processes and external entities. Although many structured development methodologies use data flow diagrams, and the formats used to represent each of these items vary, the principle is the same.

4.2 Data Flow Diagrams

As referred to previously, the four main parts of a data flow diagram are **process**, **data flow**, **data store** and **external entity**. Refer to the following extract from the description of a **Hotel Reception** system:

"When a customer telephones the hotel, Chris, the receptionist, checks the booking log for an available room, which he offers to the customer, along with the price. If the customer is happy with that room, Chris fills in a duplicate booking form with the customer's name, address and, telephone number, and the dates, room number, room occupancy and price of the booking. He then updates the booking log by writing the customer's name against the appropriate dates for the booked room. At various convenient points during the day, the receptionist sends all the original booking forms filled in so far to the customers as confirmation. He then files the duplicates in the booking form file."

Refer to Figures 4.1 and 4.2, which illustrate the two types of paperwork used in the current system.

19 March 2000			
Room	Occupancy	Price	Customer
1	2	£60	
2	4	£73	Katie Rubek
3	2	£60	Martin Walsh

Figure 4.1 One page from the booking log

BOOKING FORM			
Customer Name:	Katie Rubek		
Address:	15 Dandow Close Pelton Bucks MK13 4ST	Telephone:	01495-649735
We have pleasure in confirming the following reservation:			
Start Date:	19/3/2000	End Date:	20/3/2000
Room Number:	2	Occupancy:	4
Total Price:	£146		

Figure 4.2 A sample booking form

In order to draw a data flow diagram from a description, it is helpful first to make a rough drawing of the activities that take place. There is no specific diagrammatic standard for this approach: just draw a diagram to represent what is happening, using pictures to represent the people and files or logs, and arrows to show which way the information is flowing. It is also very useful to write down the information that is being sent or received along the arrows in your diagram. This is called a **system picture**. It can also be called a **rich picture** or a **soft system picture**. Refer to Figure 4.3 for a **system picture** of the **Hotel Reception** current working system.

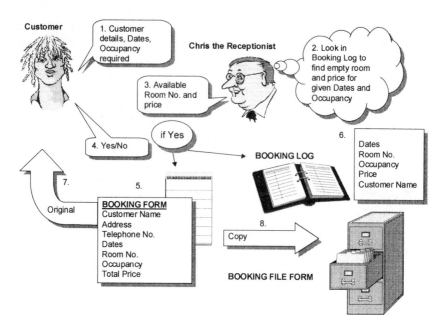

Figure 4.3 System picture of the current Hotel Reception system

Before you go any further, it is important to establish which parts of the description are actually parts of the new system. It may turn out that half of what you have described is not going to be part of your new system at all. You will need to refer to the scope of the new system section in the terms of reference which will describe how much of the current working system you need to include in your analysis and design.

In the **Hotel Reception** example above, the scope of the system would include only the tasks carried out by the receptionist. The customer, therefore is external to the system. Although this seems fairly straightforward, it is not necessarily so. Take the case of a Quotations and Orders department, which sends half-filled quotation forms to the Purchasing department to complete before returning them. Since the scope states that the Purchasing department is not part of the new system, Purchasing is therefore external to the system.

One way to illustrate which areas of the current system are external to your new system is to draw a system boundary line onto your system picture. Refer to Figure 4.4.

4.3 Start the Data Flow Diagram with the External Entities

Drawing a data flow diagram is not a procedure that can be completed in one attempt. You will find that your initial draft will quickly become untidy and confusing, as arrows will start to cross over each other and start being looped around the boxes on the page. This always happens since when you start it is never clear exactly where on the page you should position each box such that all its incoming and outgoing arrows will not cross over. It is best not to worry about this and draw the first draft freely. Once you have the first draft down on paper, it can easily be tidied up to produce a clearer version.

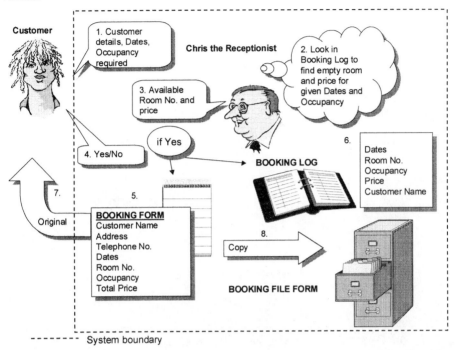

Figure 4.4 Picture of the current **Hotel Reception** system, showing the system boundary

Having examined your terms of reference carefully and established how much of your current system will be included in your new system, the easiest parts of the Data Flow Diagram to determine first are the *external entities*.

An **external entity** can be defined as a person, a group of people or an automated object that sends information to your system, or receives information from your system. A group of people can be represented by a company or a department for example, and an automated object could be a computer. Some examples of external entities:

System scope	External Entities
Functions carried out by the controller at a taxi firm	Customers, taxi drivers, repairs, workshop, manager
Booking, enquiry and cancellation functions carried out by travel agent	Tour operators, air-flight computer system, customers
Emergency admissions procedures carried out in the accident and emergency ward	Patients, patients' doctors, police

The format used to represent an external entity in this book (similar to that used in the SSADM methodology) is an oval with the name of the external entity in it.

Draw the external entities around the outside of your blank sheet. In this simple example of the **Hotel Reception** system there is only the one. Refer to Figure 4.5.

Figure 4.5 Hotel Reception system data flow diagram – external entity added

4.4 Add Data Stores to the Data Flow Diagram

Before you look at the processes, which are most complex part of the data flow diagram, it is easier to add the next simplest items to the diagram, the data stores.

A **data store** can be defined as anything that contains information in your system. This can include structured information stores such as an index file, a list on paper in a book or folder, a wall chart or a spreadsheet on a computer. Data stores can also be informal, such as small yellow notes stuck to the wall and even information stored in a person's memory. Some examples of data stores are:

System scope	Data stores
Functions carried out by the controller at a taxi firm	Pick-up log, customer address book, repairs log, driver schedule
Booking, enquiry and cancellation functions carried out by travel agent	Holiday brochures, tour operator, contact file, flight database system, bookings file
Emergency admissions procedures carried out in the accident and emergency ward	Accident log, doctor's address file, emergency doctor contact numbers, ward admissions book

In the **Hotel Reception** system example, there appear to be three data stores:

- Booking Log.
- Booking Form.
- Booking Form File.

Booking Log

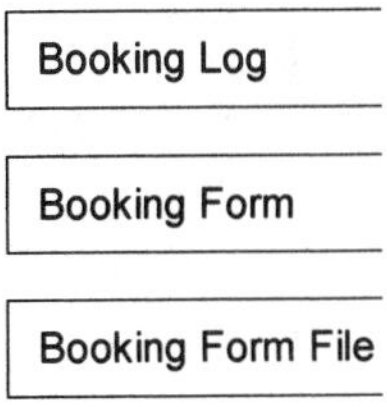

The format used to represent a data store in this book (similar to that used in the SSADM methodology) is an open-ended rectangle with the name of the data store in it.

Booking Form

Booking Form File

Draw the data stores along the right side of your data flow diagram page. Refer to Figure 4.6.

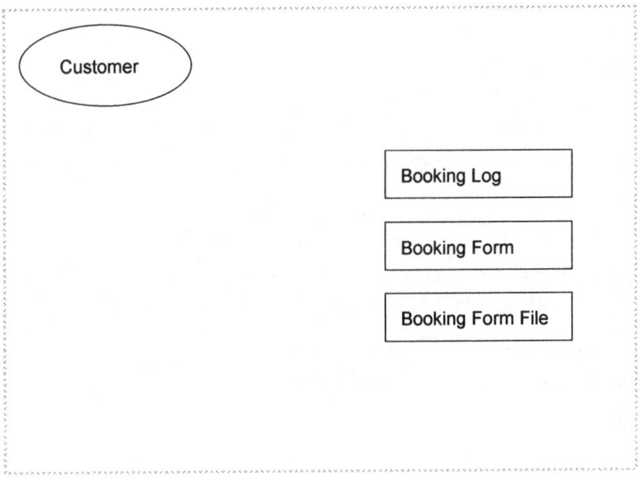

Figure 4.6   Hotel Reception system data flow diagram – data stores added

4.5   Identifying the Individual Processes, Inputs and Outputs

Identifying the processes and data flows is the most difficult part of drawing a data flow diagram – not because the processes are necessarily complex, but because there are often several different ways to split the functions in the system into separate processes.

A **process** can be defined as an action that takes place involving the transfer of information within the system. A **data flow** describes the direction in which the information is being transferred and what the information comprises.

The following method of identifying the processes from a given scenario involves splitting the given system description into separate tasks, and then breaking those tasks down into smaller instructions. Refer to the **Hotel Reception** example again:

"When a customer telephones the hotel, Chris, the receptionist, checks the booking log for an available room, which he offers to the customer, along with the price. If the customer is happy with that room, Chris fills in a duplicate booking form with the customer's name, address and, telephone number, and the dates, room number, room occupancy and price of the booking. He then updates the booking log by writing the customer's name against the appropriate dates for the booked room. At various convenient points during the day, the receptionist sends all the original booking forms filled in so far to the customers as confirmation. He then files the duplicates in the booking form file."

Step 1

Break the system description down into small sentences, each containing a task or an action. If in doubt whether a task should be split into two or left as one, split it. It can always be merged again later.

1. *When a customer telephones the hotel, Chris, the receptionist, checks the booking log for an available room, which he offers to the customer, along with the price.*

2. *If the customer is happy with that room, Chris fills in a duplicate booking form with the customer's name, address and, telephone number, and the dates, room number, room occupancy and price of the booking.*

3. *He then updates the booking log by writing the customer's name against the appropriate dates for the booked room.*

4. *At various convenient points during the day, the receptionist sends all the original booking forms filled in so far to the customers as confirmation.*

5. *He then files the duplicates in the booking form file.*

Step 2

This step involves identifying the **inputs** and **outputs** to and from each task. To do this, it helps to break the tasks down into smaller instructions. To decide which information is input and which is output, it helps to compare the information held by each item involved with in task *before* and *after* the task.

For example, if the task is for a policeman to write down the time on a speeding ticket, then the information being transferred is the *time*. To establish whether this is an input to or an output from the task, compare the amount of information known before and after the task. Before the task, the policeman knows what the time is, but the speeding ticket does not contain the time. After the task, the piece of paper now contains the time. Since the speeding ticket has *gained* information, the transfer of information was an output from the policeman to the speeding ticket.

In another example, the task is for the policeman to obtain a suspect's address from a file. The information being transferred is the address, but to establish whether that address is an input or output to the task, we must compare the before and after images. Before the task, the policeman does not know the address, but the address is held on the file. After the task, the address is still held on the file, but the policeman also knows it. Since the policeman has *gained* the information, this shows an input to the policeman who is performing the task.

For each of the tasks in your list, you will need to complete an input/output table as shown in Figure 4.7.

Task n				
Instruction	**Input**	**from**	**Output**	**to**

Figure 4.7 Input/output table

The 'Instruction' column will contain each small instruction that makes up the task. For each of these instructions, you will need to fill in what the input and/or output information is. If there is input information, as well as writing down each piece of that information in the 'Input' column, you will need to write down the source(s) of that Information in the 'from' column. This can be an external entity, a data store or another task.

If there is an output from the instruction, you will also need to write down the information being output in the 'Output' column, as well as the destination of that output. The destination must be an external entity or a data store, and must be written in the 'to' column.

Although the external entities and data stores will have been previously identified, it may be the case that you uncover a new data store or external entity that wasn't evident in your previous examination of the system. If this is the case, add it to your diagram, using the appropriate format.

Remember that when you write down the information in the input and output columns, you must not refer to the manner in which the information is being transferred. For example, when the task was for the policeman to write the time on the speeding ticket, the output information would be the *time*, and the destination (the 'to' column) would be the *speeding ticket*.

An input/output table for each of the five tasks identified for the **Hotel Reception** example is created as follows:

Task 1

"When a customer telephones the hotel, Chris, the receptionist, checks the booking log for an available room, which he offers to the customer, along with the price."

This task can be split into two smaller instructions:

"When a customer telephones the hotel,
Chris, the receptionist, checks the booking log for an available room, which he offers
to the customer, along with the price."

The first instruction is that the *customer telephones the hotel.* Although it is not stated in the text, the system picture (refer to Figure 4.4) shows the type of information the Customer provides when making an enquiry. For example, "We would like a double room for three nights from the 6th of December, please." Therefore, the information being transferred is the enquiry information: number of rooms, occupancy, start and end date of stay.

To decide whether this information is an input to the instruction or an output from the instruction, compare the amount of information known by each party before and after the instruction took place. Before the instruction took place, the Customer knew her own enquiry details, of course, but the Receptionist was unaware of them. After the instruction took place, the Customer still knows that information, but now, the Receptionist also knows the information. Since the Receptionist, who is carrying out the instruction, has gained information, the enquiry details must be an *input* to the instruction from the Customer. This information is written in a table. Refer to the first line of Figure 4.8.

The second part of the instruction is that the Receptionist *checks the booking log for an available room, which he offers to the customer, along with the price.* Again, we need to make some assumptions about the type of information the Receptionist is seeking here: presumably, it is both the available Room Number and the Price he needs. Therefore, the information being transferred is the Room Number and the Price.

As before, we need to decide whether this is an input to the instruction or an output from the instruction. Compare the amount of information known to each party before and after the instruction takes place. Before the Receptionist checks in the Booking Log, the Receptionist does not know the Room Number and Price, but the information is in the Booking Log. After looking up the information in the Booking Log, the Receptionist now knows the available Room Number and Price. Since the Receptionist has *gained* the information, the available Room Number must be an input to the Receptionist from the Booking Log.

Although this may sound strange, since the Booking Log is not physically *giving* the Receptionist the information, by his reading it the information is being transferred to the Receptionist.

This instruction also has an output as well as input. The Output here is the Room Number and the Price that the Receptionist relays to the Customer. It is clearly an output, since before the instruction the Customer did not know which room was available, but after the instruction the Customer does know. Since the Customer has *gained* information, the information is an output from the instruction to the Customer.

Refer to Figure 4.8 for the completed input/output table for Task 1.

Task 1				
Instruction	**Input**	**from**	**Output**	**to**
Customer telephones with a booking enquiry	No. rooms Occupancy Start Date End Date	Customer		
Receptionist checks the booking log for an available room, which he offers to the customer, along with the price	Room No. Price	Booking Log	Room No. Price	Customer

Figure 4.8   Task 1 input/output Table

Task 2

"If the customer is happy with that room, Chris fills in a duplicate booking form with the customer's name, address and, telephone number, and the dates, room number, room occupancy and price of the booking."

There is only one instruction here, to fill the Booking Form with the Customer and booking details. We must make an assumption again about the *dates* part of the instruction, but to stay in line with the previous task, we shall assume that the dates recorded will be start date and end date.

To determine the inputs to and outputs from the task, we must consider the before and after pictures. Before the task, the Receptionist knew the Customer and booking details, but the Booking Form was blank. After the task, the Receptionist still knows this information, but the Booking Form has been filled in with that information. Since the Booking Form has *gained* the information, we can say that the information transfer is an output from the task to the Booking Form.

Also, before the task, the Customer knew whether she was happy or not with the proposed Room Number, but the Receptionist did not. After this task, the Customer has either said 'yes' or 'no'. If it was a 'yes', then the Booking is carried out. Since the Receptionist had *gained* that yes/no information from the Customer, this is an input to the instruction. Yes/no information is often called **Confirmation** information. Refer to Figure 4.9 for the completed input/output table for this task.

Task 2				
Instruction	**Input**	**from**	**Output**	**to**
If the customer is happy, the receptionist fills in a booking form with the customer and booking details	Confirmation	Customer	Customer Name, Address, Telephone No., Start Date, End Date, Room No., Occupancy, Total Price	Booking Form

Figure 4.9 Task 2 Input/output table

Documenting the transfer of information – data flow diagrams   35

Task 3

"He then updates the booking log by writing the customer's name against the appro-priate dates for the booked room."

For this task, there is clearly an output. At the end of the task, the Booking Log will have *gained* the Customer Name. However, there is no clear input here. It does not state where the Customer Name and booking information is coming from.

When a task is identified with a missing input or output (since a task should have both), there are two options:

- The task can be combined with the previous or next sequential task in the sce-nario. It may be that you split the description incorrectly.

- The missing input or output will need to come from or go to another Task, and not an external entity or data store.

In this case, this task will be left on its own as Task 3, and will have an input from Task 2, giving it the Customer and Booking information needed to select the appropri-ate Booking Log entry and write in the Customer Name. Refer to Figure 4.10 for the completed input/output table.

Task 3				
Instruction	Input	from	Output	to
The receptionist updates the booking log by writing the customer's name against the appropriate dates for the booked room	Customer Name Start Date End Date Room No.	Task 2	Customer Name	Booking Log

Figure 4.10 Task 3 input/output table

Task 4

"At various convenient points during the day, the receptionist sends all the original booking forms filled in so far to the customers as confirmation."

There is just the one instruction here, sending the Booking Forms to the customer. It is not too difficult to see that the output from this task is the Booking Form being sent to the Customer. This is a clear output, since after the task the Customer has *gained* the Booking Form information. When we fill in the table, it is important to write down only the information that is being transferred, not the manner in which it is being trans-ferred.

For example, in this case we will write down that the output information is the Customer Name, Address, Telephone Number, Room Number, Occupancy, Start and End Date of booking and Total Price. The output will be to the Customer. No mention is made here of the Booking Form in relation to the output.

However, in order for there to be an output from a task, the information being output must come from somewhere. There should therefore be an *input* to this task. Although it may sound confusing in this example, the Input to the task is actually the Booking Form itself. Remember that in the table you do not write down the manner in which the information is being transferred, simply the information itself. The input, therefore, is the same information as the output, but it is being input from the Booking Form.

This may sound rather confusing when you are still imagining the physical actions taking place in the system, rather than the logical picture of the information being transferred. However, when you see the completed data flow diagram at the end of the chapter, it will make sense. Refer to Figure 4.11 for the completed input/output table for this task.

Task 4				
Instruction	**Input**	**from**	**Output**	**to**
At various convenient points during the day, the Receptionist sends all the original booking forms filled in so far to the customers as a confirmation	Customer Name Address Telephone No Start Date End Date Room No Occupancy Total Price	Booking Form	Customer Name Address Telephone No Start Date End Date Room No Occupancy Total Price	Customer

Figure 4.11 Task 4 input/output table

Task 5

"He then files the duplicates in the booking form file."

This task sounds the same as the previous task, except that instead of the output being sent to the Customer, the output is being put into the Booking Form File. We need to think very carefully about what is actually happening to the information here. We have already established that the customer details and booking details are stored on the Booking Form, which is one of our data stores.

However, the physical act of placing the Booking Form in a folder containing other Booking Forms is not actually transferring the information to another data store, since the information is still in the Booking Form. In this case, the Booking Form File is merely a container for the Booking Forms and no more. It therefore makes sense to remove the Booking Form File from our list of data stores and also to ignore this task, since it is not transferring information, but merely, placing the data store in a container.

4.6 Turning the Input/output Tables into Process Boxes and Data Flows on the Data Flow Diagram

The format used to represent a process in this book (similar to that used in the SSADM methodology) is a rectangle with a brief description of the task in it. Identify each process box with a unique number, in sequential order, such that the order of the process boxes resembles the order in which the tasks occur in the real system.

The format used to represent a data flow is an arrow connecting a process box with an external entity, a data store or another process box. The information being transferred must be written in brief format, above or below the arrow.

Three basic actions must be carried out when drawing the process boxes and data flows on the data flow diagram:

1. Draw a process box for each task. If there are several instructions in that task, you must combine the individual descriptions into one brief description for the whole process. The description must be written from the task's point of view and without references to physical items such as people or documents. For example, instead of writing *"Customer telephones with a booking enquiry. The receptionist checks the booking log for an available room, which he offers to the customer"* you would write *"Receive customer Booking enquiry, check the Booking Log for an available room and tell Customer"*. Another guideline for naming process boxes, is not to include the word *process*.

2. Draw on each input and output to/from the task using data flows to connect the process to external entities, data stores or other process boxes.

3. Write above/below each data flow a brief description of the information being transferred.

Refer to Figure 4.12 for a diagram of the process box, data store and data flow representing the task described previously about a policeman reading a suspect's address from a police File.

Figure 4.12 Example process box, data store and data flow

When building a data flow diagram, there are some basic rules that must be used as a guideline:

- Position the external entities around the outside of the diagram.

- Where possible, try to position the process boxes such that they are in sequential order, either from left to right, or from top to bottom.

- If possible, do not cross the data flow arrows over each other. If this is unavoidable, use the following notation: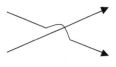

- To avoid crossing the data flow arrows, one technique that may help is to draw duplicate external entities and data stores. Make sure you mark both the duplicate and original as shown in Figure 4.13.

Figure 4.13 Duplicate external entity and data store

Remember that once you have drawn a first draft, you will probably need to tidy it up to avoid too many crossing and looping data flows.

The steps given next describe how the process boxes and data flows are added to the data flow diagram for each task from the **Hotel Reception** system.

1. Draw a process box with a brief but clear description of all the instructions included in the table for that task. Refer to Figure 4.15 for the process box for Task 1.

Task 1

Task 1				
Instruction	**Input**	**from**	**Output**	**to**
Customer telephones with a booking enquiry	No. rooms Occupancy Start Date End Date	Customer		
Receptionist checks Booking Log for an available room, which he tells that Customer, along with the Price	Room No. Price	Booking Log	Room No. Price	Customer

Figure 4.14   Task 1 input/output table

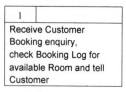

Figure 4.15 Process box for Task 1

2. Draw an arrow from each object in the 'from' column to the process box and write, over or under the arrow, a brief description of the information in the corresponding 'Input' box on the table.

   In this example, there are two inputs, one for each of the instructions; an initial input from the Customer with the basic enquiry information, the Number of Rooms required, Occupancy, Start and End Dates, and an input from the Booking Log in the second instruction with the available Room Number and Price. Refer to Figure 4.16.

3. Draw an arrow from the process box to each object in the 'to' column, and write over that arrow a brief description of the information in the corresponding 'Output' box on the table.

In this example, there is only the one output in this task, coming from the second instruction in that task. The output is to the Customer, with the available Room Number and Price. Refer to Figure 4.17.

Adding the process boxes and data flows for the remaining tasks will now complete the data flow diagram. Note that as each new process is added, the previous drawing becomes more compact to make room.

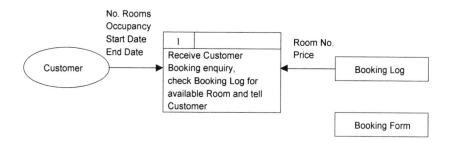

Figure 4.16 Input data flows for Task 1 added to the data flow diagram

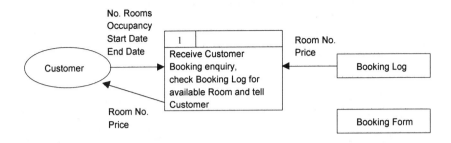

Figure 4.17 Output data flow for Task 1 added to the data flow diagram

Task 2

The process box and data flows for Task 2 are added to the data flow diagram.

Task 2				
Instruction	**Input**	**from**	**Output**	**to**
If the Customer is happy, he fills in a Booking Form with the Customer and booking details	Confirmation	Customer	Customer Name Address Telephone No. Start Date End Date Room No. Occupancy Total Price	Booking Form

Figure 4.18 Input/output table for task 2

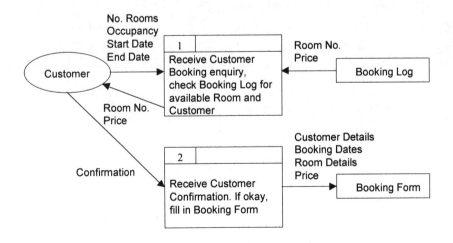

Figure 4.19 Process box and data flows for Task 2 added to the data flow diagram

Task 3

The process box and data flows for Task 3 are added to the data flow diagram. Note that the input is from the process box for Task 2. Refer to Figures 4.20 and 4.21.

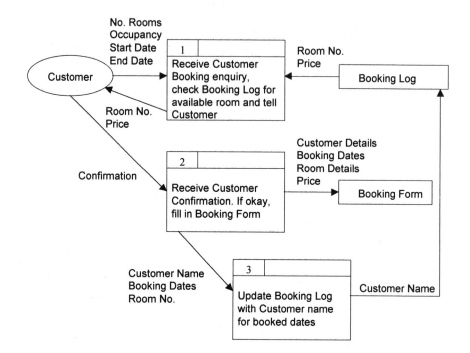

Figure 4.20   Process box and data flows for Task 3 added to the data flow diagram

Task 3				
Instruction	**Input**	**from**	**Output**	**to**
The Receptionist writes the Customer Name against the Booking Log entry for the appropriate room for each of the dates of the stay	Customer Name Start Date End Date Room No.	Task 2	Customer Name	Booking Log

Figure 4.21   Input/output table for Task 3

Task 4

The process box and data flows for Task 4 are added to the data flow diagram. Note that to avoid either crossing the data flows or displaying the process boxes out of sequence, a duplicate Booking Form data store has been added (Refer to Figures 4.22 and 4.23).

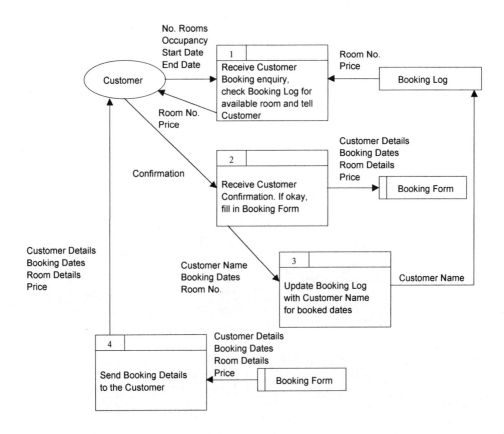

Figure 4.22 Process box and data flows for Task 4 added to the data flow diagram

Task 4				
Instruction	**Input**	**from**	**Output**	**to**
At various convenient points during the day, the Receptionist sends all the original booking forms filled in so far to the cus- tomers as a confirmation	Customer Name Address Telephone No. Start Date End Date Room No. Occupancy Total Price	Booking Form	Customer Name Address Telephone No. Start date End date Room No. Occupancy Total Price	Customer

Figure 4.23 Input/output table for Task 4

4.7 Add the System Boundary to the Data Flow Diagram

Finally, the **system boundary** shown on the system picture must be added to the data flow diagram to show clearly which part of the diagram is within the system, and which parts are outside. In this system, only the Customer is outside the system boundary. Refer to Figure 4.24.

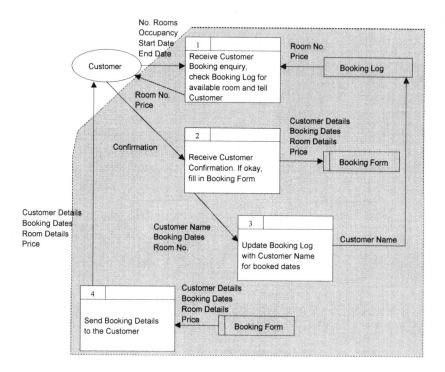

Figure 4.24 Completed data flow diagram including the system boundary

4.8 Summary

This chapter has covered the following material:

- Why drawing a current system on paper can be difficult.
- Introduction to a data flow diagram.
- Drawing a simple picture of the current system.
- Identifying external entities in the current system.
- Identifying data stores in the current system.
- Identifying individual tasks in the current system.

- Splitting tasks into instructions.
- Identifying inputs and outputs for each instruction.
- Drawing process boxes and data flows from the tasks, inputs and outputs.
- Showing the system boundary on the diagram.

4.9   Written Exercises

4.9.1   Define the following:

External entity	Data store
Process	Input to a process
Output from a process	Data flow

4.9.2   Complete an input/output table as shown below for each of the following processes:

Task 1					
Instruction	**Input**	**from**	**Output**	**to**	

(a) A customer services operator for a **Toy Manufacturer** receives a complaint about a computer game from a customer. He logs it and passes on the complaint to the computer games department.

(b) The marketing manager for a **Football Club** reads through the fans' club members list to find out how many members live within a five kilometre radius.

(c) A **Training Company** send information about new training to previous clients.

4.9.3   Answer parts (a) to (d) based on the following administration system in the **Painting and Decorating Company** referred to in the previous chapter.

"A customer rings up the administrator to request a quote for a piece of decorating work. The customer's name and address are written on a quote form and an appointment (quote date) is made for one of the decorators to go round and draw up a quote. The quote form is then passed to one of the decorators and the quotation will be carried out. The decorator fills in the quotation amount and the form is returned to the administrator. The administrator will send the original quote to the customer and place a copy in the quote folder.

If the customer rings up to confirm the job (ninety percent of the quotes result in a job), a date is agreed and written on the quote form in the folder. A copy of the updated quote form is given to the decorator to carry out the work and the quote form is transferred to the jobs folder. Once the work has been done, the decorator updates the quote form to show the final price and date of completion.

When the customer pays, the last date of payment is written on the appropriate form in the jobs folder, with the amount outstanding, if there is any.

Any materials required for a job are ordered, using an item code and quantity, from one of the company's main suppliers. A record of the order is written in the orders folder, along with the date, total price for each item and the quote reference number for that job. When the goods are delivered, the order in the folder is updated to show the delivery date."

(a) Draw a system picture, showing the system boundary, for the painting and decorating administration system. In this case, the managing director wants a computer system to replace the administration of the quotes, jobs and orders paperwork.

(b) Identify the external entities and data stores for the painting and decorating administration system.

(c) Identify the tasks in the painting and decorating administration system. Complete an input/output table for each one, making sure you split the task into smaller Instructions where appropriate.

(d) Draw a data flow diagram for the painting and decorating administration system, linking together the external entities, data stores and process boxes using labelled data flows. Show the system boundary.

5 Grouping the Information – Entity-relationship modelling

5.1 Introduction

In the previous chapter, we looked at a technique for interpreting the current system in a data flow diagram. This diagram breaks the system down into processes, data stores and external entities, as well as showing how the information is transferred to and from each process. The data flow diagram is the first step in the analysis phase, in which you try to differentiate between the processes that are taking place in the system, and the data that is being moved around the system. The processes defined in the data flow diagram will be used as the basis for designing the screens and reports, and the information flowing around the system will be used as the basis for the new database. This information needs to be collected into organised groups that will eventually become the tables in the database. That task is done using various data analysis and design techniques.

In Part I of this chapter, a technique called **entity-relationship modelling** is described. This technique involves the identification of particular items and events described by the information in the system, and identifies the relationships between these items and events. This relationship is then illustrated in a diagram, called an entity-relationship diagram. The lists of items and the diagram together make up the entity-relationship model, and is one of the main design tools used to design the database tables and relationships between them.

Part II of this chapter will enable you to put the database table designs into practice. You can work through the session, following the step-by-step instructions provided, to find out about the basic features of the database management tool, Access, and to create a database and tables with and without the table Wizard.

Part I: Database Design Theory

5.2   What is Entity-relationship modelling?

Entity-relationship modelling involves examining the information that flows around a system and identifying specific *entities* that are being described by that information. An **entity** can be described as an item, in a system, about which information is held.

In this chapter, the method for designing the entity-relationship model starts with the data. You will first group the data into sets that will then be defined as entities. Once the entities have been identified, they are tested to ensure that they obey the three basic rules described below. This may result in the model being amended with each test being carried out. Once the relationships between the entities have been tested, the original sets of information may need to be redistributed around the final set of entities.

The way in which each entity relates to the other entities in the system is illustrated in a diagram called an *entity-relationship diagram*. This, together with the lists of information for each entity, makes up the entity-relationship model.

For example, in the **University Department** system discussed in the first chapter, the three entities are STAFF DETAILS, COURSE DETAILS and TIMETABLE. The entity-relationship diagram for the university department main office system in Figure 5.1 shows each entity as a box with the entity name in it, and an arrow linking two entities together. The arrowhead will point to the entity that can have more than one occurrence for each entity in the linking box.

This diagram shows that a member of staff can be related to more than one timetable entry, and a course can be related to more than one timetable entry. Figure 5.2 show the lists of information grouped under each entity in the **University Department** main office system.

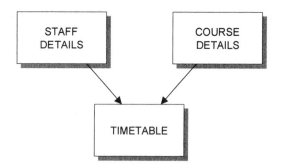

Figure 5.1   Entity-relationship diagram for university department main office system

STAFF DETAILS	COURSE DETAILS	TIMETABLE
Staff ID	Course Code	Day
Name	Course Title	Time
Address	Course Summary	Location
Salary Grade		Course Code
Holiday Entitlement		Session Type
Holiday Remaining		Staff ID

Figure 5.2 Three lists showing the information grouped under each entity in the entity-relationship model for the university department main office system

When grouping the information into entities, there are three basic rules that must be obeyed:

1. Ideally each entity should contain a key item or items of information that can be used to identify that particular entity.

2. The number of items in an entity must be the same for each occurrence in that group.

3. The relationship between two entities A and B will be such that any one occurrence in entity A may relate to more than one occurrence in entity B, but any one occurrence in entity B can relate to only one occurrence in entity A.

In the University example above, the groups and relationships between them satisfy the basic rules as follows:

Rule 1:   Ideally each entity should contain a key item or items of information that can be used to identify that particular entity.

Each occurrence of the STAFF DETAILS entity will have its own unique Staff ID. There will not be more than one occurrence of STAFF DETAILS with the same Staff ID. In the same way, each occurrence of the COURSE DETAILS entity will have a unique Course Code key. To ensure that each occurrence of the TIMETABLE entity has a unique key, the key needs to be made up of three separate items: Day, Time and Location. There will not be more than one Timetable entry with the same day, same time and same location.

An example in which this rule is not obeyed would be if the TIMETABLE entity used only Day and Time as the key, and not Location. Since it is possible for there to be two or more lectures taking place at the same time on the same day, but in different locations, there could be at least two occurrences of the TIMETABLE entity containing the same Day and Time keys. To avoid this problem, an extra item needs to be added to the key. To decide which item it should be, the other items in the entity group need to be examined. In this case, the remaining items are Location, Session Type, Course Code and Staff ID. You must decide which of these items, when combined with the Day and Time, will make the TIMETABLE occurrence unique.

Session Type clearly will not, since you can have two lectures taking place at the same time on the same day. Course Code also is not very safe to use, since there may

be a time when two tutorials or lectures for the same course need to be scheduled together. This leaves only Staff ID and Location. Both of these would be unique for a
session. A member of staff cannot be in two places at once and two or more lec-
tures/tutorials cannot be held in the same location at once. In this case, either would
do, so (with the flip of a coin) the Location is selected to become the third part of the
key.

*Rule 2:   The number of items in a group must be the same for each occurrence in
             that group.*

The number of items for the STAFF DETAILS entity will be the same for each member
of staff. Each member will have a Staff ID, Name, Address, Salary Grade, Holiday
Entitlement and Holiday Remaining, even it is zero. The same applies to the COURSE
DETAILS information and the TIMETABLE information.

An example in which this rule is not obeyed would be if the COURSE DETAILS
entity information included course textbooks. Each course occurrence might have a
different number of textbooks, ranging from none to six or more. A table cannot be
designed to allow for a variable number of items.

The way to handle this would be to split the textbook item away from the COURSE
DETAILS entity; and introduce a new entity called TEXTBOOK that contained just two
items of information: Course Code and Textbook. Both of those items would make up
the key. In this way, the course that had two textbooks would have two occurrences in
the new TEXTBOOK entity, each having the same Course Code. Since the key would
be made up of both the Course Code and the Textbook, the key would be unique for
each occurrence and would therefore obey the first rule.

*Rule 3:   The relationship between two entities A and B will be such that any one
             occurrence in entity A may relate to more than one occurrence in entity B,
             but any one occurrence in entity B can relate to only one occurrence in en-
             tity A.*

Each occurrence of the STAFF DETAILS entity can appear in more than one entry on
the timetable, since a lecturer can teach more than one class per week. However, each
occurrence in the TIMETABLE entity will correspond to only one member of staff in
the STAFF DETAILS entity, since each lecture or tutorial has only one member of staff.
This is called a **one-to-many relationship**.

If the system had been modelled on a system where a class could have more than
one lecturer in it at one time, then this relationship between STAFF DETAILS and
TIMETABLE would be called a **many-to-many relationship** and would not obey this
rule.

The following steps should be carried out to group the data in your system. The **Hotel Reception** system is used here as an example.

5.3.1   Step 1 – Identify the Entities and Relationships

1. Identify all the entities in your system. An entity is *an item in your system about which information is held.* To do this, list all the information that is flowing around your system. You can obtain this information from the data flow diagram and any documents used in the system.

<table>
<tr><td>

Booking Log
Booking Date
Room Number
Room Occupancy
Price Per Night
Customer Name

</td><td>

Booking Form
Customer Name
Customer Address
Customer Telephone Number
Start Date
End Date
Room Number
Occupancy
Total Price

</td></tr>
</table>

2. Group the information in your list so that each group is describing a particular item in your system. Try to break down the original groupings where appropriate. For example, customer details have been extracted into a customer group, since these describe a CUSTOMER entity. Examine the information and decide which items the information is describing. The names of the items being described will be the entity names.

   For example:

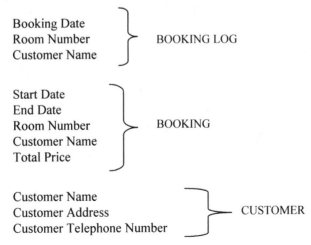

```
Room Number
Room Occupancy        }  ROOM
Price Per Night
```

The booking information has been split into two entities: BOOKING LOG and BOOKING. This is because some of the data will exist once only for the booking, such as the Start Date, End Date and Total Price, while other items such as Booking Date will exist for each day of the booking. For example, if the customer stays nine days at the hotel, there will be nine BOOKING LOG occurrences, one for each day of the stay. The other booking information, such as Start Date, End Date and Total Price, will exist, again along with Room Number and Customer Name to identify the whole booking, once only for each stay, regardless of the length of the stay. These are therefore two separate groups of information.

Note that Customer Name and Room Number have been placed in both the BOOKING LOG group and the BOOKING group. Customer Name clearly belongs to the CUSTOMER group, but also needs to be in the BOOKING and BOOKING LOG groups to identify the Bookings.

3. Examine the entities carefully to check that the first basic rule for entity-relationship modelling has been obeyed:

Each entity must contain a key item or items of information that can be used to identify that particular entity.

Check that each entity can be identified by one or more items used to describe that entity. Fill in a table as shown in Figure 5.3.

Each entry in the	*Can be identified by the*
BOOKING LOG	Booking Date and Room Number
BOOKING	Room Number, Start Date and End Date
CUSTOMER	Customer Name and Customer Address
ROOM	Room Number

Figure 5.3 Table key list

Since a customer could make two bookings for the same Start and End Dates, but one room could never be booked on the same Start and End Dates, it is important that the Room Number be included in the list of BOOKING key items. Also, both Customer Name and Address need to be included in the key CUSTOMER items, since there could be two customers with the same name.

4. Examine the items describing each entity carefully to check that the second basic rule for entity-relationship modelling has been obeyed:

The number of items in an entity must be the same for each occurrence in that group.

For each entity, check that each possible occurrence of the entity has exactly the same number of items listed in it.

In our example, this rule is obeyed. If, however, the BOOKING entity included a list of the individual dates booked, instead of just a Start Date and an End Date, this would break the above rule. The number of dates recorded could vary from one to the largest number a days the hotel will accept on a booking, maybe 30 days at a time. In this way, the entity would not contain the same number of items for each occurrence, and the days would need to be split away from the BOOKING entity into an entity of their own, called BOOKING DAYS. In fact, this is what we have already, called the BOOKING LOG.

5. Examine the entities and write down pairs of entities that you feel may have a direct relationship between them. A useful method to help you to do this is draw a small table with the entities listed along the side and across the bottom. Shade out the squares showing duplicate or self-self relationships, such as the cell joining ROOM to ROOM. Then tick the boxes representing pairs of entities you feel have direct correspondence. Refer to Figure 5.4. For example:

	CUSTOMER	ROOM	BOOKING	BOOKING LOG
CUSTOMER			✓	✓
ROOM			✓	✓
BOOKING				✓
BOOKING LOG				

Figure 5.4 Entity-relationship pairing table

In most cases, the relationships are easy to identify, like the one between the BOOKING and the BOOKING LOG. However, in some cases a relationship can be identified that does not directly link the two entities. For example, it could look as if there could be a relationship between ROOM and CUSTOMER, since when a customer makes a booking, he/she is booked into a specific room. However, in this case, the BOOKING entity is providing that relationship between CUSTOMER and ROOM via two direct relationships, between BOOKING and CUSTOMER and between BOOKING and ROOM. Therefore, no direct relationship between ROOM and CUSTOMER is required.

The entity-relationship pairing table in Figure 5.4 shows that there are five possible relationships:

1. CUSTOMER and BOOKING
2. CUSTOMER and BOOKING LOG
3. ROOM and BOOKING
4. ROOM and BOOKING LOG
5. BOOKING and BOOKING LOG

6. To test the type of relationship between the two entities, you must ask the following two questions for each pair of entities A and B:

Could one entity A correspond to more than one entity B?
Does one entity B correspond to only one entity A?

If the answer to both of these questions is *yes*, then there is a direct one-to-many relationship between entity A (one) and entity B (many).

If the answer to the first question is *no*, but the answer to the second question is *yes*, then you must assume that this is a one-to-one relationship. See a later step to handle this type of relationship.

If the answer to the first question is *yes*, but the answer to the second question is *no*, then you must assume that entity B can correspond to more than of entity A. If this is the case, the relationship is a many-to-many relationship, which will need to be converted into two one-to-many relationships in order to build the database. See a later step to handle this type of relationship.

If the answer to both these questions is *no*, then ask the same two questions again, but reverse the order of the entities. For example:

Pair 1:   CUSTOMER and BOOKING

Could one CUSTOMER correspond to more than one BOOKING?   *yes*
Does one BOOKING correspond to only one CUSTOMER?   *yes*

Since both these answers are *yes*, we can say that there is a direct one-to-many relationship between CUSTOMER (one) and BOOKING (many).

Pair 2:   CUSTOMER and BOOKING LOG

Could one CUSTOMER correspond to more than one BOOKING LOG?   *yes*
Does one BOOKING LOG correspond to only one CUSTOMER?   *yes*

Since both these answers are *yes*, we can say that there is a direct one-to-many relationship between CUSTOMER (one) and BOOKING LOG (many).

Pair 3:   BOOKING and ROOM

Could one BOOKING correspond to more than one ROOM?   *no*
Does one ROOM correspond to only one BOOKING?   *no*

Since both answers are *no*, try again swapping the order of the entities:

Could one ROOM correspond to more than one BOOKING?   *yes*

Does one BOOKING correspond to only one ROOM?   *yes*

Since both these answers are *yes*, we can say that there is a direct one-to-many relationship between ROOM (one) and BOOKING (many).

Pair 4:   ROOM and BOOKING LOG

Could one ROOM correspond to more than one BOOKING LOG?   *yes*
Does one BOOKING LOG correspond to only one ROOM?   *yes*

Since both these answers are *yes*, we can say that there is a direct one-to-many relationship between ROOM (one) and BOOKING (many).

Pair 5:   BOOKING and BOOKING LOG

Could one BOOKING correspond to more than one BOOKING LOG?   *yes*
Does one BOOKING LOG correspond to only one BOOKING?   *yes*

Since both these answers are *yes*, we can say that there is a direct one-to-many relationship between CUSTOMER (one) and BOOKING (many).

5.3.2   *Step 2 – Handle one-to-one relationships*

If there are any one-to-one relationships, you will need to decide how to handle them. A one-to-one relationship is one in which an occurrence of entity A is directly related to only one occurrence of another entity B, and that an occurrence of entity B is directly related to only one occurrence of entity A.

The relational database design protocol does not permit one-to-one relationships. As a result of this, database management systems such as Access do not recognise a one-to-one relationship and have no automatic way to police the relationship. It is possible to incorporate a one-to-one relationship into a database by 'pretending' that it is a one-to-many relationship, but there is no automatic way to stop someone entering two or more occurrences of one of the entities relating to one occurrence in the other entity. In other words, you cannot rely on the database management system to stop the one-to-one relationship turning into a one-to-many relationship.

In most cases where a one-to-one relationship is identified, the two entities are merged into one larger entity – since one occurrence of each will only relate to one occurrence of the other.

In some instances, however, it may be more efficient to use a one-to-one relationship. For example, suppose you were designing a database for a **Cruise Ship** passenger system in which there are two entities sharing a one-to-one relationship. One entity, PASSENGER, contains details about each passenger, such as address, date of birth, sex, cabin allocation, etc. The other entity, MEDICAL NEEDS, contains information about any special medical requirements a passenger might have, from medicines to be taken in an emergency, to requirements for wheelchairs and lifting aids. This entity contains various sections of information, enough to contain all the medical requirements of one passenger.

Since each MEDICAL NEEDS entity is specific to each passenger, it therefore has a one-to-one relationship with PASSENGER. If only a very small proportion of the passengers require a MEDICAL NEEDS entity, it would be wasteful to combine the PASSENGER and MEDICAL NEEDS entities into one entity, thereby holding numerous empty fields for most of the passengers. Although these do not necessarily mean wasted space on the database, the extra fields makes any work done using the combined entity more complicated since there are so many extra items to handle.

There are therefore three alternative ways to handle a one-to-one relationship:

- Double-check that the relationship between the entities is one-to-one. Re-examine your data and your identification of entities. You may have split up your data into too many groups, or you may have missed out some vital information that may indicate that this is in fact a one-to-many relationship.

- Since the relationship between the entities is so direct, the data for both entities could be grouped together into one entity. Examine your data to decide whether the two areas of data are in fact information about the same item or event. If this is the case, combine them into one entity. If they are not about a similar item or event, you can still combine them and create a new entity name.

- Do not change the entities and leave the relationship as a one-to-one relationship. You must be aware, however, that the database management system will probably treat the relationship as a one-to-many relationship, and therefore multiple occurrences of one of the two entities could be permitted. This would cause any queries, screens or reports built upon the one-to-one relationship to be inaccurate at least; and at worst the system might crash.

5.3.3 Step 3 – Handle many-to-many relationships

Although a one-to-one relationship can be accommodated, albeit strictly against the 'rules' and best avoided if possible, a many-to-many relationship cannot be incorporated into a database design. The database will not allow such a relationship to be created, and you must therefore change any many-to-many relationships so that they are represented by one-to-many relationships only.

Consider the **Cruise Ship** passenger system example. During the design, two directly related entities were identified: PASSENGER and CRUISE. Since a passenger can be booked onto many cruises over a period of time, and a cruise can contain many passengers, this is a many-to-many relationship. This relationship is illustrated in Figure 5.5.

The many-to-many relationship can be seen here, since two of the passengers are related to more than one cruise, and one of the cruises has three passengers related to it. In order to include this information in the database, the many-to-many relationship will have to be represented by two one-to-many relationships, and a new entity. The new entity will just contain the two keys of each of the pairs of many-to-many relationships in the previous diagram. Figure 5.6 shows these two one-to-many relationships.

PASSENGER   CRUISE

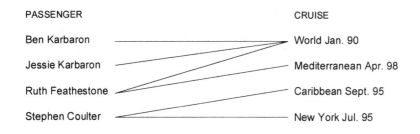

Ben Karbaron   World Jan. 90

Jessie Karbaron   Mediterranean Apr. 98

Ruth Feathestone   Caribbean Sept. 95

Stephen Coulter   New York Jul. 95

Figure 5.5   Many-to-many relationship between PASSENGER and CRUISE entities

The new BOOKING entity simply contains the combinations of passenger and cruise that were shown before by the relationships between the PASSENGER and CRUISE entities. Now, instead of each passenger having a direct relationship with the cruise he/she was booked on, the passenger has a direct relationship with their actual booking. This may seem the same as before, but only that passenger will have the relationship with that booking – no other passenger can. Therefore, this relationship is now a one-to-many relationship between PASSENGER (one) and BOOKING (many). In the same way, each cruise is related to the individual bookings for that cruise. Although a cruise may have several bookings, each booking is related to only the one cruise. This is also a one-to-many relationship between CRUISE (one) and BOOKING (many).

This approach, of breaking down a many-to-many relationship into two one-to-many relationships with a new entity in between, is the standard way to handle a many-to-many relationship.

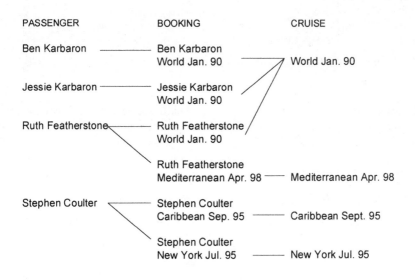

PASSENGER   BOOKING   CRUISE

Ben Karbaron   Ben Karbaron
                       World Jan. 90   World Jan. 90

Jessie Karbaron   Jessie Karbaron
                       World Jan. 90

Ruth Featherstone   Ruth Featherstone
                       World Jan. 90

                       Ruth Featherstone
                       Mediterranean Apr. 98   Mediterranean Apr. 98

Stephen Coulter   Stephen Coulter
                       Caribbean Sep. 95   Caribbean Sept. 95

                       Stephen Coulter
                       New York Jul. 95   New York Jul. 95

Figure 5.6   Two one-to-many relationships to replace the many-to-many relationship

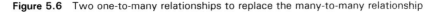

Entity-relationship modelling   57

5.3.4 Step 4 – Illustrate the Relationships in a Diagram

1. List the relationships in a table to show which is the *one* side of the relationship and which is the *many* side. Refer to Figure 5.7, which again concerns the **Hotel Reception** system.

Can exist without the other entity	One	Many	Can exist without the other entity
	CUSTOMER	BOOKING	
	CUSTOMER	BOOKING LOG	
	ROOM	BOOKING	
	ROOM	BOOKING LOG	
	BOOKING	BOOKING LOG	

Figure 5.7   Entity-relationship existence table

2. Consider both entities in each relationship carefully, to decide whether each entity can exist without the other.

   Ask the following two questions for each entity A–entity B (one-to-many) relationship. Write the answer to each question in the table:

   Could entity A (one) exist without entity B (many) existing?
   Could entity B (many) exist without entity A (one) existing?

   For example:

   Pair 1:   CUSTOMER and BOOKING

   Could the CUSTOMER exist without a BOOKING?   *no*

   Could the BOOKING exist without a CUSTOMER?   *no*

   In the current system, the only customer details stored are those written on the booking form. Therefore these cannot be a customer in the current system unless he/she has a booking.

   Pair 2:   CUSTOMER and BOOKING LOG

   Could the CUSTOMER exist without a BOOKING LOG?   *no*

   Could the BOOKING LOG exist without a CUSTOMER?   *yes*

   The booking log is basically just a diary with all Room Numbers listed for each day. Any bookings are then written in the log against the appropriate room for each day of the booking. Therefore, a booking log entry can exist with simply the date and room in it, and no booking and customer for that day.

Pair 3: ROOM and BOOKING

Could a ROOM exist without a BOOKING?	*yes*
Could a BOOKING exist without a ROOM?	*no*

Pair 4: ROOM and BOOKING LOG

Could a ROOM exist without a BOOKING LOG?	*no*
Could a BOOKING LOG exist without a ROOM?	*no*

In the same way that in the current system customer details are only recorded on the booking form when a booking is made, the room number and room details are only recorded on the booking log. Since no separate room details are held on the system currently, the room cannot exist without a written booking log entry for it.

Pair 5: BOOKING and BOOKING LOG

Could a BOOKING exist without a BOOKING LOG?	*no*
Could a BOOKING LOG exist without a BOOKING?	*yes*

A booking cannot exist without corresponding entries for the booked dates and room being made in the booking log, however, the booking log is already set up with dates and room numbers in, whether a booking is made against it or not.

Figure 5.8 shows the completed entity-relationship existence table.

Can exist without the other entity	*One*	*Many*	*Can exist without the other entity*
No	CUSTOMER	BOOKING	No
No	CUSTOMER	BOOKING LOG	Yes
Yes	ROOM	BOOKING	No
No	ROOM	BOOKING LOG	No
No	BOOKING	BOOKING LOG	Yes

Figure 5.8 Completed entity-relationship existence table

3. Draw entities as boxes in an initial entity-relationship diagram. Write the name of each entity in the centre of the box and space the boxes well apart on the diagram.

4. Draw a line between the entity boxes on the diagram to represent each relationship pair in the above table. Draw an arrow at the end of the line joining the *many* entity box. You may need to redraw the entity boxes so that the arrows point downwards or horizontally, but not upwards. Try not to cross the arrows. Refer to Figure 5.9.

Figure 5.9   Initial entity-relationship diagram

5. If an entity can exist without the other in its relationship, draw the half of the line joined to that entity as dotted, otherwise leave the line as solid.

Figure 5.10   Dotted line shows that the BOOKING LOG entity can exist without the CUSTOMER entity

6. Write a brief description at each end of the relationship line to describe the entity's relationship to the other. Refer to Figure 5.11.

Figure 5.11   Relationship descriptions

Refer to Figure 5.12 for the completed entity relationship diagram for the **Hotel Reception** System.

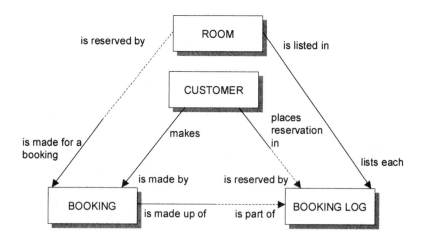

Figure 5.12   Completed entity-relationship diagram

5.3.5 Step 6 – Check for Connection Traps

Once the entity-relationship diagram is completed, although the three basic rules must have been obeyed there is still a chance that direct relationships between some entities could have been misinterpreted or omitted and therefore not added to the list of pairs of relationships.

Since all the tests for one-to-many relationships and the resulting diagram are based upon the originally selected pairings, any missing or incorrect pairings could cause problems when trying to obtain information from the database. When a problem does exist in the database, such that it is impossible to connect two logically related occurrences of two different entities together, this is called a **connection trap**.

In the **Hotel Reception** example above, there are no such traps, but the following example will illustrate such a trap. Consider this text:

"A university has three separate sites, each with over ten halls of residence. At each site, over a thousand students are registered."

If the two relationships HALL OF RESIDENCE/UNIVERSITY SITE and UNIVERSITY SITE–STUDENT were identified, the entity-relationship diagram shown in Figure 5.13 would have been drawn, obeying the three basic rules:

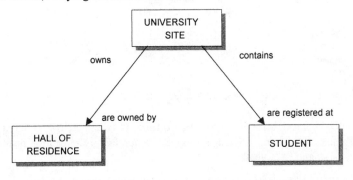

Figure 5.13 Entity-relationship diagram for example text

There is a connection trap in this model. Take the data extract shown in Figure 5.14 as an example. Although this database shows which student is at which site, and which halls of residence are at which site, it does not show us which students are in which hall of residence. This is a classic connection trap.

To untangle this diagram, the relationships between the three entities need to be re-examined. There are clearly relationships between the HALLS OF RESIDENCE and the UNIVERSITY SITE, and between the UNIVERSITY SITE and the STUDENT, but there is also a relationship between the HALL OF RESIDENCE and the STUDENT, which was overlooked before. Simply adding a one-to-many relationship between HALL OF RESIDENCE (one) and STUDENT (many) will not necessarily create the ideal model, as shown in Figure 5.15, since there may now be some unnecessary relationships in the diagram.

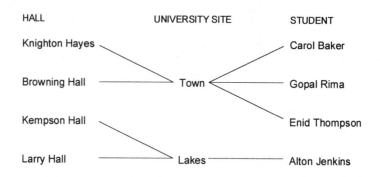

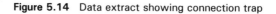

Figure 5.14 Data extract showing connection trap

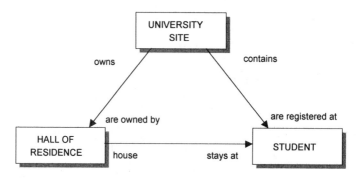

Figure 5.15 Extra relationship added between HALL OF RESIDENCE and STUDENT

Although with this model it will be possible to find out which STUDENT stays at which HALL OF RESIDENCE, there is also a possible redundant relationship now between UNIVERSITY SITE and STUDENT.

If all the STUDENTS registered to a SITE stay in one of the HALLS OF RESIDENCE on site, then the relationship between UNIVERSITY SITE and STUDENT is not required. This is because you can find the students who are registered to the SITE by first finding the HALLS OF RESIDENCE for the SITE, then finding the STUDENTS for those HALLS OF RESIDENCE. You can also find out which site a student is registered to by finding his/her Hall, then finding the SITE for that HALL OF RESIDENCE.

If, however, not all students stay at a HALL OF RESIDENCE, then the relationship between SITE and STUDENT must remain, or you would not be able to find out all STUDENTS registered to a UNIVERSITY SITE. In this case, the *stays at* end of the relationship arrow between HALL OF RESIDENCE and STUDENT would be dotted to show that a STUDENT can exist on the database without staying at a HALL OF RESIDENCE.

5.3.6 Step 7 – Re-distribute the Data to the completed Entities

In Step 1, initial lists of entities with their data and keys were drawn up. However, because of the entity-relationship modelling process, the list of entities may have changed. Although in the **Hotel Reception** example the entities have not been changed, a final list of the key items and non-key items for each entity is still put together.

Where a new entity is added, you will need to examine carefully the data in the original entities and remove those items of data that relate to the new entity, and place them in the new entity.

The completed list of entities is:

Entity	Key Items	Non-Key Items
CUSTOMER	Customer Name Customer Address	Telephone Number
ROOM	Room Number	Room Occupancy Price Per Night
BOOKING LOG	Booking Date Room Number	
BOOKING	Start Date End Date Room Number	Customer Name Total Price

Part II: Access Practical

5.4 Create a new database using Access

When you start Access, it will want to know whether you wish to open up an existing database or whether you want to create a new database. If you do want to create a *new* database, you will need to specify whether you wish to create it using your own designs, or whether you wish to use the Wizard tool to help you to create a new database based on some tables already set up in Access. If you want to open up an *existing* database, you will need to select one from the list provided.

Work through this practical session to create a new blank database, then create tables to represent the **Hotel Reception** database, detailed in Section 5.4, Step 7.

1. If there is a Microsoft Access icon on your main Windows screen, double-click it. If not, click the Start button on the task bar at the bottom of the Windows screen. Point the cursor arrow to where it says Programs and a list of available programs will be displayed. Click on Microsoft Access.

Microsoft Access

2. A dialogue box will appear: refer to Figure 5.16. In this chapter, you are going to create some tables in a blank database, so click against Blank Database and click the OK button.

Figure 5.16 Initial Access dialogue box

3. Another dialogue box will be displayed: refer to Figure 5.17. The new database has been given a default name of db1 in the default folder called My Documents on the C: disk.

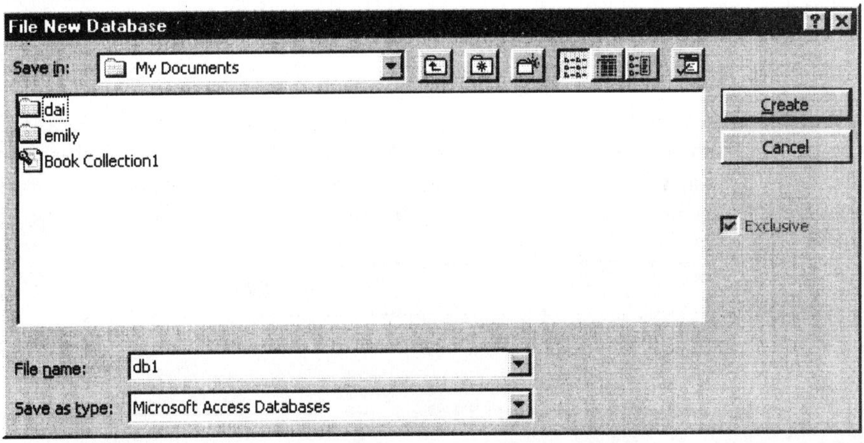

Figure 5.17 New database dialogue box

4. Select a new location for the database by clicking the 'up one level' icon repeatedly until the floppy disk icon appears in the large box under the **Save in** text. Click the floppy disk icon, then click the **Open** box. The floppy disk icon will appear in the box to the right of the text **Save in**.

5. Change the name of the file by clicking the mouse cursor at the end of the word db1 and using the backspace key to delete the text db1. Then type the text Hotel Reception and click the **Create** box. A dialogue box will be displayed. Refer to Figure 5.18.

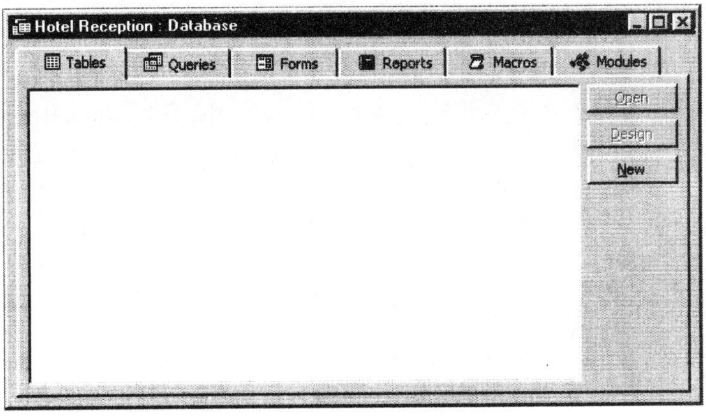

Figure 5.18 Database dialogue box for the new hotel reception database

5.5 Create a New Table using the Wizard, then amend it

A Wizard is a tool that helps you to create the various different parts that make up the database. When using a Wizard to create a table, you select one of the pre-defined tables stored on the computer as a base for your new table. You will be able to select the fields you wish to include in your new table from a list of sample fields.

If you are creating a type of table that is often used, such as for an Employee, Customer or Product, it is often much quicker to let the Wizard set up the initial table, and change it later to suit your own purposes. In this case, you are going to create a Customer table using a Wizard, based on the following table description:

Entity	Key Items	Non-Key Items
CUSTOMER	Customer Name	Telephone Number
	Customer Address	

1. Click the **New** box. The dialogue box shown in Figure 5.19 is displayed.

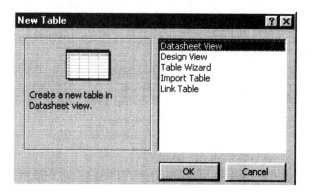

Figure 5.19 New Table dialogue box

2. Select **Table Wizard** (by clicking on it) then click the **OK** button. Refer to Figure 5.20.

3. Click on the down scroll arrow at the bottom right corner of the **Sample Tables** box to view the complete list of sample tables. Get back to the top of the list by dragging the grey square between the up and down scroll arrows as high as it will go. Since there is no Staff table, select **Customers**. Watch the list of **Sample Fields** in the centre of the dialogue box change to show sample fields for a **Customer** table.

Note that the **Sample Tables** displayed are for business-related applications. To see a list of tables for personal/home application,

click the white circle to the left of the word Personal on the dialogue box. In this case though, leave Business selected.

4. You will now need to select which fields you want in your new
    table. This is done by selecting a field in the Sample Fields list
    and clicking the single right arrow to place it in the Fields in my
    new table list. To remove a field from the Fields in my new ta-
    ble list, if you select the wrong field, simply select it and click the
    single left arrow.

Table Wizard

Which of the sample tables listed below do you want to use to create your table?

After selecting a sample table, choose the sample fields you want to include in your new table.
Your table can include fields from more than one sample table. If you're not sure about a field,
go ahead and include it. It's easy to delete a field later.

Sample Tables:

- Mailing List
- Contacts
- Customers
- Employees
- Products
- Orders
- Order Details

(• Business
(◦ Personal

Sample Fields:

- MailingListID
- Prefix
- FirstName
- MiddleName
- LastName
- Suffix
- Nickname
- Title
- OrganizationName
- Address

Fields in my new table:

Rename Field...

Cancel   < Back   Next >   Finish

Figure 5.20 Table wizard dialogue box

The double right arrow will move all the fields from the
Sample Fields list into the other list, and the double left
arrow will remove all the fields in the Fields in my new
table list.

Select the following fields as described above and add to the Fields in my new
table list as follows:

Customer ID   StateOrProvince
ContactFirstName   PostalCode
ContactLastName   Country
BillingAddress   ContactTitle
City   PhoneNumber

Note that the Customer ID field is not in the original CUSTOMER table description. This has been included since you cannot guarantee that each customer name

will be unique at a certain address. For example, in one family, there may well be two J. Browns. Therefore, in order to ensure that every row in that table has a unique key, the **primary key**, you can allow Access to create a key for you.

5. It is possible to change the names of the selected fields by selecting the field in the Fields in my new table list and then clicking the Rename Field button. You then type the new name in the box displayed on the screen and click the OK button. Rename City to become Town and rename StateOrProvince to become County. Click the Next button to continue. A dialogue box will be displayed, asking if you wish to rename the table and whether or not you wish the primary key to be automatically chosen by Access.

6. Although in this case you are going to leave the table name as Customers, if you had wanted to rename it, you would simply type over the name Customers with the new name. Since the fields you have selected include the unique CustomerID field, it is safe to let the Wizard select the key. The Wizard will select the CustomerID field as the key. Click the Next button and the last dialogue box will be displayed.

7. Click against the Modify the Table Design text, since you need to make some amendments before you can enter any data into the table. Click the Finish button. The initial table will be displayed. Refer to Figure 5.21.

▦ Customers : Table	
Field Name	**Data Type**
🔑 CustomerID	AutoNumber
ContactFirstName	Text
ContactLastName	Text
BillingAddress	Text
Town	Text
County	Text
PostalCode	Text
Country	Text
ContactTitle	Text
PhoneNumber	Text

Figure 5.21 Initial CUSTOMERS table design

8. Click on the County field name. If the Caption field in the Field Properties list at the bottom of the screen contains State/Province, delete that text.

9. Click on the PhoneNumber field and if the Input Mask field in the Field Properties list at the bottom of the screen contains any text, for example \(9999″) "00090009, delete it. The input mask can be very useful for a ensuring that a standard field such as postcode (or zip code) is always entered in the same format, but telephone number formats vary and it is better not to restrict yourself by trying to use a mask. In the same way, remove the input mask for the PostalCode field.

10. Click the **Save** icon on the tool bar, then click the **Close** icon on the top right of the table's window (make sure you don't click the **Close** icon at the top right of the screen, or you'll close down Access!). You will return to the main database screen.

5.6 Create a new table without using the Wizard

Create the remaining three tables in the **Hotel Reception** database, without using a Wizard, as follows. Create the BOOKING LOG first, based on the following table description:

Entity	Key Items	Non-Key Items
BOOKING LOG	Booking Date	Customer Name
	Room Number	

1. Click **New** on the main database dialogue box. The **New Table** dialogue box will appear as before (in Figure 5.19). This time however, select **Design View** and click the **OK** box. An empty table will be displayed.

2. Type `Booking Date` into the first empty box in the **Field Name** column and use the Tab key on the keyboard to move to the corresponding box in the **Data Type** column.

3. The default data type is **Text** but, you will need to change it. Click on the down scroll arrow that appears and select the **Date/Time** data type.

4. Press the Tab key twice to get to the next empty **Field Name** box. Type `Room Number`. Again, you will need to select a new **Data Type**, other than **Text**. As before, click the down scroll arrow and select **Number**.

5. Instead of calling the third field **Customer Name** as suggested in Section 5.4, as we have already established that a customer cannot be uniquely identified by his/her customer name and address, type the field name `CustomerID` instead. Since this Customer ID will correspond to the Customer IDs in the Customer table, you must not define it as data type **AutoNumber**. If you do this, each new Booking Log will automatically be given a new Customer ID. The automatically generated Customer ID in the **Customers** table will be a **Data Type** of **Number** (**Long Integer**, to be exact). You therefore need to set the **Data Type** of Customer ID in the Booking Log table to **Number**.

6. In this table, there are two fields that make up the key. To select the two fields together, select the **Booking Date** row by clicking on the grey box to the left of the text **Booking Date**, then hold the Ctrl key down on the keyboard. Keep the Ctrl key held down whilst you click on the grey box to the left of the text **Room Number**. Both rows should be highlighted. You can now

release the Ctrl button. Click the **Primary Key** icon on the tool bar as before and a key picture should appear to the left of each of these two fields.

7. To insert a row into a table, click on the row *below* where you want the new row to appear. In this case, you are going to create a superfluous row above the **Customer ID** row. Click anywhere on the **Customer ID** row and click the **Insert Rows** icon on the tool bar. An empty row will appear. Type the field name `Superfluous` and click on the row below to get the **Data Type** of **Text** to appear.

8. Since this **Superfluous** row has only been inserted to practise inserting and deleting rows, delete the row now by clicking anywhere on it and then clicking the **Delete Rows** icon on the tool bar.

9. Save the new table by clicking the **Save** icon on the tool bar. You will be invited to enter a new table name for the table. Type `Booking Log` and click the **OK** box. Refer to Figure 5.22.

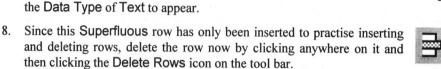

Field Name	Data Type
Booking Date	Date/Time
Room Number	Number
CustomerID	Number

Figure 5.22 BOOKING LOG table

10. Close the table design by clicking the **Close** icon at the top right corner of the table design window (not the screen).

11. Follow the same procedures to create the third and fourth new tables, BOOKING and ROOM respectively, as shown in Figure 5.23. Close all table windows.

⊞ Booking : Table

Field Name	Data Type
Start Date	Date/Time
End Date	Date/Time
Room Number	Number
CustomerID	Number

⊞ Room : Table

Field Name	Data Type
Room Number	Number
Room Occupancy	Number
Price Per Night	Currency

Figure 5.23 Completed BOOKING and ROOM tables

5.7 Data Integrity

One of the main features of a database such as Access, is that key data, such as Room Number and Customer ID, are often stored in two or more tables, linking the tables together. In this way, the BOOKING record only needs to contain the Room Number, and you can find the appropriate room details in the ROOM table by using the same Room Number as provided in the BOOKING. One advantage of this is that you save space, since you do not need to store the Price Per Night and Occupancy in each booking – you only need to store it once for the Room Number.

Another advantage not referred to so far is that once the tables have been related together, the database can check whether you are entering non-existent or erroneous data. For example, in the hotel reception system, once the relationships have been set up to link the tables, there will be a one-to-many relationship between ROOM (one) and BOOKING LOG (many). The database would not allow you to set up an entry in the BOOKING LOG for a room that does not exist in the ROOM table. In our example, we have the three rooms 1, 2 and 3. If we set these up in the ROOM table and then tried to create a BOOKING LOG entry for room 4, an error message would be displayed.

As well as prohibiting the creation of records linked to non-existent fields in other tables, you can set up the database to stop you deleting an entry that is linked to another table. For example, if you had a BOOKING LOG entry for Room 1, you would not be permitted to delete the entry for Room 1 in the ROOM table.

This ability of a database to check that related table entries are never left in a state where one of the two related records is missing is called **data integrity**. This is very important, since the database could come to an abrupt halt if it tried to find room details for a room recorded in the BOOKING LOG that never existed or has been deleted from the ROOM table.

Data integrity can only exist if the relationships between the tables have been set up. Without these, the database does not know what to check against. In a database, there are two main types of data:

- **Working data** – data that records the main functions of the system you have computerised. In other words, it is the data that is entered into your system, is then stored, maybe processed, included in various reports, calculations etc, and then is finally archived or deleted. This type of data has a finite lifespan and lasts as long as the event you are recording information about. It forms the main bulk of the data in you database. In our hotel reception database, the working data tables would be the BOOKING LOG table, the BOOKING TABLE and the CUSTOMER table.

- **System data** – data that is used to provide basic information upon which the system is based. This data changes infrequently and is stored for the life of the system. In the hotel reception example, the system data is the ROOM table. This table will only change when a new room is added, room occupancy is changed or when the room prices are changed.

In order to ensure the integrity of your database, it is important that none of the data is set up until the relationships between the tables have been created. Without the relationships between the tables, the data integrity checks cannot be performed on the data and the database could therefore include erroneous data, such as a room in a BOOKING that does not exist in the ROOM table. Remember that erroneous data can cause the database system to stop or **crash**.

5.8   Close a Database and Access

1. Close the database by clicking the Close icon at the top right corner of the Hotel Reception database window.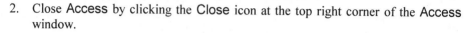

2. Close Access by clicking the Close icon at the top right corner of the Access window.

5.9   Summary

This chapter has covered the following material:

Part I: Database Theory

*   Description of what a database is and how it is constructed.
*   Introduction to entity-relationship modelling as a technique for analysing the relationships between the items and events used in the current system.
*   Step-by-step guide to carrying out entity-relationship modelling, using the hotel reception system as an example.

Part II: Access Practical

*   Creating a new database.
*   Creating a new table using a Wizard.
*   Creating a new table without using a Wizard.
*   Description of data integrity.

5.10   Written Exercises

5.10.1   Describe the three fundamental rules that must be obeyed when grouping the information into entities, giving an example for each.

5.10.2   The two entities DRIVER and CAR have been identified to contain information about the drivers and cars in a **Rally** team. In any one race, a driver can race in two or more cars, and a car can be driven by more than one driver.

(a) What type of relationship is this?
(b) Illustrate this relationship with some sample data.
(c) How can this relationship be represented on the database? Illustrate your solution with the same sample data.

5.10.3 The **Painting and Decorating** company system referred to previously uses three folders: Quotes Folder, Jobs Folder and Orders Folder. The information contained in each folder is as follows:

Quotes Folder	Jobs Folder	Orders Folder
Quote Reference	Quote Reference	Item Code
Customer Name	Customer Name	Item Description
Customer Address	Customer Address	Order date
Work Description	Quotation Date	Quantity
Quotation Date	Quotation Value	Total Price
Quotation Value	Agreed Work Date	Quote Reference
Agreed Work Date	Completed Date	Supplier Name
	Final Price	Supplier Address
	Customer Paid Date	Actual Delivery Date
	Outstanding Balance	

(a) Follow step 1 of the "Step-by-step guide to entity-relationship modelling" to group the information listed above into entity groups. Two of those are QUOTE and JOB. Identify the others and show how the data can be split up among the entities.

(b) Complete step 1 to identify the relationships between the entities.

(c) The two entities QUOTE and JOB have an unusual relationship. What is it? Discuss the different ways in which such a relationship can be handled and the merits of each approach.

(d) In this particular case, the two entities should be combined into one entity called JOB. Referring back to the text in written exercise 3 in Chapter 4, suggest why this approach was taken.

(e) Complete steps 4–7 to show the redistributed list of data for each entity, indicating the primary key for each and drawing the entity-relationship diagram.

5.11 Practical exercises

5.11.1 Create a new database called University Department. Create three tables, as follows.

(a) Create a Staff table to contain the same fields as shown in Figure 5.2, using the Employee Wizard as a base and adding and amending fields as described next.

Select the following fields from the **Employee** Wizard sample fields:

EmployeeID	Address
FirstName	City
LastName	StateOrProvince
Title	PostalCode

- Rename **EmployeeID** to become **StaffID**, rename **City** to become **Town** and rename **StateOrProvince** to become **County**.

- Rename the table to call it **Staff** and let the Wizard select the key, in this case, the renamed **StaffID** field.

- Modify the table design to add three new fields: **Salary Grade**, **Holiday Ent** and **Remain Hol**, all with a **Data Type** of **Number**.

- Change the **Data Type** of the **StaffID** field from AutoNumber to Text.

(b) Create two more tables, without using a Wizard, as follows:

Course

Field Name	Data Type	
Course Code	Text	◄————— Primary Key
Course Title	Text	
Course Summary	Text	

Timetable

Field Name	Data Type	
Day	Text	◄——— ⎰ Primary
Time	Date/Time	◄——— ⎱ Key
Location	Text	
Course Code	Text	
Session Type	Text	
Staff ID	Text	

5.11.2   Create a new database called **Rally**. Create the tables described in the 5.10.2 without using a Wizard. Add some suitable fields to each table.

5.11.3   Create a new database called **Painting** and create four tables to represent the four entities described in part (e) of 5.10.3. Use the Wizard where appropriate.

6 Grouping the Information – Normalisation

6.1 Introduction

In the previous chapter, a method of database design called entity-relationship modelling was described, enabling you to produce initial table and relationship designs. In this chapter, a second method of database design is described, normalisation. When carried out on the same system, these methods will produce similar diagrams to represent tables and the relationships between them.

Although in practice it may appear quicker to carry out only one of the two techniques referred to, because the two approaches use different methods to group and separate the data into tables, by using both methods it is possible to check whether you have omitted any relationships in one of the designs and to avoid splitting up a table into two where there are repeating items of data. This not only improves the quality of the database, but also saves time – it takes considerably less effort to add an extra table or relationship now than later on in the development when queries, screens, reports and data have been created.

In Part I of this chapter, the **normalisation** technique is described. This structured method of designing database tables uses a series of standard steps and rules to group the information. This method requires samples of data to be written down in a series of tables. Gradually these tables are divided and then merged into other tables as the steps and rules are applied. Each major step will leave the tables in a recognised state, called **normal form**. The first major series of steps will leave the tables in *first normal form*, the second series will leave the tables in *second normal form* and the third series of steps will leave the tables in *third normal form*. These tables are then combined where possible to produce the final set of tables, which will be basis for the database. A diagram similar to an entity-relationship diagram can then be drawn showing the relationships between the tables.

Once both the entity-relationship and normalisation techniques have been carried out, it is important to compare the two database designs and examine any differences. This will enable you to arrive at a final database design to reflect your current system.

Part II of this chapter will enable you to enhance your database designs using Access by adding the relationships between the tables. Work through the session, following the step-by-step instructions provided to create, delete and view table relationships.

Part I: Database Design Theory

6.2   Normalise the Information

The following steps should carried out to create normalised database table designs from the information stored in the current system.

1.   List the information used in each document or data group in the current system – these are called the **data names**.

2.   Create a table for each document or data group in the current system, with a column for each of the data names in that document. A reasonable cross-section of each type of document should be selected and the 'real' information from each of these documents should be added to the appropriate table.

3.   Remove any columns where the information is given more than once for several rows and place them in new tables. This is **first normal form**.

4.   Identify a **key** for each table. The key is a column or columns that make each row unique.

5.   Where a table has a key made up of two or more columns, remove any non-key columns of information that are dependent on only part of the key, not all of it. Place these in new tables. This is **second normal form**.

6.   Merge any newly created tables that are duplicates of other newly created tables.

7.   Remove any columns of information that are dependent on other non-key columns in the table and place them in new tables. This is **third normal form**.

8.   Merge any newly created tables that are duplicates of other newly created tables.

9.   Combine tables that have the same key columns and delete any columns containing duplicated information. This is called **rationalisation**.

This normalisation technique for grouping data to design the database tables and relationships is illustrated using the **Hotel Receptionist** system example in each of the nine steps.

6.2.1 Step 1 – List the Data Names

1.   List all the information provided on each document or group of information in the system. This information can be found in the data stores, input and output columns in input/output tables, prepared in the previous chapter. Otherwise, they can be found on the documents or other any other information receptacle in your system. For example, a manager may remember all the customers' names and addresses, rather than keep them on file. This is still information that is stored in the system.

2. Keep it logical – don't refer to physical terms such as 'photocopy'. You may decide to leave out certain items, such as the company's own name and address.

3. Give data meaningful names in their own right, e.g. not just the word 'Date', but 'Booking Date', 'Start Date' or 'End Date'. These can be abbreviated later if required. Dates and names are especially prone to confusion and must be carefully labelled. In our example, the BOOKING LOG and the BOOKING FORM both contain prices, but, the BOOKING LOG price is for one night, and the BOOKING FORM price is for the duration of the stay. It is important that they be labelled with different names.

4. The sequence in which the data is added to the list of information is not important. You may have a document such that some of the information is added at the start of the system process, and another piece of information is added at a much later stage. This later item of data must still be included in the list of information.

For example:

Document	Name
BOOKING LOG	Booking Date
	Room Number
	Room Occupancy
	Price Per Night
	Customer Name
BOOKING FORM	Customer Name
	Customer Address
	Customer Telephone Number
	Start Date
	End Date
	Room Number
	Occupancy
	Total Price

6.2.2 Step 2 – Set up a Table with Data

Carry out the following actions for each document in the list obtained in step 1:

1. Draw up a table, with each column headed by an item in the list. The item names can be abbreviated.

2. Keep the columns representing data that can be listed more than once on the document to the right hand side of the table. In the **Hotel Reception** example, the BOOKING LOG would contain several Room Numbers for each Date. The Room Number column would therefore be written on the right of the table, with the Date column on the left.

3. Obtain at least three examples of each type of document or information group used in the workplace. Select documents that represent a good cross-section of ways in which each document can be used.

4. Fill in the table with the data from the selected documents. Remember to write all dates with the year including the century, i.e. 2000 or 2001, not 99 or 01.

5. In some documents in which the data is added to the table in rows, some of the data will change for each row, whilst other parts of the data will be the same for each row. For example, the BOOKING LOG may have three Rooms listed against one Date. In the table, you will show three rows for this; the first row will show both the Date and the Room Number. The second and third rows for that date will contain only the different Room Numbers, but instead of the Date, a double quote will be used to indicate a repeat of information.

6. Draw a thick line under the last row written in the table for each document, even if there is only one row for each document. For example, a thick line will be drawn under the room 3 row for each day in the BOOKING LOG (Figure 6.1) and under the second row for the Mills Construction BOOKING FORM (Figure 6.2).

Booking Date	Room No.	Room Occ.	Price Per night	Customer Name
16/3/2000	1	2	£60	
"	2	4	£73	Katie Rubek
"	3	2	£60	Martin Walsh
17/3/2000	1	2	£60	Gina London
"	2	4	£73	
"	3	2	£60	Martin Walsh
18/3/2000	1	2	£60	Mills Construction Ltd
"	2	4	£73	
"	3	2	£60	Mills Construction Ltd
19/3/2000	1	2	£60	Mills Construction Ltd
"	2	4	£73	Katie Rubek
"	3	2	£60	Mills Construction Ltd

Figure 6.1 Initial BOOKING LOG data

6.2.3 Step 3 – Remove Repeating Groups and place them in their own Tables (First Normal Form)

Carry out the following actions for each table in turn:

1. Look at each section of rows within a table marked by a thick underline. These rows represent one document. For example, look at the first three rows in the BOOKING LOG table representing the log for date 16/3/2000.

2. If there is more than one column that contains information that is repeated within a document, indicated by double quotes, create a new table with those repeated columns. For example, in the BOOKING FORM, the first three columns can be repeated – refer to the Mills Construction Ltd rows. A new table will be created containing just those three columns. Note that the BOOKING LOG has only one repeating column, Date, and therefore, does not need to have any columns removed. Refer to Figures 6.3 and 6.4 for an example of repeated group extraction.

Start Date	End Date	Rm No.	Rm Occ.	Tot Price	Customer Name	Customer Address	Cust. Tel No.
16/3/2000	16/3/2000	2	4	£73	Miss Katie Rubek	15 Dandow Close, Pelton, Bucks, MK16 5DS	01495-649735
16/3/2000	17/3/2000	3	2	£120	Mr Martin Walsh	Flat 23B, Barrow Heights, Cambridge	01563-862645
17/3/2000	17/3/2000	1	2	£60	Mrs Gina London	Crumbly Cottage, Brook Lane, Puddlecombe, Herts, AL3 6GH	01707-568134
18/3/2000	19/3/2000	1	2	£120	Mills Construc-tion Ltd	Location 15F, Station Ind. Estate, Clapham, London	0181-451895
18/3/2000	19/3/2000	3	2	£120	"	"	"
19/3/2000	19/3/2000	2	4	£73	Miss Katie Rubek	15 Dandow Close, Pelton, Bucks, MK16 5DS	01495-649735

Figure 6.2 Initial BOOKING FORM data

Start Date	End Date	Rm No.	Rm Occ.	Tot Price	Customer Name	Customer Address	Cust. Tel No.
16/3/2000	16/3/2000	2	4	£73	Miss Katie Rubek	15 Dandow Close, Pelton, Bucks, MK16 5DS	01495-649735
16/3/2000	17/3/2000	3	2	£120	Mr Martin Walsh	Flat 23B, Barrow Heights, Cambridge	01563-862645
17/3/2000	17/3/2000	1	2	£60	Mrs Gina London	Crumbly Cottage, Brook Lane, Puddlecombe, Herts, AL3 6GH	01707-568134
18/3/2000	19/3/2000	1	2	£120	Mills Construc-tion Ltd	Location 15F, Station Ind. Estate, Clapham, London	0181-451895
18/3/2000	19/3/2000	3	2	£120	"	"	"
19/3/2000	19/3/2000	2	4	£73	Miss Katie Rubek	15 Dandow Close, Pelton, Bucks, MK16 5DS	01495-649735

Figure 6.3 Initial BOOKING FORM data, with repeated groups shaded

Grouping the information – Normalisation   79

The shaded columns represent the columns containing repeated data, which are copied into a new table.

Customer Name	Customer Address	Cust. Tel. No.
Miss Katie Rubek	15 Dandow Close, Pelton, Bucks, MK16 5DS	01495-649735
Mr Martin Walsh	Flat 23B, Barrow Heights, Cambridge	01563-862645
Mrs Gina London	Crumbly Cottage, Brook Lane, Puddlecombe, Herts, AL3 6GH	01707-568134
Mills Construction Ltd	Location 15F, Station Ind. Estate, Clapham, London	0181-451895
,,	,,	,,
Miss Katie Rubek	15 Dandow Close, Pelton, Bucks, MK16 5DS	01495-649735

Figure 6.4 Extracted Customer columns from BOOKING FORM table

3. In the original table, delete the repeating columns that have been set up in the new table, but make sure you leave one or more key columns to identify each row and to tie together the remaining information with the new table. In the case of the BOOKING FORM, the Customer Name column should be left in the BOOKING FORM table. The other two columns, Customer Address and Customer Telephone Number should be removed. The Customer Name column in the BOOKING FORM will identify each row and will tie together the BOOKING FORM table and the newly created table, since they will both have the same first column, Customer Name.

4. Once the tables have all been examined and any repeating groups removed, replace any quotes with the actual text that is being repeated. This should exist only in the remaining key columns. For example, in the BOOKING FORM the quotes representing the Customer Name for the second Mills Construction Ltd row, should be replaced by the actual Customer Name, Mills Construction Ltd, and in the BOOKING LOG, all the repeated Booking Dates should be shown, instead of double quotes.

5. Remove all thick underlines from the original table. These were only used to help to identify the repeating groups.

For example:

Start Date	End Date	Room No.	Room Occ.	Total Price	Customer Name
16/3/2000	16/3/2000	2	4	£73	Miss Katie Rubek
16/3/2000	17/3/2000	3	2	£120	Mr Martin Walsh
17/3/2000	17/3/2000	1	2	£60	Mrs Gina London
18/3/2000	19/3/2000	1	2	£120	Mills Construction Ltd
18/3/2000	19/3/2000	3	2	£120	Mills Construction Ltd
19/3/2000	19/3/2000	2	4	£73	Miss Katie Rubek

Figure 6.5 Amended BOOKING FORM table, without the Customer Address and Customer Telephone Number columns

The Customer Address and Customer Telephone Number columns have been removed and the Customer Name column has been updated to replace all double quotes with the repeated names. The thick lines denoting the end of a document have been removed. Refer to Figure 6.5.

The double quotes representing repeated Booking dates are replaced by the actual Booking Date in each row. The thick line separating the dates have been removed. Refer to Figure 6.6.

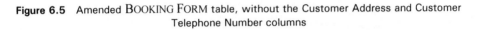

Booking Date	Room No.	Room Occ.	Price Per Night	Customer Name
16/3/2000	1	2	£60	
16/3/2000	2	4	£73	Miss Katie Rubek
16/3/2000	3	2	£60	Mr Martin Walsh
17/3/2000	1	2	£60	Mrs Gina London
17/3/2000	2	4	£73	
17/3/2000	3	2	£60	Mr Martin Walsh
18/3/2000	1	2	£60	Mills Construction Ltd
18/3/2000	2	4	£73	
18/3/2000	3	2	£60	Mills Construction Ltd
19/3/2000	1	2	£60	Mills Construction Ltd
19/3/2000	2	4	£73	Miss Katie Rubek
19/3/2000	3	2	£60	Mills Construction Ltd

Figure 6.6 Amended BOOKING LOG table, quotes replaced and thick lines removed

6. The newly created table will need a descriptive name and the old table will probably need renaming to reflect the remaining data. In this example, the new table containing the customer details will be called the CUSTOMER DETAILS table. The BOOKING FORM table will keep that name.

7. The rows in the new table may well contain several duplicated rows. In this example, there are two rows for Katie Rubek and two rows for Mills Construction Ltd. Remove the duplicated rows.

8. If there are any rows where the key column information is the same, such as the Customer Name, but other information such as the Customer Address is different,

you need to check your sources to investigate further. If the difference is an error, delete the erroneous row; if it is correct, and there are two customers with the same name, you will need to add a key column in the next step.

For example, see Figure 6.7, in which the duplicate Katie Rubek and Mills Construction Ltd rows have been deleted.

Customer Name	Customer Address	Customer Tel No.
Miss Katie Rubek	15 Dandow Close, Pelton, Bucks, MK16 5DS	01495-649735
Mr Martin Walsh	Flat 23B, Barrow Heights, Cambridge	01563-862645
Mrs Gina London	Crumbly Cottage, Brook Lane, Puddlecombe, Herts, AL3 6GH	01707-568134
Mills Construction Ltd	Location 15F, Station Ind. Estate, Clapham, London.	0181-451895

Figure 6.7 Updated CUSTOMER DETAILS table

6.2.4 Step 4 - Identify a Key in each Table

Carry out the following for each table:

1. Ideally, each row in a table should be identified by a unique key. In some tables, the unique key can be one value alone, such as the Customer Name in the CUSTOMER DETAILS table. In other tables one column is not sufficient to identify a row. For example, in the BOOKING LOG, a Booking Date of 16/3/2000 will identify three rows. To identify an individual row, the Room Number also needs to be added to the key. The key columns in the Booking Log table will therefore be the Booking Date and the Room Number.

2. In some cases where the key column is currently a textual item, such as a name or address, a unique key will need to be added, to help ensure that a row is unique. For example, in the CUSTOMER DETAILS table, the key column is the Customer Name. Although in our sample documents, the Customer Name is unique for each booking, there might be an instance where there are two bookings for a Mr P. Garner. The addresses may even be the same for the same name. The key column must be different for each customer to enable the bookings to be identified for each Mr P. Garner. When this case arises, one solution is to add new column to the left of the table with a unique code, such as Customer Code. This code will become the key for the table *instead of* Customer Number. Where the original 'unique' key column, in our example, the Customer Name column, is used in other tables, such as the Booking Log, you will need to replace it with the new key column, Customer Code.

3. The column(s) representing the key in each table are identified by underlining the column heading. It is also clearer if the key column(s) is/are the left-most column(s) in the table.

4. Where a non-key column in a table has the same column heading as a key column in another table, the non-key column must be labelled as a **foreign key**, by adding an asterisk suffix. For example the Customer Code column in the BOOKING LOG table is a foreign key, and is marked with an asterisk.

For example in Figure 6.8, a new key column is added, Customer Code, and the column is identified as a key column by the use of underline. The Booking Date and Room Number columns together are the key columns required identifying each row. The Customer Name column has been replaced with the Customer Code column. Since this column is a key in another table, a foreign key, an asterisk is added after the column name to indicate this. Refer to Figure 6.9.

Customer Code	Customer Name	Customer Address	Customer Tel No.
0012	Miss Katie Rubek	15 Dandow Close, Pelton, Bucks, MK16 5DS	01495-649735
0013	Mr Martin Walsh	Flat 23B, Barrow Heights, Cambridge	01563-862645
0014	Mrs Gina London	Crumbly Cottage, Brook Lane, Puddlecombe, Herts, AL3 6GH	01707-568134
0015	Mills Construction Ltd	Location 15F, Station Ind. Estate, Clapham, London.	0181-451895

Figure 6.8   Amended CUSTOMER DETAILS table with Customer Code key

Booking Date	Room Number	Room Occ.	Price	Customer Code*
16/3/2000	1	2	£60	
16/3/2000	2	4	£73	0012
16/3/2000	3	2	£60	0013
17/3/2000	1	2	£60	0014
17/3/2000	2	4	£73	
17/3/2000	3	2	£60	0013
18/3/2000	1	2	£60	0015
18/3/2000	2	4	£73	
18/3/2000	3	2	£60	0015
19/3/2000	1	2	£60	0015
19/3/2000	2	4	£73	0012
19/3/2000	3	2	£60	0015

Figure 6.9   Amended BOOKING LOG table

The Customer Name column is replaced with the new Customer Details key, Customer Code. Since this column is a key in another table, an asterisk is added after the column name to indicate this. Referring to the two rows for customer 0015 (Mills Construction Ltd), it is not possible to identify either of those two rows using just the Start and End Dates alone. The Room Number must also become part of the key. Refer to Figure 6.10. The tables are now in **first normal form**.

Start Date	End Date	Room No.	Room Occ.	Total Price	Customer Code*
16/3/2000	16/3/2000	2	4	£73	0012
16/3/2000	17/3/2000	3	2	£120	0013
17/3/2000	17/3/2000	1	2	£60	0014
18/3/2000	19/3/2000	1	2	£120	0015
18/3/2000	19/3/2000	3	2	£120	0015
19/3/2000	19/3/2000	2	4	£73	0012

Figure 6.10 Amended BOOKING FORM table, containing the Customer Code foreign key

6.2.5 Step 5 – Remove any Part-Key dependencies and place in their own Tables (Second Normal Form)

In any table, each row should ideally have a unique key made from one or more column values. Every column in that table should then be dependent on all parts of that key. For example, in the BOOKING LOG table, the Customer Code value is dependent not only on the Booking Date, but also on the Room Number too. This makes sense, since the customer does not simply book a date at the hotel, he/she also books a room, and in the same way, cannot just book a room, but also needs to book a date. Therefore, both parts of the key are required.

There may be, however, some non-key columns that are not dependent on all the key columns. The Room Occupancy and Price Per Night columns in the Booking Log table, for example, are only dependent on the Room Number part of the key, not on the Booking Date. Whatever the data is, the Room Occupancy and Price Per Night will always be the same for the each Room Number. This hotel always charges the same price for the same room occupancy, regardless of location or season. In this way, you can say that the Room Occupancy and Price Per Night are not dependent on the whole key, but only on part of it. These two columns in the BOOKING LOG table therefore contain a lot of repeated information. This is wasting storage space, and it would make more sense if this information were in table of its own.

A new table must be created containing the non-key column(s) from the original table that is dependent on only part of the key. Add the key column(s) it is dependent on to the left of the new table, and make that the key column of the new table. Finally, remove the non-key column from the original table. In the **Hotel Reception** example, a new table is created containing three columns: Room Number, Room Occupancy and Price Per Night. The Room Number column is the key column. The Room Occupancy and Price Per Night columns are then removed from the original table.

In our example, the BOOKING FORM also contains the Room Occupancy column that is dependent only on part of the key, the Room Number column. In the same way as above, the Occupancy column is removed and placed in a new table, along with a copy of the Room Number column as a key column. This new table does not contain the Price Per Night column, and is therefore a different table at this stage. It is given a different name, ROOM OCCUPANCY DETAILS.

Note that if a table has three or more key columns, any non-key column dependent on any groups of key columns other than the whole set of key columns is treated as described above.

Carry out the following for each table where there is more than one key column:

1. Examine each non-key column in the table to see whether any of these columns are dependent on only part of the key. The Room Occupancy and Price Per Night columns in the BOOKING LOG table are one example.

2. If a column is found to be dependent on only part of the key, remove that column and place it in a new table, along with a copy of the column(s) from the original table holding the part of the key the removed column was dependent on. The copied key column(s) will then become the key to the new table. Give the new table a suitable name.

For example, in the BOOKING LOG table shown in Figures 6.11 and 6.12, the Room Occupancy and Price Per Night columns are removed and a new table is created with the first column called Room Number. This will be the key, and the second and third columns will be Room Occupancy and Price Per Night respectively. The new table will be called the ROOM DETAILS table. Refer to Figure 6.13.

For example, in Figure 6.11, the shaded column shows the Room Occupancy and Price Per Night columns which are removed and placed in a new table. A copy of the Room Number column is added to the new table as the key. In Figure 6.12, Room Occupancy and Price Per Night columns have been removed.

3. For each new table, remove any rows with the same key as another row in the same table. The information in the two duplicate key rows should be the same. Don't worry too much at this stage if it is different, since this is only test data to help you to design the database tables. Later, however, you will need to check the data thoroughly. Refer to Figures 6.13 and 6.14.

Booking Date	Room Number	Room Occ.	Price Per Night	Customer Code*
16/3/2000	1	2	£60	
16/3/2000	2	4	£73	0012
16/3/2000	3	2	£60	0013
17/3/2000	1	2	£60	0014
17/3/2000	2	4	£73	
17/3/2000	3	2	£60	0013
18/3/2000	1	2	£60	0015
18/3/2000	2	4	£73	
18/3/2000	3	2	£60	0015
19/3/2000	1	2	£60	0015
19/3/2000	2	4	£73	0012
19/3/2000	3	2	£60	0015

Figure 6.11 BOOKING LOG tables with shaded non-key dependent columns

Grouping the information – Normalisation 85

Booking Date	Room Number	Customer Code*
16/3/2000	1	
16/3/2000	2	0012
16/3/2000	3	0013
17/3/2000	1	0014
17/3/2000	2	
17/3/2000	3	0013
18/3/2000	1	0015
18/3/2000	2	
18/3/2000	3	0015
19/3/2000	1	0015
19/3/2000	2	0012
19/3/2000	3	0015

Figure 6.12 Amended BOOKING LOG table, with Room Occupancy and Price Per Night columns removed

The columns removed from the BOOKING LOG, as well as a copy of the Room Number column, have been used to create this new table. The shaded rows are duplicates, with the same key values as the white rows. Refer to Figure 6.13.

In Figure 6.14, the duplicate rows have been deleted. In Figure 6.15, the shaded column shows the Room Occupancy column that is removed and placed in a new table. A copy of the Room Number column is added to the new table as the key.

In Figure 6.16, the Room Occupancy column has been removed. The shaded columns from the BOOKING FORM have been removed and, along with a copy of the Room Number column, have been used to create this table. In Figure 6.17, the shaded rows are duplicates, with the same key values as the white rows. In Figure 6.18, the duplicate rows have been removed. The tables are now in **second normal form**.

Room Number	Room Occ.	Price Per Night
1	2	£60
2	4	£73
3	2	£60
1	2	£60
2	4	£73
3	2	£60
1	2	£60
2	4	£73
3	2	£60
1	2	£60
2	4	£73
3	2	£60

Figure 6.13 ROOM DETAILS table – shaded rows show duplicates

Room Number	Room Occ.	Price Per Night
1	2	£60
2	4	£73
3	2	£60

Figure 6.14 ROOM DETAILS table after duplicate rows have been removed

Start Date	End Date	Room No.	Room Occ.	Total Price	Customer Code*
16/3/2000	16/3/2000	2	4	£73	0012
16/3/2000	17/3/2000	3	2	£120	0013
17/3/2000	17/3/2000	1	2	£60	0014
18/3/2000	19/3/2000	1	2	£120	0015
18/3/2000	19/3/2000	3	2	£120	0015
19/3/2000	19/3/2000	2	4	£73	0012

Figure 6.15 BOOKING FORM table, with shaded column dependent on part-key

Start Date	End Date	Room No.	Total Price	Customer Code*
16/3/2000	16/3/2000	2	£73	0012
16/3/2000	17/3/2000	3	£120	0013
17/3/2000	17/3/2000	1	£60	0014
18/3/2000	19/3/2000	1	£120	0015
18/3/2000	19/3/2000	3	£120	0015
19/3/2000	19/3/2000	2	£73	0012

Figure 6.16 Amended BOOKING FORM table, with the part-key dependent column removed

Room No.	Room Occ.
2	4
3	2
1	2
1	2
3	2
2	4

Figure 6.17 ROOM OCCUPANCY DETAILS table, with duplicate rows shaded

Room No.	Room Occ.
2	4
3	2
1	2

Figure 6.18 ROOM OCCUPANCY DETAILS table, after duplicates have been removed

6.2.6 Step 6 – Remove Duplicated Newly Created Tables

In some instances, during the normalisation procedure, when you remove columns from a table and create a new table for them, you may create two or more new tables with the same key. If the column headings for these tables are the same, they can be merged into one table. For example, if the newly created ROOM DETAILS and ROOM OCCUPANCY DETAILS tables had had identical column headings, the two tables would be merged to contain all the information, duplicate rows would be removed, and a suitable name given to the merged table. In our example, however, the two tables do not have identical column headings and cannot be merged here.

Follow the following step for the tables created in the previous step:

1. Examine the new tables you have created. If there are any two or more identical tables, you must combine those tables into one table. You will need to make sure that there are no duplicated rows of data.

In our example, we do not need to do this.

6.2.7 Step 7 – Remove any columns that are not dependent on the key and place in their own Tables (Third Normal Form)

You will have already removed columns that are dependent on part of the key, but there may still be some columns of data that are not directly dependent on the key at all. For example, the Price Per Night column in the Room Details table is not directly dependent on the Room Number column, but is directly dependent on the Room Occupancy column. This is the case since the hotel charges a set price for its rooms based upon their occupancy, regardless of the location or season. This column can therefore be removed along with a copy of the column it is dependent on. In this case, the Price Per Night column is removed and a new table is set up with the first column called Room Occupancy, and the second column called Price Per Room.

The new table must then be given a key. The column that has been copied from the original table, the one containing the values upon which the removed column was dependent, will be the key. In this case, the Room Occupancy column will be the key to the new table. Give the new table a suitable name. In our example, the new table will be called ROOM PRICE.

The column in the original table containing the values that are in the key column in the new table, in this case the Room Occupancy column, will now be referred to as a foreign key column. The column heading will be given an asterisk suffix to indicate a foreign key.

Once the non-key dependent columns have been removed into their own tables, the new tables may well contain several rows of duplicated data. Remember that the key value(s) in any table must be unique for each row. For example, in the new ROOM PRICE table created from the ROOM DETAILS table, there are two rows with same key of Room Occupancy 2. Since the rows both contain the same information (if they don't, then your information needs to be checked), only one version of the row is required, so the duplicate row must be removed.

Carry out the following steps for each table:

1. Examine each column to determine whether the values in the column are dependent directly upon the key to the row, or are dependent on another value in that row. Refer to Figure 6.19.

2. If the column is dependent on a non-key column, remove that column and create a new table with that removed column and a copy of the column with the non-key value it is dependent on. That copied column will become the key to the new table. Refer to Figure 6.20.

3. The column heading of the copied column in the original table will have an asterisk suffix added to it to indicate that this column represents a foreign key to another table. Refer to Figure 6.21.

4. For each new table, remove any rows with the same key as another row in the same table. The information in the two duplicate key rows should be the same. Don't worry too much at this stage if it is different, since this is only test data to help you to design the database tables. Later, however, you will need to check the data thoroughly. Refer to Figure 6.22.

Room Number	Room Occ.	Price Per Night
1	2	£60
2	4	£73
3	2	£60

Figure 6.19   ROOM DETAILS table with a shaded non-key dependent column

Room Occ.	Price Per Night
2	£60
4	£73
2	£60

Figure 6.20   New ROOM PRICE table – the shading shows a duplicate row

Room Number	Room Occ.*
1	2
2	4
3	2

Figure 6.21   Amended ROOM DETAILS table, with the Price Per Night column removed

The shaded Price Per Night column in the ROOM DETAILS table shown in Figure 6.19 is removed, along with a copy of the Room Occupancy column, and placed in a new, ROOM PRICE table. Refer to Figure 6.20. The remaining Room Occupancy column title in the ROOM DETAILS table has been suffixed with an asterisk to show that it is a foreign key. Refer to Figure 6.21.

The shaded row in the ROOM PRICE table shown in Figure 6.20 is a duplicate, with the same key as the first row. This row is removed. Refer to Figure 6.22. The duplicate row has been deleted in Figure 6.22.

Room Occupancy	Price Per Night
2	£60
4	£73

Figure 6.22 ROOM PRICE table with duplicate row removed

6.2.8 Step 8 – Remove Duplicated Newly Created Tables

In some instances, when you remove non-key dependent columns from a table and create a new table for them, you may create two or more new tables with the same key. In the same way you merged duplicate tables created in step 6, you must merge any duplicate tables created in step 7. In our example, after the Price Per Night column was removed from the ROOM DETAILS table, this table now has identical column headings to the ROOM OCCUPANCY DETAILS table created previously. These two tables can be merged and renamed, Room Occupancy Details. Refer to Figure 6.23, 6.24 and 6.25.

Carry out the following step for the tables created in the previous step:

1. Examine the new tables you have created. If there are any two or more tables with identical column headings, you must combine those tables into one table. You will need to make sure that there are no duplicated rows of data. Make sure you indicate whether a column heading is a foreign key or not.

Room Number	Room Occ.*
1	2
2	4
3	2

Figure 6.23 ROOM DETAILS table

Room No.	RoomOcc.
2	4
3	2
1	2

Figure 6.24 ROOM OCCUPANCY DETAILS table

Combine into one table

Room Number	Room Occ.*
1	2
2	4
3	2

Figure 6.25 COMBINED ROOM and ROOM OCCUPANCY DETAILS tables

In our example, this resulting table is basically the ROOM DETAILS table with a new title, since the contents of the two tables were identical. The tables are now in **third normal form**.

6.2.9 Step 9 – Rationalise the Tables

At this point, the tables should all be in third normal form and all tables with the same keys and columns will have been merged. However, there may be some tables that have identical keys (made up of one or more columns) but that do not have the same non-key columns. These tables must also be merged together, since they are effectively both holding rows of information about the same item, indicated by the unique key. In this way, you are minimising duplication of information, which reduces the chance of errors as well as the space needed to store the database. In our example, the new tables all have different keys.

Although the tables at this point are fully normalised, there is still the possibility that there could be some information stored more than once on them. This is not because they were not normalised correctly, but because the current working system can often store the same item of information in several locations, associated with several different actions. At this point, you need to ignore the current physical system, and consider only how the information is stored on the tables.

If a piece of information is held in two different places, then it needs to be entered twice. Most importantly, if the information is stored in two or more places and needs to be updated, it is possible that not all the duplicate pieces of information will be updated. Another possible problem that can arise when there is duplicate information is that this doubles the chance of an error being made when entering the information, or trebles it if the information is stored in three separate places.

To rationalise the tables, the following steps must be carried out:

1. Compile a list of your tables, with their keys. Refer to Figure 6.26.

2. Examine the list and if two or more tables have the same key, made up of one or more columns, the tables should be merged as follows:

   * Create a new table with the same columns as all the tables you are merging, but no duplicates. If a column heading is labelled as a foreign key using an asterisk, the column heading in the merged table must also show it as a foreign key.

   * Fill in the table, making sure you include all the rows from the tables. Each row may well contain information for more than one table.

   * If you find conflicting information – for example, that a Customer Address for the same Customer is different in two tables, but has the same key – you will need to investigate to find the correct version. It doesn't matter too much at this point, since this is only the database design, but when you set up your correct data later on you will need to correct any erroneous information.

3. Decide on an appropriate name for your merged tables. Try to keep the name short.

4. Rename non-merged tables if necessary, using the same naming criteria as above.

5. Rename non-merged table columns, to clarify possible instances where two columns have the same or similar column names, but actually contain different information.

6. Where non-key columns contain the same data in more than one table, it may be the case that one of these entries of information will be redundant. Examine the tables to find any non-key columns of information that are providing the same information that can be found via another table. Remove the redundant column.

In our example, we only need to go as far as to compile a list of tables with their keys. Refer to Figure 6.26.

Table Name	Key
BOOKING LOG	Booking Date, Room Number
BOOKING FORM	Start Date, End Date, Room Number
CUSTOMER DETAILS	Customer Code
ROOM PRICE	Room Occupancy
ROOM OCCUPANCY DETAILS	Room Number

Figure 6.26 List of tables with their keys

Since there are no tables sharing the same keys and no redundant duplicated columns of information, we do not need to carry out any rationalisation.

6.2.10 Step 10 – Draw Completed Table Designs

During normalisation, the data is used to group the tables. Once the normalisation is complete, the data is no longer required. Draw the completed table designs without the data, listing the column headings under each table name. Underline the keys and use asterisks to identify foreign keys as before.

ROOM PRICE table
Room Occupancy
Price Per Night

ROOM OCCUPANCY DETAILS table
Room Number
Room Occupancy*

BOOKING FORM table
Start Date
End Date
Room Number
Customer Code*
Total price

BOOKING LOG table
Booking Date
Room Number
Customer Code*

CUSTOMER DETAILS table
Customer Code
Customer Name
Customer Address
Customer Telephone Number

6.3   Identify and Draw the Relationships between Tables

6.3.1   Step 11 – Find the Relationships between the Tables

When you first draw up the tables, there may well be very little information in common between them. But as you split the tables up to break down the levels of repeated and dependent information, you will find that that most of the tables will relate to one or other of the tables by having one or more column in common. When the database is used in your system to display information on a screen or to produce a report, it is important that all the required information can be found, 'hopping' from one table to another via the relationships between them. This is called **navigating** around the database.

In the **Hotel Reception** system, imagine a scenario whereby the hotel was going to undergo some emergency repair work for the month of December. The receptionist would need to contact each customer who had booked a room for December and arrange an alternative hotel. Currently, the receptionist would need to look in the booking log to find all the names, dates and room numbers of customers who had booked rooms in December. He would then need to look through all the booking forms to find the addresses or telephone numbers for the customers for those dates and room numbers. This is a form of navigation whereby, armed with a piece of information, you search through an initial source of information to find out more information. With that new piece of information, you search through subsequent sources and so on.

A fully normalised database will store the information in a form such that you can navigate around the database to find various different types of information combinations. The navigation around a database is carried out using the relationships between one table and another, which is why it is important to identify and illustrate these clearly.

To do this, apply the following rules:

1. Draw up a list similar to that drawn up in the previous step, showing each table name with its key and foreign keys. Remember that the main key can be made up of more than one column, and that there can be more than one foreign key.

2. Add a fourth column called "Relates to more than one entry in ...". Refer to Figure 6.27.

For example:

Table Name	Key	Foreign Key	Relates to more than one entry in ...
BOOKING LOG	Booking Date, Room Number	Customer Code	
BOOKING FORM	Start Date, End Date, Room Number	Customer Code	
CUSTOMER DETAILS	Customer Code		
ROOM PRICE	Room Occupancy		
ROOM OCCUPANCY DETAILS	Room Number	Room Occupancy	

Figure 6.27 Initial normalised tables relationship diagram

3. Examine the list one table at a time. Carry out the following steps for each table:

- Look at the key in the current row. The key could be made up of one or more column headings. Call that the "current key". For example, the current key for the ROOM OCCUPANCY DETAILS table is just Room Number, whereas the current key for the BOOKING LOG table is both Booking Date and Room Number.

- Search through the other entries in the "Key" column for the other tables to find any other keys that include the "current key". Remember that the current key could include more than one value. For example, if you were examining the ROOM OCCUPANCY DETAILS row, you would look through the "Key" column to find any other keys containing Room Number. In this case, both the BOOKING LOG and the BOOKING FORM table keys both contain Room Number.

- Write the names of any tables whose keys contain the current key in the "Relates to more than one entry in ..." column for the current row. For example, you would write "Booking Log" and "Booking Form" in the "Relates to more than one entry in ..." column for the ROOM OCCUPANCY DETAILS row, since both keys for these two tables contain the Room Number current key. Refer to Figure 6.28.

- In cases where the key is made up of more than one column heading, you should search through the list to find any keys that contain *all* the column headings in your current key, as well as additional column headings.

For example:

Table Name	Key	Foreign Key	Relates to more than one entry in ...
BOOKING LOG	Booking Date, Room Number	Customer Code	
BOOKING FORM	Start Date, End Date, Room Number	Customer Code	
CUSTOMER DETAILS	Customer Code		
ROOM PRICE	Room Occupancy		
ROOM OCCUPANCY DETAILS	Room Number	Room Occupancy	**Booking Log** **Booking Form**

Figure 6.28 Normalised tables relationship diagram after searching through the key columns

Bold text shows the table names added in this version of the table.

- Carry out the same procedure to find any entries in the "Foreign Key" column that match or contain the current key, and write the names of the tables of the matching foreign keys in the "Relates to more than one entry in ..." column. For example, if you were examining the CUSTOMER DETAILS table row, after having searched through the "Key" column, you would search through the "Foreign Key" column to find Customer Code listed as a foreign key for the BOOKING LOG and BOOKING FORM tables. You would then write "Booking Log" and "Booking Form" in the "Relates to more than one entry in ..." column for the CUSTOMER DETAILS table row. Refer to Figure 6.29.

For example:

Table Name	Key	Foreign Key	Relates to more than one entry in ...
BOOKING LOG	Booking Date, Room Number	Customer Code	
BOOKING FORM	Start Date, End Date, Room Number	Customer Code	
CUSTOMER DETAILS	Customer Code		**Booking Form** **Booking Log**
ROOM PRICE	Room Occupancy		**Room Occupancy Details**
ROOM OCCUPANCY DETAILS	Room Number	Room Occupancy	Booking Log Booking Form

Figure 6.29 Completed normalised tables relationship diagram

6.3.2 Step 12 – Illustrate the Relationships in a Diagram

Although the table shows how the tables link together by the keys they have in common, it is not very easy to use to navigate around the database. To show the relationships between the tables as clearly as possible, a diagram is drawn up from the information in the table.

Do the following:

1. Use a pencil to draw the diagram since it will need adjusting as it develops!

2. Draw a box for each table in the "Table Name" column of your completed list. Include the keys and foreign keys in the box under the table name. The table name should be in upper case, the keys should be underlined and the foreign keys should be marked with an asterisk. Refer to Figure 6.30.

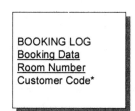

Figure 6.30   BOOKING LOG table in diagram

3. Refer back to the completed list for each table box. Draw a line between each table box and each box representing the tables listed in the "Relates to more than one entry in …" column for that row. The lines should have an arrow pointing to the "Relates to more than one entry in …" box. For example, you would draw two lines from the CUSTOMER DETAILS box, one pointing to the BOOKING FORM box and the other pointing to the BOOKING LOG box. Refer to Figure 6.31.

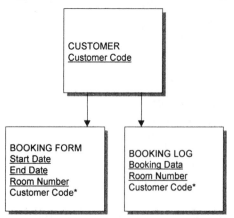

Figure 6.31   CUSTOMER, BOOKING FORM and BOOKING LOG tables and relationships in diagram

4. Two common protocols when drawing a relationship diagram are:

- Do not cross any lines, if possible.
- Try to draw the diagram such that the lines all have the arrows pointing downwards or horizontally. You should avoid having arrows pointing upward.

Refer to Figure 6.32 for the completed normalised tables and relationships diagram.

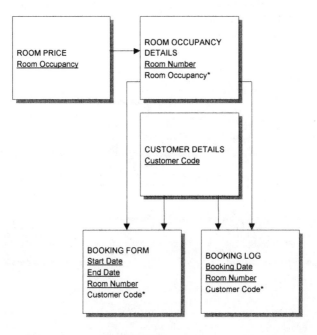

Figure 6.32 Completed normalised tables and relationships diagram

6.4 Compare Entity-Relationship Design with Normalisation Design

In practice, you may have decided not to carry out both types of design technique. At this point, therefore, you will have to trust that you have not made any omissions or incorrect assumptions about the information. If, however, you *have* used both techniques, you can check your designs by comparing the two.

1. Compare the two designs, using the same format of diagram that has been constructed for both techniques.

In the **Hotel Reception** example, the entity-relationship diagram and the normalisation diagram are shown in Figures 6.33 and 6.34.

2. Identify any differences between the two diagrams.

In the example, there are only two differences between the two diagrams:

a) The ROOM entity in the entity-relationship diagram has been split into two tables in the normalisation diagram, ROOM PRICE and ROOM OCCUPANCY DETAILS.

b) There is a direct relationship between the BOOKING entity and the BOOKING LOG entity in the entity-relationship diagram which is not shown in the normalisation diagram.

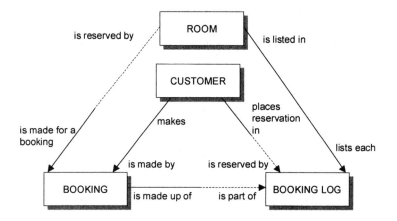

Figure 6.33 Entity-relationship diagram

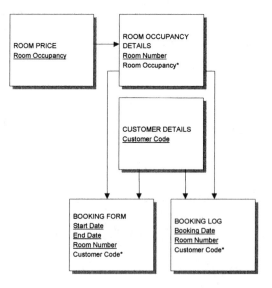

Figure 6.34 Normalised tables and relationships diagram

3. Examine each difference and decide which design is the most appropriate for your system.

In the **Hotel Reception** example, the two differences were considered as follows:

a) The normalisation procedure has created two tables to represent the ROOM PRICE and ROOM OCCUPANCY DETAILS. There are two tables here, since the ROOM PRICE is dependent on room occupancy in this hotel. For example, every room with a room occupancy of two has the same price. It would make sense to hold the room price information separately from the individual room details for the following reasons:

- Since the price for all rooms with the same occupancy will be the same, it is wasting storage space to repeatedly store the price for all rooms with the same occupancy.

- If room details are all in one entity and the room prices change, the details for every room will need to be changed. However, if the price is held in a separate table, only the price table will need to be changed.

- If the price is held for each room, there is a possibility that a price could be entered incorrectly for one of the rooms. Holding the price once only in a ROOM PRICE table reduces the number of times the price needs to be entered into the system, and therefore reduces the possibility of errors.

b) Although the entity-relationship diagram shows a direct relationship between a BOOKING and BOOKING LOG entities for the same booking, the normalisation diagram cannot show this relationship. This is because there is no key or foreign key field that can link the two tables in every case. Imagine a BOOKING for Room 3 with a start date of 1/5/2000 and an end date of 5/5/2000. There would be five BOOKING LOG entries relating to this BOOKING, each for Room 3 for the dates 1/5/2000, 2/5/2000, 3/5/2000, 4/5/2000 and 5/5/2000. How can a link be made between the original BOOKING entry and the BOOKING LOG entry 3/5/2000, since the only dates held in the BOOKING table are Start Date and End Date? Access cannot form a relationship based on the fact that the Booking Date in the BOOKING LOG is *between* the Start and End dates on the BOOKING.

It does make sense, however, to relate these two tables. There may be several instances when the receptionist may look at the BOOKING LOG for a particular day, find that it is booked, and instead of searching through the BOOKING LOG to find the end of the booking, simply look at the corresponding BOOKING to find the end date. The way to link two tables in this type of example is to introduce an item that is unique to the BOOKING so that the BOOKING LOG can be related to that. A *Booking Code* would be the ideal solution here.

The Booking Code would become the primary key in the BOOKING table. The Start and End Dates would no longer be keys and the Room Number would become a foreign key. The Booking Code would be added to the BOOKING LOG as a foreign key. In this way, a booking was made against a room for a particular date in the BOOKING LOG, the Booking Code would relate that BOOKING LOG entry to the corresponding BOOKING.

Since there is now a relationship between BOOKING and BOOKING LOG, the relationship between CUSTOMERS and BOOKING LOG is redundant. If the receptionist wanted to find out which customer made a booking, he could simply look up the BOOKING corresponding to the Booking Number in the BOOKING LOG. The BOOKING contains the Customer Code, which could in turn be used to find the Customer Details via the relationship between BOOKING and CUSTOMERS. The foreign key Customer Code in the BOOKING LOG can be removed, along with the relationship between BOOKING LOG and CUSTOMERS. The relationship between ROOM and BOOKING LOG must still remain, since the BOOKING LOG can still exist if there is no BOOKING against it.

4. Combine the two diagrams to give one database diagram for the tables and relationships as follows:

   - Use the normalisation diagram as a base.
   - Change the table names to be most like those in the entity-relationship diagram, rather than referring to the actual documents, as in the normalisation diagram. Avoid the word *Details*.
   - Show dotted half arrows where an end of the relationship is not obligatory.
   - Make any changes to the relationships and table contents arising from the differences examined in step 3. Refer to Figure 6.35 for the resulting diagram.

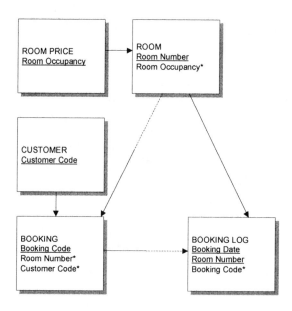

Figure 6.35 Resulting diagram

5. Update the table designs by using the normalised table design as a base, and apply any changes detailed above.

In the example, the Room Price and Room Occupancy details remain, and a Booking Code is added to the BOOKING table as primary key. It is also added to the BOOKING LOG as a foreign key. The Customer Code foreign key is removed from the BOOKING LOG.

ROOM PRICE

Room Occupancy
Price Per Night

ROOM

Room Number
Room Occupancy*

BOOKING

Booking Code
Room Number*
Customer Code*
Start Date
End Date
Total Price

BOOKING LOG

Booking Date
Room Number
Booking Code*

CUSTOMER

Customer Code
Customer Name
Customer Address
Customer Telephone Number

Part II: Access Practical

Work through this practical session to create a new table, ROOM PRICE, and amend the existing tables to reflect the completed table designs made in step 6.4. Then continue to create relationships between the tables.

6.5   Retrieve an existing database using Access

1.   Start Microsoft Access as described in Section 5.4.

2.   When the main Access dialogue box is displayed, click against Open an Existing Database. Insert your floppy disk and select the a:\Hotel Reception database shown in the list in the dialogue box. The main Hotel Reception dialogue box should now be displayed, as in Figure 6.36.

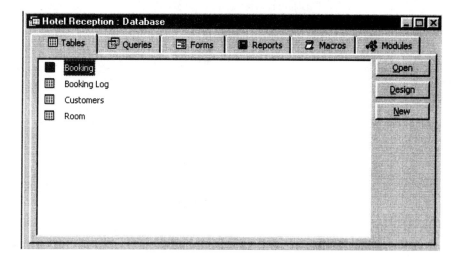

Figure 6.36   Main Hotel Reception dialogue box

6.6   Amend the Tables to represent the final Current Database Design

This section adds a ROOM PRICE table and amends the ROOM, BOOKING and BOOKING LOG tables to reflect the completed current database tables shown in step 5 of Section 6.4.

1. Create a new table, ROOM PRICE, by clicking the New box on the dialogue box. Select Design View, then click OK.

2. Add Field Names and Data Types shown in Figure 6.37 to the table. Set Room Occupancy as the primary key. Click the Save icon on the tool- bar and name the table Room Price. Click the OK button. Close the table by clicking the Close icon for the Room Price : Table window.

	Room Price : Table	
	Field Name	Data Type
🔑	Room Occupancy	Number
	Price per Night	Currency

Figure 6.37 New ROOM PRICE Table

3. Change the ROOM table to remove the Price Per Night field by selecting the Room table, then click Design to see the Field Names and Data Types. Click on the Price Per Night row and click Edit on the menu bar. Select Delete Rows. If a dialogue box is displayed, asking whether you want to delete the row, click Yes. Refer to Figure 6.38. Click the Save icon and close the table by clicking the Close icon for the Room : Table window.

	Room : Table	
	Field Name	Data Type
🔑	Room Number	Number
	Room Occupancy	Number

Figure 6.38 Amended ROOM table

4. Select the Booking table and click Design. Leave the cursor highlighting the top row and click Insert on the menu bar, then click Rows. A row will be inserted at the top of the ROOM table.

5. Type the text Booking Code into the Field Name column and select a Data Type of AutoNumber, since this is not a code that the current sys- tem uses. Still with the top row current, click the Primary Key icon and the new Booking Code row will become the primary key. The primary key icons against the other three rows will be removed. Refer to Figure 6.39. Click the Save icon and close the table by clicking the Close icon for the Booking : Table win- dow.

6. Select the Booking Log table and click the Design box. Delete the CustomerID row as before by selecting the row, then clicking Edit, then Delete Rows. Click on Yes when asked if you are sure you want to delete it.

7. Add a third row to the table with Field Name `Booking Code` and a Data Type of **Number**. This is because any number created using the **AutoNumber** facility must be given a data type of **Number** in all tables other than the one where it was created. Refer to Figure 6.40.

8. Click the **Save** icon and close the table by clicking the **Close** icon for the **Booking Log** : **Table** window.

▦ Booking : Table	
Field Name	Data Type
⑨ Booking Code	AutoNumber
Start Date	Date/Time
End Date	Date/Time
Room Number	Number
CustomerID	Number
Total Price	Currency

Figure 6.39 Amended BOOKING Table

▦ Booking Log : Table	
Field Name	Data Type
⑨ Booking Date	Date/Time
⑨ Room Number	Number
Booking Code	Number

Figure 6.40 Amended BOOKING LOG Table

6.7 Create Relationships between Tables

Refer back to the completed database diagram created in section 6.4, Figure 6.35, and create the relationships between the tables using Access as follows:

1. Open the **Relationships** window by clicking the **Relationships** icon on the toolbar. A **Show Table** dialogue box will be displayed. Refer to Figure 6.41.

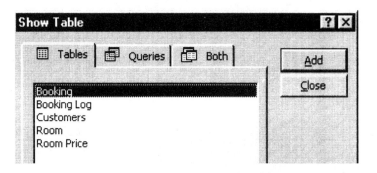

Figure 6.41 Show Table dialogue box

2. Select **Room Price** and click the **Add** box. The ROOM PRICE table will appear in the **Relationships** window. Then select **Room** in the same way. Click the **Close** box to get rid of the **Show Table** dialogue box. Refer to Figure 6.42.

Figure 6.42 ROOM and ROOM PRICE in the Relationships window

3. These two tables are related together via the Room Occupancy field, in a one-to-many relationship from ROOM PRICE to ROOM. To create the relationship in Access, click on the connecting field in the 'one' table, in this case the **Room Occupancy** field in the **Room Price** table, and keep the left mouse button depressed while moving the cursor to point at the **Room Occupancy** field in the **Room** table. A small white rectangle will appear over each field as you move the cursor. Release the mouse button. A **Relationship** dialogue box will be displayed. Note that it is automatically set up as a one-to-many relationship. Refer to Figure 6.43.

4. Click on the white box next to the text **Enforce Referential Integrity**. Once this box is selected, Access will ensure that all Room Occupancy values entered in the ROOM table correspond to existing **Room Occupancy** values in the ROOM PRICE table.

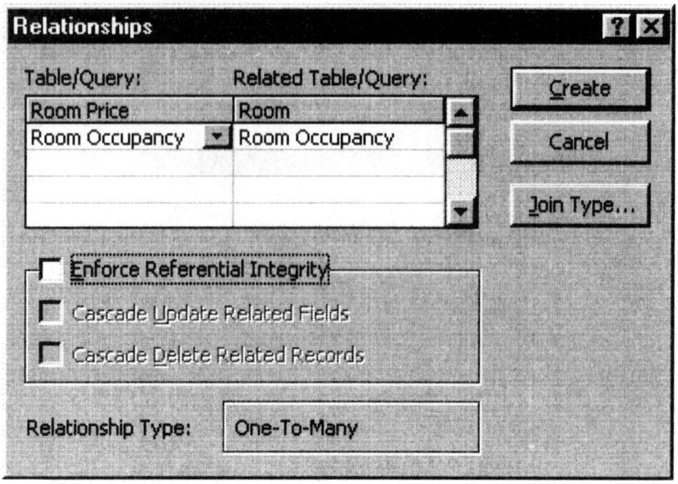

Figure 6.43 Relationships dialogue box

5. The two boxes and text below **Enforce Referential Integrity** will become highlighted now. These boxes carry out additional integrity functions, as follows:

- **Cascade Update Related Fields** – This means that if a Room Occupancy value changes in the ROOM PRICE table, all the same Room Occupancy values in corresponding ROOM tables will also be changed.

- **Cascade Delete Related Records** – This means that if you were to delete the ROOM PRICE table entry for a particular Room Occupancy, then all corresponding ROOM table entries for that Room Occupancy would also be deleted.

6. Do not select either of these boxes, but click the **Create** box. The relationship between the ROOM PRICE and ROOM tables will be displayed. Refer to Figure 6.44.

7. Add the remaining tables to the window by clicking the **Show Table** icon  on the toolbar. Select and add the **Customers, Booking** and **Booking Log** tables to the window as before. Then click the **Close** box to remove the **Show Tables** dialogue box. Tables such as the **Customers** table that contain more fields than can be shown in the table box will contain a scroll bar. To enlarge the table box, click and drag the bottom of the table box. The scroll bar will disappear.

8. Click and drag the tables into a similar position to those in the database diagram in Figure 6.35.

9. Create a one-to-many relationship from **CustomerID** in the **Customers** table to the **CustomerID** in the **Booking** table. Select **Enforce Referential Integrity** as before and click **Create**.

10. Create a one-to-many relationship from **Room Number** in the **Room** table to the **Room Number** in the **Booking** table. Select **Enforce Referential Integrity** as before and click **Create**.

Figure 6.44 Relationship between ROOM PRICE and ROOM tables

11. Create a one-to-many relationship from Room Number in the Room table to the Room Number in the Booking Log table. Select Enforce Referential Integrity as before and click Create.

12. Create a one-to-many relationship from the Booking Code in the Booking table to the Booking Code in the Booking Log table.

Refer to Figure 6.35 and note that the relationship between the BOOKING and BOOKING LOG tables is dotted at the BOOKING LOG end. This means that a BOOKING LOG table entry can exist without a corresponding BOOKING. In other words, a BOOKING LOG can be set up with no Booking Code. A one-to-many relationship must still be set up, so that the database can obtain the BOOKING LOG entries that correspond to each BOOKING record and vice versa: however, that relationship must not be subject to referential integrity, otherwise each BOOKING LOG entry would have to have a Booking Code.

In this case, leave the Enforce Referential Integrity box empty and click Create. Note that the relationship line is thin to indicate that there is no referential integrity.

13. Click and drag the tables to avoid the lines crossing where possible. Refer to Figure 6.45 for the completed relationship window.

14. Click the Save icon.

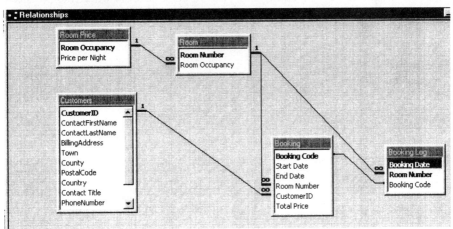

Figure 6.45 Completed relationships between tables

6.8 Delete a Relationship

To demonstrate this tool, you are going to delete the relationship between the ROOM PRICE and ROOM tables, and then re-create it.

1. Delete the relationship between Room Price and Room, by clicking on the relationship line. The line will appear slightly thicker to show that it is selected. Click on Edit on the menu bar, then select Delete on the pull-down menu. A dialogue box will be displayed asking you if you want to delete the relationship. Click Yes.

2. Create the relationship as before by clicking and dragging the Room Occupancy in the Room Price table over to the Room Occupancy in the Room table. Click against Enforce Referential Integrity and click the Create box.

3. Close the Relationships window by clicking its Close icon, then close the database and Access in the same way.

6.9 Summary

This chapter has covered the following material:

Part I: Database Design Theory

- Introduction to normalisation and third normal form.
- Step-by-step instructions for normalising a database.
- Identifying the relationships between the tables.
- Construction of the 'entity-relationship' type diagram from the normalised tables.
- Comparing the entity-relationship and normalisation database designs to produce a 'best fit' design.

Part II: Access Practical

- Amending existing tables.
- Creating a relationship between two tables.
- Deleting a relationship between two tables.

6.10 Written Exercises

6.10.1 Briefly, describe each of the nine steps carried out when normalising tables of data.

6.10.2   Normalise the following three sets of sample data, shown in Figures 6.46, 6.47 and 6.48, from the **Painting and Decorating Company** administration system, and illustrate the relationships between the normalised tables in a diagram.

Quotation for Job	**Quote Ref.:** 100
Customer Name: J. Barratt	**Quote Date:** 15/10/2000
Customer Address: 15 Long Way, Barlow, Bucks	**Description:** Painting front sash window (external)
Quote Value: £250	**Agreed Work Date:**
Completion Date:	**Final Price:**
Customer Paid Date:	**Outstanding Balance:**

Quotation for Job	**Quote Ref.:** 101
Customer Name: J. Barratt	**Quote Date:** 25/11/2000
Customer Address: 15 Long Way, Barlow, Bucks	**Description:** Painting all windows (external) in house
Quote Value: £720	**Agreed Work Date:** 10/1/2000
Completion Date:	**Final Price:**
Customer Paid Date:	**Outstanding Balance:**

Quotation for Job	**Quote Ref.:** 103
Customer Name: L. Lorna	**Quote Date:** 20/11/2000
Customer Address: 153 Friary Road, Inswold, Herts, A5F 6RR	**Description:** Renovating old barn
Quote Value:	**Agreed Work Date:**
Completion Date:	**Final Price:**
Customer Paid Date:	**Outstanding Balance:**

Quotation for Job	**Quote Ref.:** 105
Customer Name: K. Bradley	**Quote Date:** 22/11/2000
Customer Address: Mill Cottage, Tumbleweed Road, Hants	**Description:** Painting External walls of House
Quote Value: £950	**Agreed Work Date:** 2/1/2001
Completion Date:	**Final Price:**
Customer Paid Date:	**Outstanding Balance:**

Quotation for Job	Quote Ref.: 106
Customer Name: L. Lorna	Quote Date: 23/11/2000
Customer Address: 153 Friary Road, Inswold, Herts, A5F 6RR	Description: Painting kitchen
Quote Value: £540	Agreed Work Date:
Completion Date:	Final Price:
Customer Paid Date:	Outstanding Balance:

Figure 4.46 Samples from the Quotation Folder

~~Quotation for Job~~ Agreed Job	Quote Ref.: 99
Customer Name: J. Barratt	Quote Date: 10/10/2000
Customer Address: 15 Long Way, Barlow, Bucks	Description: Painting front door (internal)
Quote Value: £160	Agreed Work Date: 20/10/2000
Completion Date: 30/10/2000	Final Price: £185
Customer Paid Date: 20/11/2000	Outstanding Balance: £100

~~Quotation for Job~~ Agreed Job	Quote Ref.: 102
Customer Name: J. Barratt	Quote Date: 25/11/2000
Customer Address: 15 Long Way, Barlow, Bucks	Description: Painting internal woodwork
Quote Value: £720	Agreed Work Date: 10/1/2001
Completion Date: 5/2/2000	Final Price: £1020
Customer Paid Date:	Outstanding Balance: £1020

~~Quotation for Job~~ Agreed Job	Quote Ref.: 104
Customer Name: P. Black	Quote Date: 26/11/2000
Customer Address: ATF Limited, Farm Industrial Estate, Banbury	Description: Painting external woodwork
Quote Value: £3650	Agreed Work Date: 2/12/2000
Completion Date: 20/1/2000	Final Price: £3000
Customer Paid Date: 27/1/2000	Outstanding Balance: £0

Figure 6.47 Samples from the Jobs Folder

Item Code	Item Description	Order Date	Qty	Total Price	Quote Ref.	Supplier Name	Supplier Address	Actual Delivery Date
RG	Red Gloss Paint	30/11/2000	20	£120	104	Leith Paints	Site 56, Farm Indust. Estate	1/12/2000
WG	White Gloss Paint	2/11/2000	3	£12	85	Leith Paints	Site 56, Farm Indust. Estate	
BG	Black Gloss Paint	30/11/2000	15	£150	104	Artist Paints	102 Abbey Road, Green-slade	2/12/2000
RG	Red Gloss Paint	5/1/2000	6	£36	102	Leith Paints	Site 56, Farm Indust. Estate	10/1/2000
LS	Lily Stencil	2/2/2000	1	£15	102	Artist Paints	102 Abbey Road, Green-slade	

Figure 6.48 Sample order sheet from the Orders folder

6.10.3 Compare the diagram showing the relationships between the normalised tables produced in the previous question with the entity-relationship diagram produced in 5.10.3 (e). Discuss any differences and explain which design you prefer to use. Produce a *final* entity-relationship diagram and list of tables (showing the primary key and contents of each).

6.10.4 Make up or find some sample data from a paper-based system. Normalise the data to produce table layouts and a diagram to show the relationships between the tables.

6.11 Practical Exercises

6.11.1 Create a new database called **Video** and create the following tables and re-lationships.

Create three tables, FILM, APPEARANCE and ACTOR. FILM will contain the four fields: Film Title (primary key), Description, Duration and Director. ACTOR table will contain the three fields Actor Name (primary key), Nationality and Date of Birth. APPEARANCE will contain the two fields Film Title and Actor Name only.

Determine the relationships between the tables and create them on the database.

6.11.2 Update the **Rally** database created in 5.10.2 to include the relationships between the tables.

6.11.3 Update the **Painting and Decorating Company** database in 5.10.3 to reflect the changes made to the table structures, and to add the relationships described in 6.10.3.

6.11.4 Update the **University Department** database to add a one-to-many relationship between the STAFF and TIMETABLE tables, via the StaffID field, and between the COURSE and TIMETABLE tables, via the Course Code field.

7 Enhancing the Current Model to include New System Requirements

7.1 Introduction

The techniques we have used so far to analyse the system have used information from the *current* system to group and link the data into what have become the database tables and relationships. The database, as it is at this stage, should reflect the system being used currently within in the specified scope. There may be *additional* functions that need to be incorporated into the database system and the inclusion of these new functions may well have been the reason for building the database system in the first place. Even if there are no additional functions, it is unlikely that any current system is without area for improvement or indeed without its problems regarding the type of information stored and passed around.

Once the database for the current system has been modelled, any additional functions or improvements to the current system should be added to the model, before the screens and reports are designed. The model will then be called the **required system model**.

In Part I of this chapter, the origins of the new requirements and requests for changes are examined and the way in which the changes are documented will also be described.

Part II of this chapter will enable you to update the tables and relationships created using Access to reflect the changes made to create the required system models.

Part I: Database Design Theory

7.2 New Requirements from the Feasibility Report

Any additional functions and improvements that need to be made to the current system will have been detailed in the **feasibility report**. This document should have been put together and agreed upon before the commencement of the database design.

The areas in the feasibility report where additional requirements and improvements will have been documented are:

- Terms of reference.
- Problems with the present system.
- Requirement of a new system.

The requirements detailed in these sections of the feasibility report should provide you with the information you need to change the database designs you have so far. In some cases, you may have to obtain further information and sample data for new functions to enable the already normalised and designed database to be changed.

7.3   New Requirements via Change Requests

As well as the pre-defined new requirements to the system, it is often the case that during the database analysis work carried out so far, problems are discovered in the current system that were not documented in the feasibility report. Small problems that can be easily solved without causing significant delays or changes to the present design can be incorporated into the new system along with the documented changes in the feasibility report.

Any problems or requirements that have been discovered that may require signifi-cant changes to the system should ideally be documented in a document similar to a *small-scale* feasibility report. This type of document is often called a **change request** form. Each change request should describe the problem, offer a variety of proposals (if possible) for solving it and provide, most importantly, the related costs and benefits for the proposed solution(s). A proposed solution for each change request must then be agreed upon by the person(s) responsible for the system.

It is important that this procedure is carried out, since one of the main reasons that computer systems in development have gained the reputation of always being behind schedule and over budget is that the analysis phase of systems development will al-ways reveal new problems that require solving before the system can be completed. This extra work will not have been included in the original plans and budgets for the system, although some level of **contingency** should have been included, and therefore without careful control of these extra requirements, the development of the system takes longer and longer.

Imagine, for example, you have ordered a new washing machine and have been told that it will be delivered in one week. You would maybe allow a couple of days extra – just in case – but could assume that you would be able to use the washing machine in about nine days. The *just in case* days are called contingency. This allows a little extra time for unforeseen circumstances, such as sickness and emergencies.

The washing machine arrives in a week as stated, but to your dismay, you find out once you plug the washing machine into the electric socket, that it does not work. You call the electrician, who says it will take only an hour to re-wire the plug, but he his not free to come round for three days. This then adds an extra day to your original estimate. When the electrician arrives, he inspects the socket, and announces that the ground floor of the house will need re-wiring. This will take at least two weeks and cannot be started for another week. Although this is an extreme example, it illustrates how unforeseen problems can be discovered whilst carrying out the tasks, which can then lead to further problems.

By their very nature, unforeseen problems cannot be predicted. The effects and number of unforeseen problems can be minimised, though, by carrying out as much investigation into the system as possible before drawing up the estimates and plans. Another way to minimise the effects of these problems on a project is to include a large amount of contingency in your original plan. The amount of contingency allowed for in a plan is often a **standard percentage**, such as 15%, 20% or 25%, but could be changed depending on the circumstances of the project.

Any problem documented in a change request should be given some indicator or code to suggest how severe the problem is. The codes used should be decided before any change requests are written, so that all change requests refer to the same code or wording for the same level of problem. Some example codes could be:

Code	Meaning
1	Must be corrected before system development can continue.
2	Will need to be corrected within a week, but other areas of the system can still be developed in the mean time.
3	Only affects a small and rarely used function in the system.

These codes will help the person responsible to prioritise the work needed to correct the problems. The three most usual outcomes for a change request are:

- Incorporate the appropriate solution to the problem in the new system design, and make plans for any extra time the development may take.

- Do not include the solution to the problem in the system design, but plan to include the solution as a new requirement in a later phase of the system development.

- Do not include the solution to the problem in this or any later system designs.

The second and third options can only be carried out if the problem is one that will not cause difficulties to the system once it is completed and that can be overcome by the installation of special operational procedures for the system. Although this may not be the perfect solution, it may be that the problem is not one that will arise very often, can easily be controlled using manual procedures, and would take a lot of resources and time to solve in the system itself.

Each change request must be documented, with the decision made regarding correction of the problem.

7.4   Documenting the New Requirements

The documentation drawn up and used to build the current system database must be amended to incorporate the new requirements, coming from either the feasibility report or the change requests. The main documents are:

- Data flow diagram.
- Entity-relationship model.
- Normalised table designs and relationship diagram.

The best way to amend the documents is to keep the original documents, labelled as **current system** documents, and amend a copy of each document, labelling them as **required system** documents. In this way, you can always refer back to the original system design if needed. In a perfect development project all the current system documents should be copied and amended to become required system documents. However, if you have used both data grouping methods to produce the table designs (entity-relationship modelling and normalisation) you may only need to change the entity-relationship style diagram and table designs produced after comparing the two methods' designs.

You may be asked just to update the database tables directly to incorporate the changes without updating any of the analysis models carried out so far. This may be the faster option at this stage, but it means that as soon as you have put those changes in, documentation you have about the system so far will no longer reflect the system. This could result in problems later during the development, testing and maintenance of the system, and can be very risky option.

In all cases, you will need to update any database tables and relationships built using your database management tool (in our case, Access) to reflect the changes made in the required system documents.

7.5   Change Control

During this stage, the current system models have been amended to incorporate the new requirements from the feasibility study and any change requests. It is likely, however, that further change requests will be produced during the later stages of the development, such as when designing queries, screens and reports. Sometimes change requests are produced after the system has been completed and is being used.

These change requests should be documented and actioned in the same way as those addressed during the new requirements phase, detailed above, but the changes made to the documentation and the actual database system must be controlled very carefully.

It is no good one designer changing a table to extend a particular field, if another designer is about to remove that field altogether. The changes must be administered very carefully to avoid such problems. Version numbers should be used on each version of the documents, and be related to the appropriate change request(s). This type of administration is called **change control**. This is a very important area of systems development and, as referred to previously, can make the difference between a system being completed on time and within budget, and delivered late and over budget.

7.6 New Requirements in the Hotel Reception System Example

Although a feasibility report has not been included in this book for the **Hotel Reception** system example, imagine that the following new requirements had been made and agreed upon:

1. Customer fax number and e-mail address should be stored along with the customer address and phone number.
2. The room information should be extended to show whether or not a room has an en-suite bathroom.
3. The room pricing should depend on the room occupancy and whether or not the room has an en-suite bathroom.

The current system data flow diagram will be copied and updated to produce the required system data flow diagram, as shown in Figure 7.1. The changes have been highlighted in bold. Since the words *Customer Details* have been used to include address, telephone number, fax and e-mail, and *Room Details* have been used to describe room number, occupancy and now en-suite, this diagram differs little from the current system data flow diagram. The changes have been highlighted in bold.

Customer Details = Customer Name, Customer Address, Customer Telephone Number, Customer Fax Number, Customer **Email Address**

Room Details = Room Number, Room Occupancy, **EnSuite** flag.

Since in our example, both the entity-relationship modelling and normalisation techniques were used, we will only create a required system entity-relationship model and required system table designs based upon the current system designs put together after the entity-relationship model and normalised tables were compared. Refer to Figures 7.2 and the list of table designs given next. The changes have been highlighted in bold.

ROOM PRICE	ROOM	BOOKING LOG
Room Occupancy	Room Number	Booking Date
EnSuite	Room Occupancy*	Room Number
Price per Night	**EnSuite***	Booking Code*

BOOKING	CUSTOMER
<u>Booking Code</u>	<u>Customer Code</u>
Room Number*	Customer Name
Customer Code*	Customer Address
Start Date	Customer Telephone Number
End Date	**Customer Fax Number**
Total Price	**Customer Email Address**

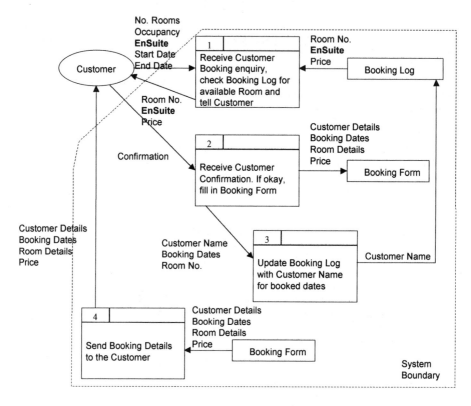

Figure 7.1 Required system data flow diagram

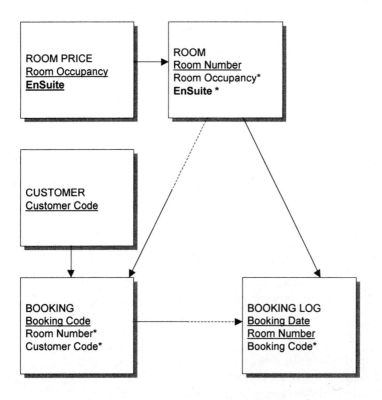

Figure 7.2 Required system entity-relationship diagram

Part II: Access Practical

Work through this practical session to reflect the changes made to the current system model in to produce the required system model. The following amendments must be made to the CUSTOMER, ROOM and ROOM PRICE tables:

- Add Fax Number and Email to the CUSTOMER table.
- Add EnSuite to the ROOM table.
- Add EnSuite to the ROOM PRICE table as part of the primary key with Occupancy.
- Add the EnSuite field to the relationship between the ROOM PRICE and ROOM tables, giving a two-field relationship.

7.7 Amending Database Tables

1. Start Microsoft Access as described in Section 5.4.

2. When the main Access dialogue box is displayed, click against Open an Existing Database. Insert your floppy disk and select the a:\ Hotel Reception database shown in the list in the dialogue box. The main Hotel Reception dialogue box should now be displayed.

3. Click on the Customers table name and click Design. Add the Fax Number and Email fields as shown in Figure 7.3.

4. Click the Save icon and close the changes by clicking the Close icon on the top right corner of the Customers : Table window.

5. Click on the Room table name and click Design. Add an EnSuite field as shown in Figure 7.4. Since this field will only contain either a Yes or a No, set the Data Type to be Yes/No.

Customers : Table	
Field Name	Data Type
CustomerID	AutoNumber
ContactFirstName	Text
ContactLastName	Text
BillingAddress	Text
Town	Text
County	Text
PostalCode	Text
Country	Text
Contact Title	Text
PhoneNumber	Text
FaxNumber	Text
Email	Text

Figure 7.3 Updated CUSTOMERS table

⊞ Room : Table	
Field Name	Data Type
🔑 Room Number	Number
Room Occupancy	Number
EnSuite	Yes/No

Figure 7.4 Updated ROOM Table

6. Click the **Save** icon and close the changes by clicking the **Close** icon on the top right corner of the **Customer : Table** window.

7.8 Amend an Existing Primary Key where the Table is part of a Relationship

Whenever you need to amend or add to the primary key for a table, if there is a relationship between this table and another table, involving the existing primary key, you must delete that relationship first. Once you have amended the primary key, you can then re-create the relationships between the two tables.

1. Before adding the **EnSuite** field to the existing primary key in the **Room Price** table, you will need to remove the existing relationship between that table and the **Room** table. Click the **Relationships** icon on the toolbar. The relationships between the tables will be displayed.

2. Click once on the relationship between the **Room Price** table and **Room** table. The relationship line will become a little thicker to show that it has been selected.

3. Click **Edit** on the menu bar, then click **Delete**. You will be asked if you want to delete it. Click **Yes**. The relationship will be removed.

4. Click the **Close** icon on the top right corner of the **Relationships** window to remove it.

5. Click the **Room Price** table, then click **Design**. Click at the left end of the **Price per Night** row to highlight the whole row. Click the **Insert Rows** icon on the toolbar to insert a row.

6. Insert the **EnSuite** field name with a field type of **Yes/No** as shown in Figure 7.5.

7. To apply the primary key symbol to both the **Room Occupancy** and **EnSuite** fields, you must select both together. To do this, click the grey box to the left of the **Room Occupancy** row, then hold the **Ctrl** key down whilst you do the same to select the **EnSuite** row. Both rows should be highlighted. Release the **Ctrl** key. Click the **Primary Key** icon on the toolbar. The primary key symbol should appear to the left of both rows. Refer to Figure 7.5.

⊞ Room Price : Table	
Field Name	Data Type
🔑 Room Occupancy	Number
🔑 EnSuite	Yes/No
Price per Night	Currency

Figure 7.5 Completed ROOM PRICE table with a two-part primary key

8. Click the Save icon and close the changes by clicking the Close icon on the top right corner of the Room Price : Table window.

7.9 Creating a Two-Field Relationship

1. The relationship between the Room Price and Room tables can be restored. This time the relationship involves two the fields Room Occupancy and EnSuite. Click the Relationships icon.

2. To create a relationship joining more than one primary key field, you must first click and drag just one of the two primary key fields. Click on the Room Occupancy field in the Room Price table and whilst holding down the left mouse button, move the mouse pointer until it is over the Room Occupancy field in the Room table. Release the mouse button. A Relationships dialogue box will be displayed as in Figure 7.6.

Relationships [?] [X]

Table/Query:	Related Table/Query:	
Room Price	Room	
Room Occupancy ▼	Room Occupancy	

Create

Cancel

Join Type...

☐ Enforce Referential Integrity
☐ Cascade Update Related Fields
☐ Cascade Delete Related Records

Relationship Type: Indeterminate

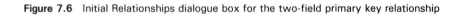

Figure 7.6 Initial Relationships dialogue box for the two-field primary key relationship

3. To add the second part of the primary key to the relationship, click in the row under the **Room Occupancy** field in the **Room Price** list. A scroll arrow will appear. Click on it and select the **EnSuite** field name.

4. Repeat this procedure to add the **EnSuite** field name to the **Room** list.

5. Click the **Enforce Referential Integrity** box and click **Create** (Figure 7.7).

6. The relationship will be added to the **Relationships** window (Figure 7.8). Although this looks like two relationships, it is in fact only the one, but between two fields in each table.

7. Click the **Save** icon to save the relationship changes and click the **Close** icon on the top right of the **Relationships** window.

8. Close the database by clicking the **Close** icon on the top right corner of the **Hotel Reception : Database** window and then close Access by clicking the **Close** icon on the top right corner of the Access window.

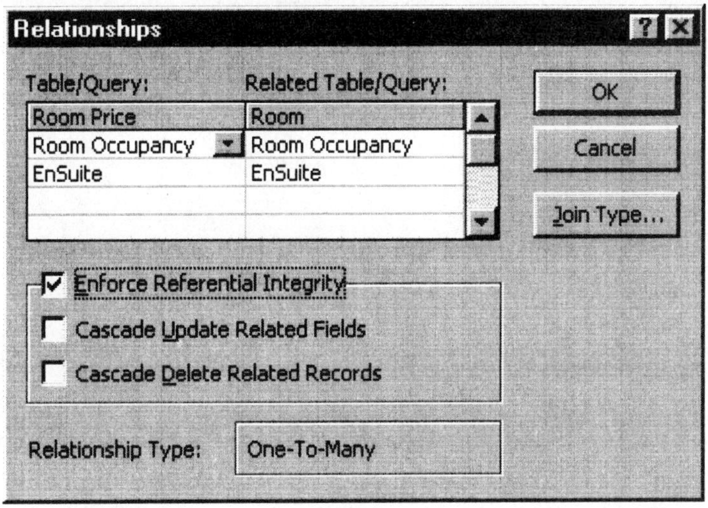

Figure 7.7 Completed Relationships dialogue box for the two-field primary key

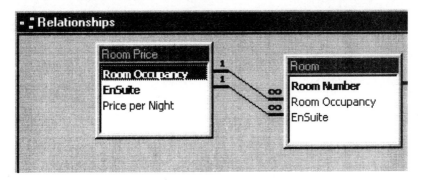

Figure 7.8 Two-part primary key relationship between tables ROOM PRICE and ROOM

7.10 Summary

This chapter has covered the following material:

Part I: Database Design Theory

- Identifying new requirements from the feasibility report.
- Identifying new requirements from change requests.
- How to document the new requirements.
- Change control.
- Example of new requirements in the **Hotel Reception** system.

Part II: Access Practical

- Amending database tables.
- Amending a primary key where the table is part of a relationship.
- Creating a two-field relationship.

7.11 Written Exercises

7.11.1   Describe the two main sources of new requirements for a system.

7.11.2   Explain why change control is such an important area of systems development.

7.11.3   Refer to the *final* set of table layouts and entity-relationship model in Section 6.10.3, and apply the appropriate changes for the following new system requirements:

The managing director wants the quotes to each be given a Work Category, to indicate whether the work being quoted for: for example, PI (painting interior), PIE (painting exterior) and PB (painting both interior and exterior). Each Work Category will have a description to explain the type of work that is included in that category and an hourly rate to be charged.

The administrator also wants to be able to hold the telephone number and fax number for each customer and supplier.

7.12 Practical Exercises

7.12.1   Update the **Painting and Decorating Company** database to reflect the changes in 7.11.3.

7.12.2 Create a new database called **Car Rental**. Create four tables: CAR, CUSTOMER, RENTAL and RATES as follows:

- CAR will contain the five fields Car Registration (primary key), Make, Model, Type and Seats.
- CUSTOMER will contain the three fields Customer Name (primary key), Customer Address and Customer Phone.
- RENTAL will contain the six fields Rental Number (primary key), Car Registration, Customer Name, Start Date, End Date and Price.
- RATES will contain Type, Seats and Daily Rate. The primary key in the Rates table is made up of the two fields Type and Seats.

Determine the relationships between the tables and create them on the database. Note that a relationship between two of the tables uses a two-field primary key.

7.12.3 Update the **Video** database created in Section 6.11.1 to allow for the fact that an actor could appear in two films of the same name. James Garner, for example, appeared in two versions of *Maverick*. To do this, add a Release Date field to both the FILM table and the APPEARANCE table and add it to the Film primary key.

Change the relationship between the FILM and APPEARANCE tables to include this new field as well as the Film Title field.

8 Data dictionary

8.1 Introduction

By now, the database tables and their relationships to each other will have been designed by analysing the current system and incorporating any new requirements into the model. This makes up the main structure of your database. In practice, you may well have created your tables in Access and linked them together by creating relationships between them.

You may have heard of the **GIGO** principle in computing, which stands for *garbage in, garbage out*. This means that a system is only as good as the data that is entered. If there are errors in the data being entered, the quality of the output will be poor. No matter how complex and brilliant the system is, if the data being entered into it is incorrect, there is very little value in the output from that system, since it will be based upon incorrect information.

In a database system there are two main controls that can be applied to the data simply by the way in which the database is set up are. These are:

- **Data integrity**. As explained previously, if a piece of data is entered into a table, and if that field is linked via a relationship to the same field in another table, the data system will check that the field in the other table exists and has the same value. This control is applied by creating relationships between tables and selecting the Enforce Referential Integrity feature.
- **Field properties**. These are rules that can be associated with a field in a table. In this way when data is entered into that field, it must obey those rules. These rules can describe the **type of data** that can be entered, for example numeric or date format, or even describe a **range of values** that can be permitted, for example, between 10 and 15.

At this stage, the relationships to enable the data integrity control have been set up, but the field properties in the tables have not. It is important, therefore, that no data is entered into the database until the field properties are completed.

As well as defining the field properties for the tables to enable the input data to be checked, it is important for two reasons to provide a brief description of each field in the table:

- To provide documentation for your system, thus enabling someone other than

126

yourself to find out what each field represents. In some cases, it may be obvious, but in other cases, it may not be so clear.

- When the field is used in a screen, called a **Form** in Access, if the cursor is placed on that field, its field description will be displayed at the bottom of the screen. This will therefore provide useful information about the field to any user trying to enter data into it. It is important, therefore, to remember that the description should provide some outline as to the type of data that can be entered as well as what the field represents.

Since some fields appear in more than one table – for example in the **Hotel Reception** system Customer Code appears in both the CUSTOMERS and BOOKING tables – it is important that the description and field properties for these fields do not vary from table to table. They must be the same in all tables. To ensure that this is the case, a list of all fields in the database must be put together, and the field description and field properties listed for each. The tables in which the fields appear are not referred to. Since the field names are ordered alphabetically, and cover the whole database, this source of information is called a **data dictionary**.

In Part I of this chapter, the most useful criteria that can describe a field are outlined and a data dictionary is built for the **Hotel Reception** example. The importance of the sequence in which that data is entered into the database is explained, and the **Hotel Reception** system database table entry sequence is identified.

In Part II of this chapter you can work through the step-by-step guide, using Access to amend the tables to include the data dictionary criteria for the **Hotel Reception** database. You will then enter data into the database in the order specified in Part I. Once the data has been entered into the database, you will be able to try some sort and filter techniques on the tables.

Part I: Database Design Theory

8.2 Data Dictionary Criteria

The data dictionary will list all field names in the database in alphabetical order, and against each field will be listed a set of criteria that describe the data in the field. The criteria listed below reflect the type of field properties available in Access. There may be alternative properties available in other database management systems.

Data Type   Can be one of Text, Number, Date/Time, Currency, Auto-

Number, Yes/No or Hyperlink. An example of each: Text = elephant, Number = 56.871; Date/Time = 28/8/1965; Currency = £16.89; AutoNumber = a unique number generated automatically by the computer, often used for key fields that are not viewed by the user and only used as part of the database. Yes/No = Yes, Hyperlink = http:// www.comcentral.com/

Description	A brief description of the field, including a guide to its layout and if it is a required field. E.g. Order date = The date on which the order was placed by the customer, dd/mm/yyyy, must be entered.
Field size	The length of the field. Some field data types will have an automatic field size, such as Date/Time and AutoNumber, but others need you to enter a size. The default size for text in Access is 50, although you can enter up to 255 in Access. It is best to consider the longest the field can possibly be. The number data type will usually require a field size of Long Integer.
Format	For some data types, it is possible to outline a format for each entry. The Date/Time data type allows you to select a date or time format. E.g. Long Date, 19 June 1994.
Default value	In some instances it is useful to be able to specify a default value for a particular field. This is the value set in a field for a new entry in the table if a value is not entered into it. For example, in the case of a Yes/No field, you may want every new entry in a table to be set to No, unless changed to Yes. This would stop the field being left blank.
Validation rule	In some instances it is useful to impose a validation rule, such as "<100". Using a validation like this can be useful and can stop invalid data being entered. Once data has been entered, the validation rule can be changed, as long as any existing data does not become invalid under the new rule.
Validation text	The text that will appear when the validation rule specified above is broken, such as "must be less than 100".

8.3   Compile a list of Field Names

To construct the data dictionary, the field names from each table must be listed together in alphabetical order, removing any duplicate entries of the field names. If the database is large, it would be easier to use a spreadsheet package such as Excel to do this, in which case you would type all the field names from each table into one column, without worrying about duplicates or order. Then sort the column in ascending alphabetical order and remove duplicates.

Note that some items, such as addresses and names, are often easier to use in database applications such as reports if they are split into separate parts – for example, Address, Town, County, Postcode, or First Name, Last Name and Title. An address is an especially difficult item to use in one long line, and very difficult to write correctly on a letterhead or envelope unless it has been stored in separate lines.

For example, the field names in alphabetical order (across the page), without duplicates, from the **Hotel Reception** database are:

BillingAddress	Booking Code	Booking Date	ContactFirstName
ContactLastName	Contact Title	Country	County
Customer ID	Customer Email	End Date	EnSuite
Customer Fax Number	Customer Phone Number	PostalCode	Price per Night
Room Number	Room Occupancy	Start Date	Total Price
Town			

There may be some instances where the same field name is used in two or more tables, but these are not connected via a relationship, and in fact represent different pieces of information. For example, in the **Painting and Decorating Company** system, you may have a Phone Number field in both the CLIENT and SUPPLIER tables in a database. If the Phone Number description and field properties are the same for both tables, then the one Phone Number entry can remain on the data dictionary. However, if the Phone Number in the two tables requires different descriptions or properties, then it would be sensible to give these two fields different field names in the two tables to avoid confusion later on when using the screens.

8.4 Agree Description and Field Properties for each Field Name in the Data dictionary

The description and any other field properties required for each field name in the data dictionary must be agreed upon. Often this task needs to be carried out by the people who are going to use the system, rather than by the analyst who will only use the data samples provided as a source for this information.

A table, such as the one in the following **Hotel Reception** example, should be set up to show this information. Where a criterion is not applicable, such as field size for a Date/Time data type, or is not required, such as a validation rule for an Acknowledgement date, leave the box blank. Refer to Figure 8.1.

8.5 Determine the Entry Sequence for the Table Data

Once the tables have been amended to contain all the criteria described in the data dictionary, you can finally enter the data into the database. However, when setting up data in a database, in order that the referential integrity referred to previously is used to ensure that the data entered into one table corresponds to the data entered in a relating table, it is important that data is added in the correct sequence.

Field Name	Data Type	Description	Field Size	Format	Default Value	Validation Rule	Valid Text
BillingAddress	Text	First line of Customer's Address	50		Unknown		
Booking Code	Auto-Number	Code to identify each Booking					
Booking Date	Date/Time	Log Date					
ContactFirst Name	Text	First name of Customer	30				
ContactLast Name	Text	Last name of Customer	30				
Contact Title	Text	Title of Customer	5				
Country	Text	Country in Customer's Address	30		UK		
County	Text	County in Customer's Address	30				
Customer ID	Auto-Number	Code to identify each Customer					
Email	Text	E-mail address of Customer	30				
End Date	Date/Time	Last date of stay at Hotel		d/m/yyyy			
EnSuite	Yes/No	Indicates whether the room has an en-suite bathroom (yes/no)					
Fax Number	Text	Fax number of Customer	20				
Phone Number	Text	Telephone number of Customer	20				
PostalCode	Text	Postcode in Customer's Address	10				
Price per Night	Currency	Price charged for one night					
Room Number	Number	Number of Room				Range 1-100	Must be range 100
Room Occupancy	Number	Max Number of people permitted in Room				Range 1-4	Must be range
Start Date	Date/Time	Start date of stay in Hotel		d/m/yyyy			
Total Price	Currency	Total price charged for the stay					
Town	Text	Town in Customer's Address	30				

Figure 8.1 Completed data dictionary table

System data must be entered first into the database, since these tables are the tables that store the basic information against which the other tables will be checked, such as Room Number. Working data can then be entered into the database.

As well as considering whether the data is system data or working data it is important that whenever data is added to any table, if that table is part of a one-to-many relationship, the data must be added to the 'one' end of the relationship first.

In the **Hotel Reception** example, the system data tables are ROOM PRICE and ROOM. Since the ROOM PRICE table is at the 'one' end of the one-to-many relationship it has with ROOM, the data in the ROOM PRICE table must be entered first. The data in the ROOM table will then be added.

The working data tables in the **Hotel Reception** example are the CUSTOMERS, BOOKING and BOOKING LOG tables. Again, considering the one-to-many relationships and the way in which the tables will be used, the BOOKING LOG table entries must be set up for the BOOKING to be able to enter a Booking Code against the BOOKING LOG entries. CUSTOMERS data must also exist entered before the BOOKING can be created.

The order for entering data into the **Hotel Reception** tables is therefore as follows:

ROOM PRICE   ROOM   BOOKING LOG   CUSTOMERS   BOOKING

Part II: Access Practical

Work through this practical session to amend the tables in the **Hotel Reception** database to include the field descriptions and field properties detailed in the data dictionary in Part I. Then continue to enter data into the tables in the appropriate sequence and finally sort and filter that data.

8.6   Amend the Tables to Include the Data Dictionary Information

1. Start **Microsoft Access** as described in Section 5.5. Insert your floppy disk and open the **Hotel Reception** database as described in Section 6.5. Then click on the **Room Price** table and click the **Design** box.

2. Type the following text into the **Description** for **Room Occupancy** field: Max Number of people permitted in Room.

3. Make sure that the cursor is still on the **Room Occupancy** row. Type the following text into the **Validation Rule** box in the **Field Properties** section at the bottom of the screen: >=1 And <=4.

    Type the following text into the **Validation Text** box: Must be in range 1-4. Refer to Figure 8.2.

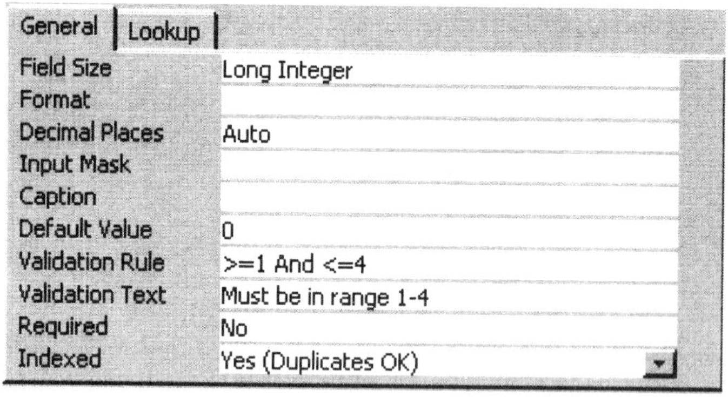

General	Lookup	
Field Size	Long Integer	
Format		
Decimal Places	Auto	
Input Mask		
Caption		
Default Value	0	
Validation Rule	>=1 And <=4	
Validation Text	Must be in range 1-4	
Required	No	
Indexed	Yes (Duplicates OK)	▼

Figure 8.2   Field properties for Room Occupancy

4. Type the following into the **Description** for the **EnSuite** field:

    Indicates whether the room has an en-suite bathroom (yes/no)

Type the following into the **Description** for the **Price per Night** field: `Price charged for one night`. Refer to Figure 8.3.

Room Price : Table		
Field Name	**Data Type**	**Description**
Room Occupancy	Number	Max Number of people permitted in Room
EnSuite	Yes/No	Indicates whether the room has an en-sute bathroom (yes/no)
Price per Night	Currency	Price charged for one night

Figure 8.3 Updated ROOM PRICE descriptions

5. Click the **Save** icon to save the updated table, then close the table by clicking its **Close** icon.

6. Click on the **Room** table name, then click the **Design** box.

7. Update the **Description** of the **Room Number** field with the text: `Number of Room`. Then type the following text into the **Validation Rule** box in the **Field Properties** section at the bottom of the screen: `>=1 And <=100`.

   Type the following text into the **Validation Text** box: `Must be in range 1-100`.

8. Update the **Description** of the **Room Occupancy** field to: `Max number of people permitted in room` and update the **Validation Rule** and **Validation Text** for that field as with the **Room Price** table. Type the following into the **Description** for the **EnSuite** field: `Indicates whether the room has an en-suite bathroom (yes/no)`.

   Refer to Figure 8.4. **Save**, then **Close** the table.

Room : Table		
Field Name	**Data Type**	**Description**
Room Number	Number	Number of room
Room Occupancy	Number	Max number of people permitted in room
EnSuite	Yes/No	Indicates whether the room has an en-sute bathroom (yes/no)

Figure 8.4 Updated ROOM descriptions

9. Click on the **Customers** table, then click the **Design** box. Update the **Description** for each field with the description in the data dictionary for the same field name. Refer to Figure 8.5.

10. Change the **Field Size** value of the **Contact Last Name** field to `30`.

11. Update the **Field Properties** of **Billing Address** by entering the text `Unknown` into the **Default Value** box. Set the **Field Size** to `50`.

12. Change the **Field Size** values of the **Town, County** and **Country** fields to `30`, **PostalCode** to `10` and **PhoneNumber** to `20`. Set the **Default Value** for **Country** to `UK`. **Save**, then **Close** the table.

Field Name	Data Type	Description
🔑 CustomerID	AutoNumber	Code to Identify each customer
ContactFirstName	Text	First name of Customer
ContactLastName	Text	Last name of Customer
BillingAddress	Text	First line of Customer's Address
Town	Text	Town in Customer's Address
County	Text	County in Customer's Address
PostalCode	Text	Postcode in Customer's Address
Country	Text	Country in Customer's Address
Contact Title	Text	Title of Customer
PhoneNumber	Text	Telephone number of Customer
FaxNumber	Text	Fax number of Customer
Email	Text	E-mail address of Customer

Figure 8.5 Updated CUSTOMER descriptions

13. Click on the **Booking** table and click **Design**. Update the **Description** for each field with the description in the data dictionary for the same field name. Refer to Figure 8.6.

Field Name	Data Type	Description
🔑 Booking Code	AutoNumber	Code to identify each booking
Start Date	Date/Time	Start date of stay iin Hotel
End Date	Date/Time	Last date of stay in Hotel
Room Number	Number	Number of Room
CustomerID	Number	Code to identify each customer
Total Price	Currency	Total price charged for the stay

Figure 8.6 Updated BOOKING descriptions

14. Click on the **Start Date** row, then click on the **Format** field property box. A down scroll arrow will appear. Click on it. A selection of date formats will appear.

15. It is important that any system developed these days considers the year part of any date format very carefully to allow for the 21st century dates. Any formats used should include all four date digits, i.e. 2001 rather than 01. The only date format provided with four date digits is **Long date**. Since the date format we need is 2/5/2001, you must type in your own format into this field.

Click to the right of the format box that has appeared to remove it, and type the following into the **Format** box: d/m/yyyy. The single d and m characters imply that the day and month values will be displayed without leading zeros if they are 1 - 9. For example, the 5th of May 2001 will be 5/5/2001 (not 05/05/2001), whereas the 10th of November 2001 will be 10/11/2001.

16. Update the **End Date** field properties by typing d/m/yyyy into the **Date Format** box.

17. Update the **Validation Rule** box of the **Room Number** field with the text: >=1 And <=100.

    Type the following text into the **Validation Text** box: Must be in range 1-100. **Save**, then **Close** the table.

18. Click on the **Booking Log** table and click **Design**. Update the **Description** for each field with the description in the data dictionary for the same field name. Refer to Figure 8.7.

19. Update the **Booking Date** field **Format** box with the format d/m/yyyy. Then update the **Validation Rule** box of the **Room Number** field with the text: >=1 And <=100.

    Type the following text into the **Validation Text** box: Must be in range 1-100. **Save**, then **Close** the table.

Field Name	Data Type	Description
Booking Log : Table		
Booking Date	Date/Time	Log Date
Room Number	Number	Number of Room
Booking Code	Number	Code to identify each Booking

Figure 8.7 Updated BOOKING LOG descriptions

8.7 Enter Data into the Tables

Now that the descriptions and field properties for the tables have been updated, the data can be entered. The sequence in which the data should be entered into the tables was identified in Section 8.5 as ROOM PRICE, ROOM, BOOKING LOG, CUSTOMER, BOOKING.

The data is entered first into the ROOM PRICE table as follows:

1. Click the **Room Price** table name on the **Main Database** dialogue box, then click the **Open** box. An empty table will be displayed, with the column headings corresponding to the field names in the **Room Price** table.

   To widen the columns so that you can see the complete headings for each column, place the cursor on the right edge of each of the column heading boxes and, whilst holding down the left mouse button, drag the cursor to the right. The rows in a database table are referred to as **records**. Refer to Figure 8.8. Note that since the **Room Occupancy** field is defined as numeric, a default value of zero displayed in it. The Yes/No box of the **EnSuite** field will be displayed as an empty tick box. The **Price per Night** field, as a currency field, shows a default value of £0.00.

Room Price : Table		
Room Occupancy	**EnSuite**	**Price per Night**
]	☐	£0.00

Figure 8.8 Empty ROOM PRICE table

2. To enter data into the table, simply position the cursor in the appropriate box and type in the text. Press the Tab key to get to the next box. Press the Enter/Return key at the end of the record to get a new record displayed. Fill in the Room Price data as shown in Figure 8.9.

Room Price : Table		
Room Occupancy	**EnSuite**	**Price per Night**
2	☑	£60.00
2	☐	£50.00
4	☑	£73.00
4	☐	£63.00

Figure 8.9 ROOM PRICE data

3. Test out the Room Occupancy validation rule, by changing the first Room Occupancy from 2 to 5. The validation message Must be in range 1-4 should be displayed. Click OK, then change it back to 2.

4. Save, then Close the table. Note that when you add data to a table, the data is saved automatically. You only needed to save the table this time because you changed the layout of the display.

5. Following the same procedures as explained in steps 1-3 to enter data into the remaining four tables Room, Booking Log, Customers and Booking in that order, as shown in Figures 8.10, 8.11, 8.12 and 8.13.

Room : Table		
Room Number	**Room Occupancy**	**EnSuite**
1	2	☑
2	4	☑
3	2	☐

Figure 8.10 ROOM data

Booking Log : Table

Booking Date	Room Number	Booking Code
16/3/1996	1	0
16/3/1996	2	1
16/3/1996	3	2
17/3/1996	1	3
17/3/1996	2	0
17/3/1996	3	2
18/3/1996	1	4
18/3/1996	2	0
18/3/1996	3	5
19/3/1996	1	4
19/3/1996	2	6
19/3/1996	3	5

Figure 8.11   BOOKING LOG data

Customers : Table

Customer ID	Contact First Name	Contact Last Name	Billing Address
1	Katie	Rubek	15 Dandow Close
2	Martin	Walsh	Flat 23B Barrow Heights
3	Gina	London	Crumbly Cottage, Brook Lane
4	Mills Construction Ltd		Location 15F, Station Industrial Estate

Customers : Table

Town	County	Postal Code	Country	Contact Title	Phone Number
Pelton	Bucks	MK165DS	UK	Miss	01495-6499735
Cambridge	Cambs		UK	Mr	01563-862645
Puddlecombe	Herts	AL3 6GH	UK	Mrs	01707-568134
Clapham	London		UK		01881-451895

Customers : Table

FaxNumber	Email
01495-649733	Rubek@homeways.co.uk
01881-450000	compsec@millscon.co.uk

Figure 8.12   CUSTOMER data (shown in three parts)

Booking : Table

Booking Code	Start Date	End Date	Room Number	CustomerID	Total Price
1	16/3/1996	16/3/1996	2	1	£73.00
2	16/3/1996	17/3/1996	3	2	£120.00
3	17/3/1996	17/3/1996	1	3	£60.00
4	18/3/1996	19/3/1996	1	4	£120.00
5	18/3/1996	19/3/1996	3	4	£120.00
6	19/3/1996	19/3/1996	2	1	£73.00

Figure 8.13   BOOKING data

Data dictionary   137

Note that although it looks as if the BOOKING LOG should be created after the BOOKING entries, since the BOOKING LOG contains Booking Code, in the live system, the BOOKING LOG entries are created with no Booking Codes in them. The Booking Codes are added to the BOOKING LOG after the BOOKINGS have been set up. To save time here, the Booking Code is added to the BOOKING LOG first. You can only do this because the referential integrity marker is switched off on the relationship between BOOKING and BOOKING LOG to accommodate the way in which the Booking Code will be added to the BOOKING LOG table in the live system.

6. Click the **Booking Log** table and click **Open**. Position the cursor on the first record in the table. At the bottom left of the window there are some arrows and a number to show which record the cursor is currently on. Refer to Figure 8.14.

Figure 8.14 Current record position

7. Click the single right scroll arrow a few times to move through the records, making each one current. The box at the bottom of the screen will show you which record number is current out of a total number of records.

8. Click the single left scroll button with a vertical line it. The first record will become the current record. Likewise, clicking the single right scroll arrow with the vertical line in will make the last record current.

9. Click the single right scroll arrow with an asterisk in to make the empty record at the end of the table current. Type in a new row of data, with the intention of deleting it in the next step, as follows:

    20/3/1996 1 5

10. Click anywhere on this new record and click **Edit** on the menu bar. Click **Delete Record**. A dialogue box will appear to ask you to confirm the deletion. Click **Yes**. The new record will disappear.

11. To test out the integrity of the database, make the following changes to the first row of the table:

    • Change the **Room Number** to 2. This will mean that there are duplicate keys values in rows 1 and 2. Press the Tab key to get to the next row. An error box will be displayed. Click **OK** and change the Room Number back to 1.

    • Change the Room Number in the same row to 4. There is no Room Number 4 in the **Room** table, and since there is a one-to-many relationship between Room and Booking Log, with referential integrity, when you press the Tab key to get to the next row, an error box will appear. Click **OK** and change it back to 1.

12. Close the table by clicking the **Close** icon on the **Booking Log : Table** window.

8.8 Sorting Data in a Table

The order in which data is entered and stored in a table is not important. Once in a table, the data can be sorted into ascending or descending order, using one of the columns as the sort order column. For example, you may wish to view the Customer Rows in the CUSTOMERS table in ascending alphabetical order of the Customer Last Name. This can be done as follows:

1. Click on the **Customers** table and click the **Open** box to view the data in the CUSTOMERS table.

2. Click on the **Contact Last Name** column heading text. The whole column should become highlighted. Click the **Sort Ascending** icon and the table will be sorted into ascending Contact Last Name order. Note that the fourth customer, Mills Construction Ltd., is sorted to the top since a space character comes before any alphabetic character in an ascending sort. Refer to Figure 8.15.

3. To revert to the previous order, sort the table into ascending CustomerID order in the same way. **Close** the table without saving it.

Customer ID	Contact First Name	Contact Last Name
4	Mills Construction Ltd	
3	Gina	London
1	Katie	Rubek
2	Martin	Walsh

Figure 8.15 Sorted CUSTOMERS table

8.9 Filtering Data in a Table

As well as being able to sort the table data into an order, it is also possible to apply a simple filter to a table to specify which rows of data are displayed. For example, you can filter the table to view only those BOOKING LOG rows for 17/3/1996, as follows:

1. Click the **Booking Log** table and click on **Open** to view the table data.

2. Highlight one of the three **17/3/1996** dates and click the **Filter by Selection** icon. The three rows for that date will be displayed.

3. To remove the filter and view all rows again, click the **Remove Filter** icon. Note that once the filter has been removed, it can be applied again by

clicking the same icon you clicked to remove it. This icon will now be called the Apply Filter icon. To apply a different filter, you will need to select the field and click the Filter by Selection icon as you did before.

4. Close the table without saving it.

It is also possible to filter by part of a field. For example, to view only customers in the Customers table that have a Contact First Name starting with an M do as follows:

5. Click on the Customers table again and click the Open box to view the data in the Customers table.

6. Select the M only in the Contact First Name of Martin and click the Filter by Selection icon. Only the two rows for Customer IDs 2 and 4 will be displayed.

7. Remove the filter and Close the table without saving it.

8.10 Summary

This chapter has covered the following material:

Part I: Database Design Theory

• What a data dictionary is and how it is used.
• Criteria described in the data dictionary.
• Compiling a list of field names to be used in the data dictionary.
• Define description and field properties for each field in the data dictionary.
• Determine the entry sequence for table data.

Part II: Access Practical

• Amending tables to include data dictionary criteria.
• Enter data into the tables.
• Sorting data in a table.
• Filtering data in a table.

8.11 Written Exercises

8.11.1   What is *data integrity*? Describe the main ways in which data integrity can be maintained in a database.

8.11.2 Draw up a data dictionary for the **University Department** database described in Section 5.11.1. Refer to Figure 8.16 for an example of the data. Include the following criteria:

Field Name   Data Type
Description   Field Size
Format   Default Value
Validation Rule   Validation Text

8.11.3 (a) Draw up a data dictionary for the **Painting and Decorating Company** database described in Section 7.11.3. Include the following criteria:

Field Name   Data Type
Description   Field Size
Format   Default Value
Validation Rule   Validation Text

Make sure you include at least one Format, Default Value and Validation Rule and Validation Text pair in your dictionary.

(b) Determine the entry sequence for the data being entered into the **Painting and Decorating Company** database.

8.11.4 Determine the entry sequence for the data being entered into the following database. Note that the arrow end of the relationship is the *many* end, and the tables marked Sys hold system data and those marked Wrk hold working data.

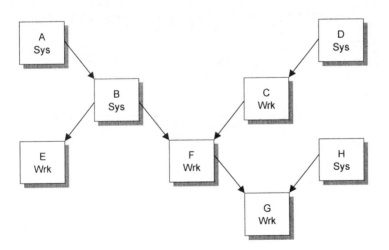

8.12 Practical Exercises

8.12.1 Update the **Painting and Decorating Company** database to include the data dictionary criteria listed in Section 8.11.3.

8.12.2 Enter the following data (Figure 8.16) into the COURSE DETAILS, STAFF DETAILS and TIMETABLE tables in the **University Department** database.

STAFF DETAILS (primary key Staff ID)

Staff ID	Name	Address	Salary Grade	Holiday Entitlement	Remaining Holiday
F123B	Mr David Holding	15 Wood Close, Barton, Manchester	7	20	5
F126G	Mrs Amanda Davidson	Bootles Cottage, Hempton Lock, Bucks MK15 3DZ	8	22	18
G452S	Dr Phillip Goodson	45 Wells Drive, Great Hanslope, Hants HT6 7GT	12	25	12

COURSE DETAILS (primary key Course Code)

Course Code	Course Title	Course Summary
WP1	Basic Word Processing	Basic features of word processing: creating, saving, formatting and printing documents.
DBD1	Database Design	Principles of data analysis: data flow diagrams, entity-relationship modelling and normalisation.
INT1	Introduction to the Internet	How to search for information, use e-mail and set up a web site.

TIMETABLE

Day	Time	Location	Course Code	Session Type	Staff ID
Monday	09:00	Hall 3	INT1	Lecture	F123B
Monday	11:00	Hall 3	DBD1	Lecture	F126G
Tuesday	14:00	Comp 3	WP1	Practical	G452S
Tuesday	14:00	Comp 1	INT1	Practical	F123B
Tuesday	14:00	Room 25F	DBD1	Tutorial	F126G
Wednesday	09:00	Comp 1	INT1	Practical	F126G
Wednesday	11:00	Comp 1	WP1	Practical	G452S
Wednesday	11:00	Comp 1	WP1	Practical	G452S

Figure 8.16 STAFF DETAILS, COURSE DETAILS and TIMETABLE table data

8.12.3 Enter data into the updated **Painting and Decorating Company** database, following the data entry sequence specified in Section 8.11.3. Use data from the samples provided in Section 6.10.2. You will need to make up some data for the new WORK CATEGORY table and the Customer and Supplier telephone and fax numbers. Make sure you test the validation, default and format values set up in the tables.

8.12.4 Create a new database called **Stock** and create a table using the Table Wizard called PRODUCTS. Select the following fields: Product ID, Product Name, Unit price, Discontinued and Units in Stock. Add the data shown in Figure 8.17.

Carry out the following sorts on the data:

(a) Sort the table into ascending Product Name order.

(b) Sort the table into descending Unit price order, to see the most expensive at the top of the list.

(c) Sort the table back into ascending Product ID order.

(d) Filter the data in the table to show just those products that start with the word Antiseptic.

(e) Remove the filter.

(f) Filter the data in the table to show just the discontinued products.

(g) Remove the filter.

Products : Table

Product ID	Product Name	Unit Price	Discontinued	Units In Stock
1	Sun Cream	£5.56	No	6
2	After-sun Lotion	£4.50	No	4
3	Shampoo	£1.50	No	9
4	Conditioner	£2.00	No	5
5	Antiseptic Cream	£1.90	No	0
6	Antiseptic Spray	£2.50	Yes	0
7	Antiseptic Liquid	£2.10	No	5
8	Hairbrush(gents)	£2.99	No	10
9	Comb (gents)	£0.50	Yes	0
10	Hairbrush (ladies)	£2.99	No	6
11	Comb (ladies)	£0.80	No	0
12	Comb (novelty)	£1.50	Yes	0

Figure 8.17 PRODUCTS table

9 Designing Queries

9.1 Introduction

In the previous chapter, we looked at how data in a table can be presented in a specific order by *sorting* the table and how some of the data can be selected by *filtering* the table. Useful as these techniques are for displaying the table data, they have the following limitations:

- A *sort* can only be applied using one column as the sort key.

- A *filter* can only be applied on one field.

- It is not possible to link tables when carrying out a sort or a filter. You cannot, in our **Hotel Reception** example, carry out a filter so that only the bookings made for customers who live in London can be displayed. This would involve linking both the BOOKING and CUSTOMER tables.

- You cannot save sort or filter instructions with the intention of carrying them out again.

All of these limitations can be overcome by using a **query**. A query is a combination of a filter and a sort that can select data from one or more related tables, using specific selection criteria, and display that data in a specified order. The query can be given a name and be saved, so that the query can be used repeatedly.

In Part I of this chapter, we are going to look in detail at what a query is and how to construct one. You are also going look at how to decide which way to navigate around the database, and how to use complex selection criteria, such as calculations in a query.

In Part II you will be shown how to create a query using Access, using both the Query Wizard and the Design View. You will also be shown how to modify a query in the Design View to change its function.

144

Part I: Database Design Theory

"A query is a combination of a filter and a sort that can select data from one or more related tables, using specific selection criteria, and display that data in a specified order. The query can be given a name and be saved, so that the query can be used repeatedly."

In the **Hotel Reception** database, an example of a query on the database could be:

"Display all room numbers, along with the dates they are booked for, for any en-suite rooms booked during December 1998, in Room Number, then Booking Date order."

The ROOM and BOOKING LOG tables shown in the steps below contain some sample data that will be used in the query. If you were to tackle the query yourself from the tables set up so far on the database, you would need to carry out the following steps (note that the shaded rows in the tables show the selected data at each step):

1. Search through the ROOM table to find all rooms where the **EnSuite** field is **Yes**. Refer to Figure 9.1.

2. For each Room Number selected in 1, find the corresponding rooms in the Booking Log table. Refer to Figure 9.2.

Room Number	Room Occupancy	EnSuite
1	4	Yes
2	2	Yes
3	4	No

Figure 9.1   Room data – selected rows are shaded

Booking Date	Room Number	Booking Code
30/12/1998	1	20
30/12/1998	2	22
30/12/1998	3	
31/12/1998	1	20
31/12/1998	2	
31/12/1998	3	
1/1/1999	1	24
1/1/1999	2	
1/1/1999	3	

Figure 9.2   Booking data – selected rows are shaded

3. Keep the Room Number and Booking Date of any of the selected Booking Log entries that have a Booking Date in December 1998 where the Booking Code is not empty (i.e. a booking has been made). Refer to Figure 9.3.

4. Once the selected Room Numbers and Booking Dates have been identified in the previous step, sort them into ascending Room Number, then ascending Booking Date order, and display them. Refer to Figure 9.4.

Booking Date	Room Number	Booking Code
30/12/1998	1	20
30/12/1998	2	22
30/12/1998	3	
31/12/1998	1	20
31/12/1998	2	
31/12/1998	3	
1/1/1999	1	24
1/1/1999	2	
1/1/1999	3	

Figure 9.3 Booking data - selected rows are shaded

Room Number	Booking Date
1	30/12/1998
1	31/12/1998
2	30/12/1998

Figure 9.4 Query result

These four instructions can be merged into one query using a database management tool such as Access, and can be saved so that this query can be used, or amended and used repeatedly.

Although the example in the previous section is a simple query, it illustrates the three main features that need to be considered for each query:

- Field Names
- Selection Criteria
- Sort Order.

9.3 Identify the Field Names for a Query

The field names used in a query are defined for one of the following reasons:

1. The data in the field is to be used as part of the selection criteria and is also displayed in the result (e.g. the Booking Date).

2. The data in the field is to be used as part of the selection criteria, but is not displayed as part of the result (e.g. the En-Suite flag).

3. The data in the field is not part of any selection criteria, but must be displayed in the result (e.g. the Room Number).

4. The data in the field is neither displayed in the result nor part of the selection criteria, but is required to allow the database manager to find the connection between one table of data and another. (E.g. Even if the Room Number was not required to be displayed in the result, it would still be needed in the query to connect the ROOM and BOOKING LOG tables, although not part of any selection criteria.)

9.4 Identify the Selection Criteria for a Query

There can be many different fields, with selection criteria applied to each one. The selection criteria will enable the query to decide whether the record containing that item of data should be included in the resulting query or not. For example, one of the selection criteria used above was that the En-Suite flag in the ROOM table record is Yes. There are also two other selection criteria in that query: that the Booking Date is in December 1998, and that the Booking Code is not spaces.

There are several simple types of criteria that can be applied to a field:

= value	equal to	> value	greater than
>= value	greater than or equal to	< value	less than
<= value	less than or equal to	<> value	not equal to

You can have more than one criterion for a particular field. For example, one way to determine whether the date is in December 1998, would be to apply these two criteria to the Booking Date:

```
>= 1/12/1998
<1/1/1999
```

Another example of multiple criteria is if you wanted to extract all bookings for either room 1 or room 3. The two criteria for the Room Number would be:

```
= 1
= 3
```

It is very important, once you have identified the two or more criteria, that you connect them together with either an **And** or an **Or**.

In the first example, to identify a date in December 1998, the date range applied must have an And between the two criteria. This gives the single criterion for the Booking Date:

```
>=1/12/1998 And < 1/1/1999
```

If the two criteria were joined using an Or, then any date before 1/12/1998 and any on or after 1/1/1999 would be selected. 28/8/1987 would be selected, for example.

In the second example, where the Room Number must be 1 or 3, the two criteria for

Room Number can be joined together using an Or:

```
=1 Or =3
```

If you use an And then *no* Room would ever be selected, since a Room Number cannot be both a 1 and a 3!

It is also possible to use three or more criteria, taking care to link them together using Ands and Ors and carefully placed brackets.

For example, if the Booking Date in a query had to be 5/3/1997, 6/3/1997 or any date in April 1997, there are actually three sets of criteria for Booking Date here:

```
=  5/3/1997
=  6/3/1997
>= 1/4/1997
<  1/5/1997
```

To decide how these will be grouped, it helps to rewrite the query criteria, paying special attention to the Ors and Ands:

A Booking Date is selected if …

the Booking Date = 5/3/1997   *or*
the Booking Date = 6/3/1997   *or*
the Booking Date is in April 1997

This shows that there are really three Or criteria that must be grouped together as follows:

```
= 5/3/1997 Or = 6/3/1997  Or (>= 1/4/1997  And < 1/5/1997)
```

Note that the third Or option here requires brackets around it.

9.5 Identify the Sort Order for a Query

When the resulting information is displayed in the query, it is possible to specify in which order the data should be shown. In our example, the data was sorted first by Room Number, then by Booking Date – both ascending.

When you define a query, you can specify which fields the resulting data should be sorted by. If more than one field is used to sort the data, you must specify in which order the data must be sorted. You must also specify whether the field should be sorted ascending or descending.

The easiest way to determine the sort order is to draw out an example of the data you expect to see in your resulting query, in the order in which you would like to see it.

In the following example, a query will list data as follows:

Town	Cinema	*Film Title*
Bradford	Astoria	Ant Eater II – The Revenge
Bradford	UCC	Your Worst Nightmare IV
Leeds	Astoria	Ant Eater II – The Revenge
Leeds	Astoria	Fifteen Seconds to Zero
Leeds	Astoria	Sent to France
Leeds	Empire	Ant Eater II – The Revenge
Leeds	Empire	Molly's Dream World

The Sort Order for this query will be:

1st	Town (ascending)
2nd	Cinema (ascending)
3rd	Film Title (ascending)

In a similar query, the same data could be sorted into a different order as follows:

Town	Cinema	*Film Title*
Bradford	Astoria	Ant Eater II – The Revenge
Leeds	Astoria	Ant Eater II – The Revenge
Leeds	Empire	Ant Eater II – The Revenge
Leeds	Astoria	Fifteen Seconds to Zero
Leeds	Empire	Molly's Dream World
Leeds	Astoria	Sent to France
Bradford	UCC	Your Worst Nightmare IV

This time, the sort order would be:

1st	Film Title (ascending)
2nd	Cinema (ascending)
3rd	Town (ascending)

9.6 Putting the Query together

The three parts that can specify a query: field names, selection criteria and sort order, can be written down in a query table as shown in Figure 9.5 (similar to an Access query design screen).

The Show Field column will indicate whether you wish to see the field in the resulting query or not. A field used to help connect one table to another, or used in the selection criteria, will not necessarily be displayed on the resulting query.

Field	Table	Show Field	Selection Criteria	Sort Order

Figure 9.5 Query layout table

The original query was as follows:

"Display all Room Numbers, along with the dates they are booked for, for any en-suite rooms booked during December 1998, in Room Number, then Booking Date order."

This will be written in the layout as shown in Figure 9.6.

Field	Table	Show Field	Selection Criteria	Sort Order
Room Number	Room/Booking Log	Yes		1
EnSuite	Room	No	= Yes	
Booking Date	Booking Log	Yes	>= 1/12/1998 And < 1/1/1999	2
Booking Code	Booking Log	No	<> zero	

Figure 9.6   Query layout table showing selection criteria and sort order

9.7   Calculations in Queries

As well as producing a selected, sorted list of data, a query can also calculate its own data from data provided in one or more fields in the query. For example, a query to display the Room Number and Room Price could also display the price for a week's booking in each room, by performing a calculation on the Price per Night. The resulting query would be as shown in Figure 9.7.

Room Number	Price per Night	Price per Week
1	£60.00	£420.00
2	£73.00	£511.00
3	£50.00	£350.00

Figure 9.7   Weekly price query results

To produce a query to simply display the Room Number and Price per Night for each room, in Room Number order, the query layout table as shown in Figure 9.8 will be written.

Field	Table	Show Field	Selection Criteria	Sort Order
Room Number	Room	Yes		1
Room Occupancy	Room/Room Price			
EnSuite	Room/Room Price			
Price per Night	Room Price	Yes		

Figure 9.8   Query layout table showing the nightly room rates for each room

Note that the Room Occupancy and EnSuite fields are also required, but not displayed in the result, since these two fields together connect the ROOM table with the ROOM PRICE table, in which the price is stored.

To add a calculation to the query, add a new row to the query layout table, since the result of the calculation will be displayed as if it were a field. Refer to Figure 9.9.

Field	Table	Show Field	Selection Criteria	Sort Order
Room Number	Room	Yes		1
Room Occupancy	Room/Room Price			
En-Suite	Room/Room Price			
Price per Night	Room Price	Yes		
Price per Week = Price per Night * 7		Yes		

Figure 9.9 Query table to show the nightly and weekly room rates for each room

Note that the arithmetic operators used in calculations are:

+   add
-   subtract
*   multiply
/   divide

Part II: Access Practical

Access provides two ways of creating queries, using a Query Wizard or the Design View. Before creating a query, however, it is important that you have described the query in the query layout sheet, as shown in Section 9.6.

Note that in Access you do not need to specify any fields in a query that are required simply to connect two tables together via a relationship. Access will be able to work that out for itself. This means that if a field name is included in the query layout sheet that has a No in the **Show Field** column, and does not have any **Selection** criteria or **Sort Order**, this field can be omitted from the query. If however, a field that is in two tables is required to be displayed in the query, you only need to select that field from one of the two tables.

You are going to create the original query described in this chapter using a Query Wizard. Since the Query Wizard will not set up selection criteria or a sort order, the resulting data displayed in the query will simply be the Room Number, EnSuite flag, Booking Date and Booking Code for every BOOKING LOG entry in the database. After you have used the Wizard to set this up, you will then apply the selection criteria and sort order in the Design View.

The original query was to *"display all Room Numbers, along with the dates they are booked for, for any en-suite rooms booked during December 1998, in Room Number, then Booking Date order."*

This query will be changed slightly to allow for the Booking dates already set up in the Access database. The selection criterion for the Booking Date will be that it is either 18/3/1996 or 19/3/1996. The amended query is described in the query layout table in Figure 9.10.

Field	Table	Show Field	Selection Criteria	Sort Order
Room Number	Room/Booking Log	Yes		1
En-Suite	Room	No	= Yes	
Booking Date	Booking Log	Yes	= 18/3/1996 Or = 19/3/1996	2
Booking Code	Booking Log	No	◇ zero	

Figure 9.10   Query table for the en-suite booking query

9.8   Creating a Query using a Wizard

Use the Query Wizard to create a basic query, listing the Room Number, Booking Date and Booking Code for all BOOKING LOG entries, along with EnSuite flag for the corresponding Room entry. You will add selection criteria in the next section.

1. Start **Microsoft Access** as described in Section 5.5. Insert your floppy disk and open the **Hotel Reception** database as described in Section 6.5. Then click on the **Queries** tab.

2. Click the **New** box and a **New Query** dialogue box will appear. Refer to Figure 9.11.

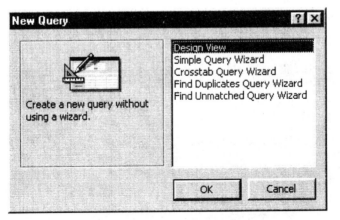

Figure 9.11 New query dialogue box

3. Click on **Simple Query Wizard**, then on **OK**. The **Simple Query Wizard** dialogue box will be displayed. Refer to Figure 9.12.

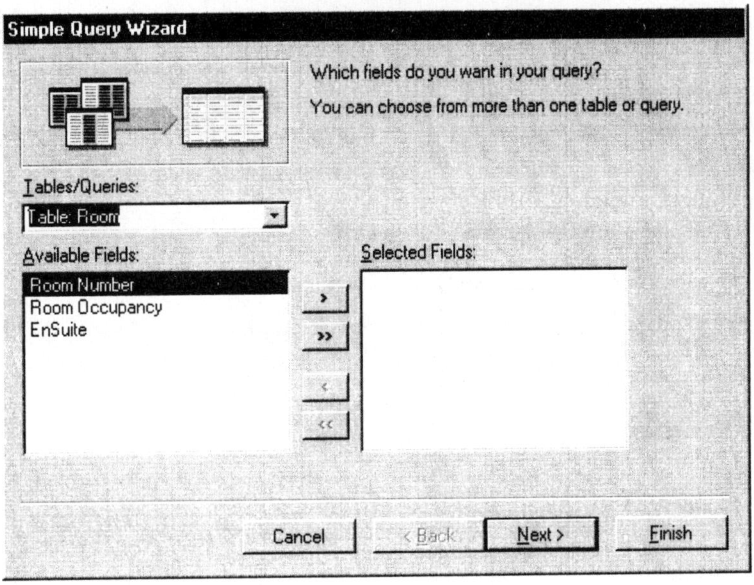

Figure 9.12 Simple query wizard dialogue box

4. You must now select each table that you require fields from for your query, and add those required fields to the **Selected Fields** list. Click on the down scroll

button on the right of the Tables/Queries box. Select the Table: Room table. The fields in the Room table will appear in the Available Fields box.

5. Click on Room Number and click on the single right arrow box to add the field to the Selected Fields list.

6. Carry out the same procedure to add EnSuite to the Selected Fields list. Alternatively, since you wanted all but one of the fields, you could have clicked the double right arrow box to add all the fields to the Selected Fields list, and then use the single left arrow to remove the Room Occupancy field.

7. You must now add the fields from the Booking Log table. You do not need to add the Room Number again, since it is already in the Selected Fields list. Click on the down scroll arrow on the Tables/Queries box again, and this time select Table: Booking Log.

8. Add the fields Booking Date and Booking Code to the Selected Fields list as before.

9. Click Next >.

10. The next dialogue box asks you whether you want to see a Detailed Query or a Summary Query. A Detailed Query will list every row that satisfies the query, as we have done so far in this chapter. A Summary Query will not display every row, but can perform calculations on various groups of rows, for example adding up certain values in each row to display a total row for the group. In this case, leave the selection on Detail and click Next>.

11. You can now change the name of your query if you wish. Change the name to EnSuiteBook. Click Finish.

The resulting query will show the Room Number, EnSuite flag, Booking Date and Booking Code for all Booking Log entries since no selection criteria have yet been applied. Refer to Figure 9.13.

Room Number	EnSuite	Booking Date	Booking Code
1	☑	16/3/1996	0
1	☑	17/3/1996	3
1	☑	18/3/1996	4
1	☑	19/3/1996	4
2	☑	16/3/1996	1
2	☑	17/3/1996	0
2	☑	18/3/1996	0
2	☑	19/3/1996	6
3	☐	16/3/1996	2
3	☐	17/3/1996	2
3	☐	18/3/1996	5
3	☐	19/3/1996	5

EnSuiteBook : Select Query

Figure 9.13 EnSuiteBook query created using a Query Wizard

9.9   Modifying a Query – Applying Selection Criteria

Now that the basic query has been constructed using the Wizard, you need to modify it to include the selection criteria and a sort order shown in Figure 9.10. To do this, you will need to use the Query Design View.

1. Click the (Design) View icon to see the design view of the Query. Refer to Figure 9.14. Note that the relationship between the two tables, Room and Booking Log, has been recognised by Access and is shown on the screen, although this information was not provided in the Query Wizard.

Field:	Room Number	EnSuite	Booking Date	Booking Code
Table:	Room	Room	Booking Log	Booking Log
Sort:				
Show:	✓	✓	✓	✓
Criteria:				
or:				

Figure 9.14   EnSuiteBook query in Design View

2. The top half of the screen shows the selected tables and the relationships between them. The bottom half shows the fields and the selection and sort criteria for each.

3. To apply the selection criteria for the EnSuite flag, type the following text into the Criteria box in the EnSuite column: = Yes.

4. Since the EnSuite flag should not be shown in the final query (they will all be Yes anyway), click on the Show box in the EnSuite column to remove the tick.

5. Apply similar changes to the Booking Code column as follows: Type the following text into the Criteria box: <> 0.

    Then click on the Show box to remove the tick.

6. To apply the date selection to the Booking Date, type the following text into the Criteria box for the Booking Date column: =18/3/1996 Or =19/3/1996.

Leave the Show box with a tick in, since we want to display this field in the query. Note that there are extra rows below the first Criteria row, labelled Or. These rows can be used if there is more than one Or criterion for your query. In our example, we only have the one criterion, that each Booking Log entry must have a non-zero Booking

Code, a room with an en-suite flag and be on either the 18/3/1996 or 19/3/1996. If the criteria for the query were that the room had to be en-suite and booked for the 18/3/1996 OR the room had to be not en-suite and booked for the 19/3/1996, this would represent two sets of criteria, linked together by an Or. In this case the first criteria would be written on the Criteria row, the second would be written on the Or row.

9.10 Modifying a Query – Applying a Sorting Order

In Access, it is not possible to allocate a particular sort order number to a field. The order in which the query will sort the selected rows of data is determined by how far to the left of the Query Design the field is placed. For example, since we want the data sorted first by Room Number, then by Booking Date, the Room Number field needs to be to the left of the Booking Date field in the Query Design.

You can also allocate a sort direction to the field of either Ascending or Descending. Although the two sort fields are in the correct order in the Query Design, to practise moving a field column in the design, you are going to move the Booking Date column next to the Room Number column.

1. Click the mouse pointer just above the top of the Booking Date field name column to select the whole column.

2. Click the Cut icon on the toolbar.

3. Create a new column between the Room Number and EnSuite columns by selecting the EnSuite column in the same way as you selected the Booking Date column, and click Insert on the menu bar, then click Columns.

4. Click the Paste icon on the toolbar to insert the Booking Date column.

5. To set both the sort fields to be Ascending, click on the Sort box in the Room Number column. A scroll arrow will appear. Click on that and select Ascending. Do the same to select Ascending for the Booking Date column too.

9.11 Running a Query

1. Click the Run icon on the toolbar to run the query. Only three Booking Log entries should be displayed. Refer to Figure 9.15. Note that the data is displayed in Room Number, then Booking Date order.

2. Save the modified query by clicking the Save icon on the toolbar. Then Close the query by clicking the Close icon on the top right corner of the EnSuiteBook : Select Query window.

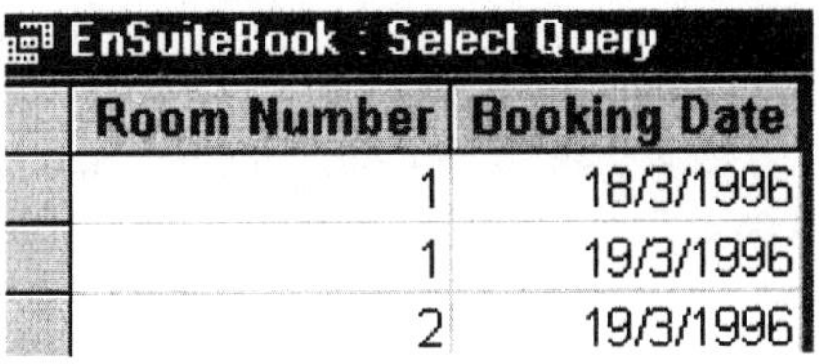

EnSuiteBook : Select Query

Room Number	Booking Date
1	18/3/1996
1	19/3/1996
2	19/3/1996

Figure 9.15 EnSuiteBook query result

9.12 Creating a Query using the Design View

You are now going to create a query without using a Wizard, just using the Design window that you used to modify the previous query. The query that will be used is that described in an earlier section in this chapter. Refer to Figure 9.16. Note that this query includes a calculation.

Field	*Table*	*Show Field*	*Selection Criteria*	*Sort Order*
Room Number	Room	Yes		1
Room Occupancy	Room/Room Price			
EnSuite	Room/Room Price			
Price per Night	Room Price	Yes		
Price per Week = Price per Night * 7		Yes		

Figure 9.16 Query table to show the nightly and weekly room rates for each room

1. Click New on the Queries section of the Hotel Reception : Database window.
2. Click on Design View, then click OK.
3. The Show Table dialogue box will be displayed listing all the tables in your database that can be included in the query. Click on Room, then click Add. The Room table will appear at the top of the query screen.
4. Add the Room Price table to the query screen in the same way. (Click on Room Price, then click on Add.)
5. Click Close to get rid of the Show Table dialogue box.

Note that when modifying a query, if you need to add an additional table to the query screen, click the Show Table icon on the toolbar to display the Show Table dialogue box. You can then select table names and add them to the screen, then close it as above.

6. You now need to select the appropriate fields from each table for the query. Click on the Room Number field of the Room table and, whilst keeping the left mouse button depressed, drag the mouse so that it is on the first Field box of the first column in the query table. Release the mouse button and the field name Room Number and the table name Room will appear in the first column.

7. The Show box will automatically be set to a tick, so leave it like that. Click on the Sort box for that column, then click on the down scroll arrow that appears and select Ascending.

Note that since neither the Room Occupancy nor the En-Suite fields are being displayed in the query, and since neither is part of the sort order or the selection criteria, they do not need to be defined in the query table. Access knows that there is a relationship between the two tables based upon the Room Occupancy and EnSuite fields and will be able to link the two tables without being told which field to use.

8. Click and drag the Price per Night field from the Room Price table into the Field box in the second column. The Show box will display a tick. Leave it like that.

9.13 Adding a Calculation to a Query

In our query, we need to create a field called Price per Week that shows the result of the calculation Price per Night * 7. When you add a calculation field such as this to a query, you must type the whole calculation into the Field box in the first empty column in the format:

Calculation Field Name:Calculation

Note that when you include a field name in the calculation, as well as making sure you have spelled it correctly, you must place brackets around it.

In our example, the Field box in the third column will be:

```
Price per Week:[Price per Night]*7
```

You can then apply the Sort, Show or Criteria information to that column as with any other field that you had obtained from a table.

1. Type the following into the **Field** box of the third column:

```
Price per Week:[Price per Night]*7
```

Note that when you click on another box, the **Show** box will have a tick in it.

2. Run the query by clicking the **Run** icon on the toolbar. Refer to Figure 9.17.

RoomWeekPrice : Select Query

Room Number	Price per Night	Price per Week
1	£60.00	£420.00
2	£73.00	£511.00
3	£50.00	£350.00

Figure 9.17 RoomWeekPrice query including calculation

3. Click the **Save** icon to save the query. When asked for a query name, type RoomWeekPrice over the default **Query1** name. Click **OK**. Close the RoomPriceWeek : **Select Query** window as before.

4. Close the **Hotel Reception** : **Database** window, then close **Access**, each time by clicking the **Close** icon in the top right corner of the window.

9.14 Summary

This chapter has covered the following material:

Part I: Database Design Theory

- Explanation of what a query is and what it can do.
- Field names in a query.
- Selection criteria in a query.
- Sort order in a query.
- Putting a query together.
- Calculations in a query.

Part II: Access Practical

- Creating a query using a Wizard.
- Modifying a query.

- Applying selection criteria to a query.
- Applying a sort order to a query.
- Running a query.
- Creating a query using Design View.
- Adding a calculation to a query.

9.15 Written Exercises

9.15.1   Using the database shown in Figure 9.18, complete a query table (refer to Section 9.6) for each query (a), (b) and (c).

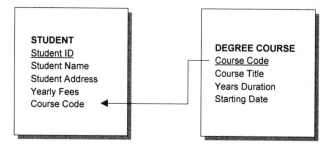

Figure 9.18   Degrees database

(a) Display all the Student Names and Addresses for all students whose Yearly Fees are at least £3000.

(b) Display all Student Names of students studying on Degree Courses that started before the start of the year 2000 and have a duration of four years.

9.15.2   Using the database shown Exercise 9.16.1, complete a Query table to include a calculation for the following query:

"Display the Name and the Total Fees for the duration of the course, for all students studying for a French degree, whose course started in September 1998."

9.15.3   Refer to the **Painting and Decorating Company** database design last updated in Section 7.11.3. Design a query table (refer to Section 9.6) for each of the following queries:

(a) List the Quote Ref., Quote Date, Quote Value and Category Description for all JOBS that have not had an agreed date set yet.

(b) The supplier Leith Paints is having financial difficulties. All undelivered orders from that supplier will not be supplied, therefore, and the jobs that are waiting for those supplies may be delayed. Produce a list showing the Quote Ref., Customer Name and Telephone Number for all JOBS that have orders placed for Items supplied by Leith Paints that have not yet been delivered.

(c) List the Quote Ref., Final price and Outstanding Balance for all completed jobs where the Outstanding Balance is more than 50% of the Final Balance (you will need to include a calculation in this).

9.16 Practical Exercises

9.16.1 (a) Create a new database called **Degrees** and use the Design View to create two tables: Students and Degree Course as described in the first written exercise in this chapter. Create the relationships between the tables as shown. Enter the following data into the tables:

Student ID	Student name	Student address	Yearly fees	Degree code
501	Thomas Brown	Rampart Hall, Rainer Campus	£2500	215
502	Matthew South	Gate Hall, Edward B. Campus	£3000	217
503	Kate Surreal	Beamer Hall, Rainer Campus	£4000	200
504	David Partner	Holding Hall, Rainer Campus	£3200	217
505	Norma Colder	Rampart Hall, Rainer Campus	£2000	215
506	John Colder	Rampart Hall, Rainer Campus	£2200	218
507	Robert Talcum	Powder Hall, Bradgate Campus	£3200	219
508	Davina Talcum	Powder Hall, Bradgate Campus	£2500	218

Degree code	Course title	Duration (years)	Starting Date
214	French	3	6/9/1997
215	French	4	15/9/1998
217	Lingerie Design	4	2/9/1999
218	French	3	6/9/1999
219	Theology	4	9/9/2000
200	Computing	4	6/9/1999

(b) Create and run the query described in Section 9.15.1, part (a). Save as StudentFees.

(c) Create and run the query described in Section 9.15.1, part (b). Save as PreMillen4Year.

(d) Create and run the query described in Section 9.15.2. Save as French-Sept1998.

9.16.2   Using the Degrees database created in the previous exercise, create the following queries:

(a) Display the Student Name and Student Address fields from the Student table in Student Address (ascending), then Student Name (ascending) order.

(b) Display all the fields from the Degree Course table in Course Title (ascending), then Starting Date (descending) order.

9.16.3   Using the Painting database, create the three queries described in Section 9.15.3, parts (a), (b) and (c), calling them NoAgreedDate, LeithPaintJobs and OutstandBal respectively.

10 Building Screens and Reports

10.1 Introduction

By now, you should have designed and built a database as well as some queries to help you view the data. You can enter and amend data in the database using the open view of each table and you can carry out complex queries to view the data in one or more tables in many different ways.

For some people, this is all they want from a database. However, to make the database more user-friendly and more like a tailor-made computer system, you need to add specially designed interfaces between the user and the database. These interfaces can be introduced whenever the user needs to access the database in any way, whether to add, modify or delete data or to read the data from the tables or queries.

There are two types of user interface: screen and report. A screen could be used to allow the user to type in booking information, for example, instead of filling in a booking form manually. The fields on the screen would match fields in the booking table on the database. A screen can also contain fields from two or more tables at once.

The easiest way to identify which screens and reports are required in the system is to refer back the data flow diagram drawn up at the start of the database project. Although screen and report design is an important issue and could fill a book on its own, a few of the important issues will be addressed in this chapter.

In Part I of this chapter, you will look back to the data flow diagram to decide where screens and reports need to be added to the database to create a fully working system. A few important guidelines for screen and report design will also be discussed, with some examples from the case study.

In Part II of this chapter, you will be shown how to use Access to create screens, called *forms* in Access, and reports, both using the Wizard tool.

Part I: Database Design Theory

10.2 Deciding which Screens and Reports are Required

When designing the screens and reports for your database, you must look at two important areas:

- the required system data flow diagram to show how the database is used in everyday working practice
- the tables in your database.

Let us look first at the data flow diagram. This diagram illustrates the way in which data flows around the current working system, and identifies various processes carried out in the current system. The screens and reports will be used in all instances in the system where the data in the database is created, changed, viewed or printed onto paper.

When examining the data flow diagram, the primary sources of screens and reports are the processes.

1. Refer back to the data flow diagram for your database. In our **Hotel Reception** example, the data flow diagram is shown is Figure 10.2.

2. Examine each process box in turn to determine whether a screen or report is required to enter or view data in the database. It is possible for one process box to contain more than one screen or report.

Refer to the table in Figure 10.1 to decide what type of screen or report is required for each process.

Example text in process box	Process description	Type of screen/report
Check/look/refer	View data	Screen displaying data using search criteria
Fill in/tick/change/ cross off/update/	Add/amend/delete data	Data entry screen
Send/write out/put together	Produce written documentation	Report

Figure 10.1   Types of screen/report for each type of process

The data flow diagram for the **Hotel Reception** system example, including new system requirements, is shown in Figure 10.2.

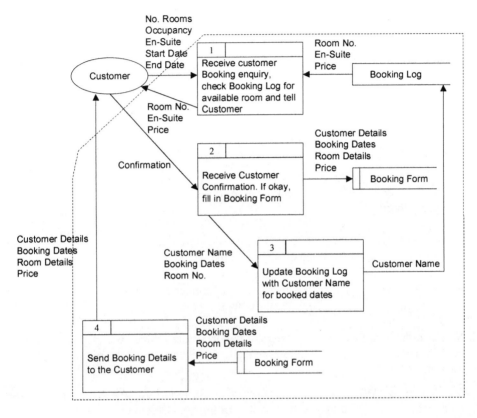

Figure 10.2 Required system data flow diagram

Process 1: Receive Customer Booking Enquiry, check BOOKING LOG for available room and tell Customer.

In this process, no data is added to the database yet, but the database is referred to to find out whether there is an available room to match the customer's enquiry. This is a good example of the first type of interface in our table above, the *screen displaying data using search criteria.*

Process 2: Receive Customer Confirmation. If OK, fill in booking form.

In this process, the customer confirmation can only be carried out by the member of staff, not by the database system. Once the confirmation has been accepted, the member of staff will fill in a booking form. This is a good example of the second type of interface in our table above, the *data entry screen.*

Process 3:   Update Booking Log

In this process the BOOKING LOG entries for the appropriate Booking Dates and Room are updated with the Booking identification, the Booking Code.

Process 4:   Send Booking Form to Customer

In this example, the Booking Form is a completed form that is printed out and sent to the customer. This is therefore, a good example of the third type of interface, a *report*.

10.3 Defining each Screen or Report

Once each screen or report has been identified from the data flow diagram, it is important to describe each one in detail. There are five important issues to consider for a screen or report:

- which fields of data from which tables must be referred to
- which of these fields will be displayed on the screen or report
- which of these fields have selection criteria
- which of the selection criteria must match user entered information
- what is the sort order (if any) for the output.

Note that the data flow diagram refers to the data stores, which will now be part of a table or tables. You will need to refer to the table designs to find the relevant fields for each interface.

To help you define and document each screen or report, fill in a screen/report definition table as shown in Figure 10.3. Note that the Sort Order column is only required for reports or for screens where the order is not the same as the key order. For such a screen, a query rather than a table would need to be used as the base.

Screen/Report Title:_____

Table	Field	Selection Criteria	Display/ Enter	Sort Order

Figure 10.3 Screen/report definition table

The screens and reports for the **Hotel Reception** case study system are defined below.

Screen 1: *Find Available Room*

This screen will require the user to type in the Room Occupancy and the Start and End Dates of the stay. If the customer requires more than one room with different Occupancy or Start and End dates, the screen will simply need to be issued again by the user as if it were for a second enquiry.

To obtain the information, the ROOM table must be accessed to obtain the Room Numbers that have the required Room Occupancy. Once the Rooms have been identified, all BOOKING LOG entries for those rooms between the Start and End Dates inclusive, with a blank Booking Code (in other words, not booked) will be displayed, along with the Price for the Room to relay back to the Customer. Refer to Figure 10.4.

Screen/Report Title: Screen – <u>Find Available Room</u>

Table	Field	Selection Criteria	Display/ Enter	Sort Order
Room	Room Number		Display	
Room	Room Occupancy	= User Entered Room Occupancy	Enter	
Room	EnSuite		Display	
Room Price	Price per Night		Display	
Booking Log	Booking Date	>= User Entered Start Date And <= User Entered End Date	Enter	
Booking Log	Booking Code	= zero	Neither	

Figure 10.4 Screen/report definition table for Find Available Room screen

Screen 2: *Bookings*

Note that the title of this screen refers only to bookings, not to whether the booking is being completed. This is because the user may use this screen to type the bookings into the database as well as for viewing the bookings to answer a customer enquiry, for example. It is important therefore, to give the screen a name relating to the *information* displayed on it, not to how the screen should be *used*.

This screen appears to be a simple data entry screen, requiring the user to type in information about the Customer and Booking. You must consider, though, that although there will only be one set of Customer Details per Customer, there may be dozens of Booking Details per Customer. The best way to handle this is to use a two-part screen set – displaying the Customer Details on the first screen and then allowing the user to click a button on the screen to display a second screen to view or enter the Booking Details on a *linked* screen.

This way, if the Customer is new, his/her details can be entered, followed by the Booking Details. If the Customer already exists, the Customer Details can be found using his/her name or ID, and then the Booking Details can be entered. Two types of data entry are needed here, but linked together under the one screen name.

The Customer screen will allow the user to either enter Customer Details into it, or to use it to search for a Customer. A database management system like Access will allow a user to *enter* data into a screen as well as to *search* for data. In other systems, you may need to design one screen to enquire about a Customer and another to enter the new Customer Details.

Although there are going to be two *linked* screens, they are defined as one screen, since you cannot get to the second one without going through the first screen. Refer to the Screen/Report Definition table in Figure 10.5.

Screen/Report Title: Screen - <u>Customer Bookings</u>

Table	Field	Selection Criteria	Display/ Enter	Sort Order
Customer	Customer Name	= User Entered Customer Name	Enter/Display	
Customer	Customer Code		Enter/Display	
Customer	Customer Address		Enter/Display	
Customer	Customer Telephone Number		Enter/Display	
Customer	Customer Fax Number		Enter/Display	
Customer	Customer Email Address		Enter/Display	
Linked Screen				
Booking	Booking Code		Display	
Booking	Room Number		Enter/Display	
Booking	Customer Code		Enter/Display	
Booking	Start Date		Enter/Display	
Booking	End Date		Enter/Display	
Booking	Total price		Enter/Display	

Figure 10.5   Screen/report definition table for the Customer Bookings screen

Screen 3: *Booking Log*

Note that in the case of the BOOKING LOG, the table entries will already be set up for each room for each day. All the user needs to do is to enter the Booking Code against each day of the Booking. There could be many hundreds of BOOKING LOG entries on the database at one time, so to avoid the user having to scroll through those BOOKING LOG entries to find the ones he/she needs for the booking, the screen could be designed so that the user enters the Start Date and Room for the Booking. Refer to Figure 10.6.

Screen/Report Title: Screen - <u>Booking Log</u>

Table	Field	Selection Criteria	Display/ Enter	Sort Order
Booking Log	Room Number	= User entered Room Number	Display	
Booking Log	Booking Date	>= User entered Start Date	Display	
Booking Log	Booking Code		Enter/Display	

Figure 10.6 Screen/report definition table for the Booking Log screen

Report 1: *Booking Confirmation*

This report will contain the same information as was previously written on the Booking Form.

Screen/Report Title: Report - <u>Booking Confirmation</u>

Table	Field	Selection Criteria	Display/ Enter	Sort Order
Customer	Customer Name		Display	
Customer	Customer Code		Display	1
Customer	Customer Address		Display	
Customer	Customer Telephone Number		Display	
Customer	Customer Fax Number		Display	
Customer	Customer Email Address		Display	
Booking	Booking Code	= User Entered Booking Code	Enter	
Booking	Room Number		Display	
Room	Room Occupancy		Display	
Booking	Start Date		Display	2
Booking	End Date		Display	
Booking	Total price		Display	

Figure 10.7 Screen

The screen/report definition table in Figure 10.7 shows that the Booking Code is used to identify which booking is to be printed out on the report.

10.4 Adding further Screens to allow data entry not already considered

The processes in your data flow diagram will enable you to identify the screens and reports required to enter, amend and view the data used in the everyday working life of your system. This type of data has been referred to in previous chapters as *working data*. However, some of the data in your database, referred to previously as *system data*, will not be created or amended during the everyday running of your system, and must therefore be set up before the system is operational. Once this data is set up, it can be amended, but usually not very often. There are two ways to enter and amend system data:

- Create screens to enter and amend the data.
- Do not create special screens for this, but use the database management system directly to set up this data.

Although an obvious advantage of the second approach is that it will take less time than producing screens for each system data table in the database, the advantages of the first option are that whole system is now consistent and on the same operational platform.

Depending on the database management system you use, there are often security measures that can be applied to stop non-authorised personnel from entering or amending system data tables via a screen. This option also means that you are not relying on the user being able to use the database management system. It may be the case that the current users are happy to use the database management system, but a user employed later or in an emergency may not.

To decide which screens are required to enter any remaining system data, carry out the following steps:

1. List all the tables and fields the database.

2. Cross out each field that has data entered into it via a screen defined in the previous section.

ROOM PRICE
Room Occupancy
EnSuite
Price per Night

ROOM
Room Number
Room Occupancy
EnSuite

BOOKING LOG
Booking Date
Room Number
~~Booking Code~~

BOOKING
~~Booking Code~~
~~Room Number~~
~~Customer Code~~
~~Start Date~~
~~End Date~~
~~Total price~~

CUSTOMER
~~Customer Code~~
~~Customer Name~~
~~Customer Address~~
~~Customer Telephone Number~~
Customer Fax Number
Customer Email Address

Although the user does not enter the Booking Code and Customer Code, these are created by the database system as automatic numbers and can be crossed off the above list. The fields remaining are therefore *system data* and will have screens designed to create and amend the data held in them.

The Booking Log screen is designed to allow the entry of the Booking Code only, not the Dates and Room Number. Refer to Figures 10.8, 10.9 and 10.10 for the Screen/Report Definition tables for the three remaining screens.

Screen/Report Title: Screen – Room Pricing

Table	Field	Selection Criteria	Display/ Enter	Sort Order
Room Price	Room Occupancy		Enter	
Room Price	EnSuite		Enter	
Room Price	Price per Night		Enter	

Figure 10.8 Screen/report definition table for the Room Pricing screen

Screen/Report Title: Screen – Room Details

Table	Field	Selection Criteria	Display/ Enter	Sort Order
Room	Room Number		Enter	
Room	Room Occupancy		Enter	
Room	EnSuite		Enter	

Figure 10.9 Screen/report definition table for the Room Details screen

Screen/Report Title: Screen – Booking Log Set Up

Table	Field	Selection Criteria	Display/ Enter	Sort Order
Booking Log	Booking Date		Enter	
Booking Log	Room Number		Enter	

Figure 10.10 Screen/report definition table for the Booking Log Set Up screen

The nature of the BOOKING LOG table, containing just the combination of Room Numbers and Dates, may lend it to being more efficiently filled up using an imported file created by an application such as Excel which can create infinite dates in repeating groups that can easily be adapted to a database table.

Part II: Access Practical

Work through the following practical session to create screens, called *forms* in Access, and reports for the **Hotel Reception** database.

There are three ways to create a form: AutoForm, Form Wizard and in Design View. In the same way, there are three ways to create a report: AutoReport, Report Wizard and Report Design View. In this session, you will use the AutoForm and Form Wizard methods of creating a form, and, since the AutoForm and AutoReport tools are so similar, just the Report Wizard to create a report. The Design View for both can be used to create complex forms and reports, but this is not covered in this book. You will however use the Design View to modify forms and reports.

It is worth noting that as well as displaying data from tables in the database, forms and reports can also display data produced as the result of a *query*, rather than a table. This way, you can view data combined from more than one table with certain selection criteria and add calculated values on a form or report. The easiest way to construct forms and reports is:

- When you wish to view or enter data from all the records in one or more related tables on a form or report, base that form or report on a table or related tables directly.

- When you wish to view only specific data that matches certain selection criteria and to display calculations, you must first create a query to satisfy the requirements, then base the form or report upon this query, not the tables.

10.5 Create a Form using AutoForm

AutoForm is the fastest way to create a simple form, displaying fields from any table or query. The only drawback with this method is that all the fields from the selected table or query are displayed on the screen. You cannot select which ones you wish to see.

To practise creating a form that refers to a single table, you will create a form that displays the CUSTOMERS details only. This form will allow the user to view and enter all the Customers' details. This form was not designed in the previous sections, since the Customer details are going to be entered into the Customers Booking form. You will create that in Section 10.7.

1. Start Microsoft Access as described in Section 5.4. Insert your floppy disk and open the Hotel Reception database as described in Section 6.5.

2. Click on the Forms tab. Then click the New box. The New Form dialogue box will appear. Refer to Figure 10.11.

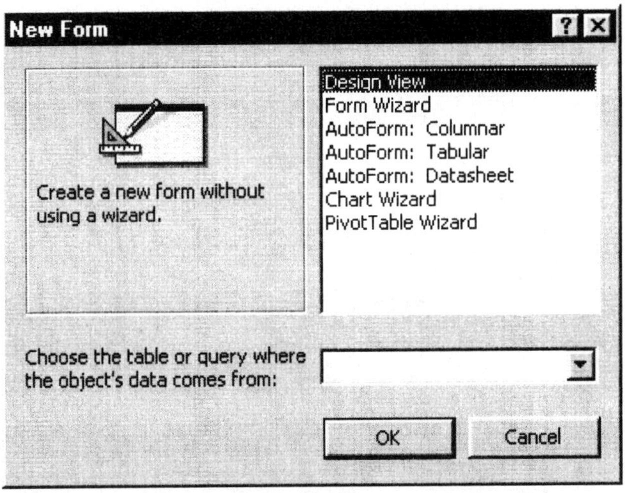

Figure 10.11 New Form dialogue box

3. Click AutoForm:Columnar. The Columnar layout will display the information in two columns on the screen; field names on the left and data on the right. This layout is suitable for a form where you want to view or enter data into one record at a time. The Tabular layout displays the field names across the top of the form, and the data below in rows, one row for each record, similar to Table Open View. This type of layout is useful if you need to view or enter data in more than one record at a time. Datasheet layout is similar to this, but looks more like a spreadsheet.

4. Click the down scroll arrow on the right of the table/query selection box below to view a list of available tables and queries in the database. Click Customers. Then click OK. After a short while, a Customers Form will be displayed, containing the first record of data from the Customers table. Refer to Figure 10.12.

5. To view the Customer records in this form, you must click one of the scroll arrows at the bottom of the form. Note that the number displayed at the bottom of the form between the scroll arrows represents the position of the record being displayed in the table. Try clicking the scroll arrows to view all the records in the Customers table. Refer to Figure 10.12.

I◀	Displays the first record	**◀**	Displays the previous record
▶	Displays the next record	**▶I**	Displays the last record
▶*	Displays an empty new record at the end of the table		

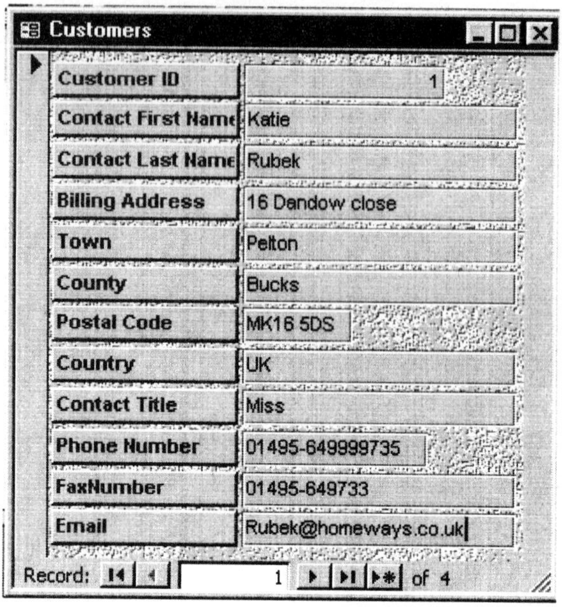

Figure 10.12 Customers form

10.6 Enter Data into a One-Table Form

As well displaying the data currently in a table, the form can display an empty record for you to type data into. Create a new Customer as follows:

1. Click the Insert New Record scroll arrow. A new empty record at the end of the table will be displayed. Note that the AutoNumber field, Customer ID, does not permit you to type a value in.

2. Type the text Matilda into the Contact First Name field. Press the tab key on the keyboard to get to the next field.

3. Type the remainder of the record as shown in Figure 10.13.

4. Once all the fields have been typed in, click the Close icon on the top right of the Customers window.

5. You will be asked if you wish to Save the form. Click Yes. The default name Customers should be displayed. Click OK. You will return to the database, Forms window.

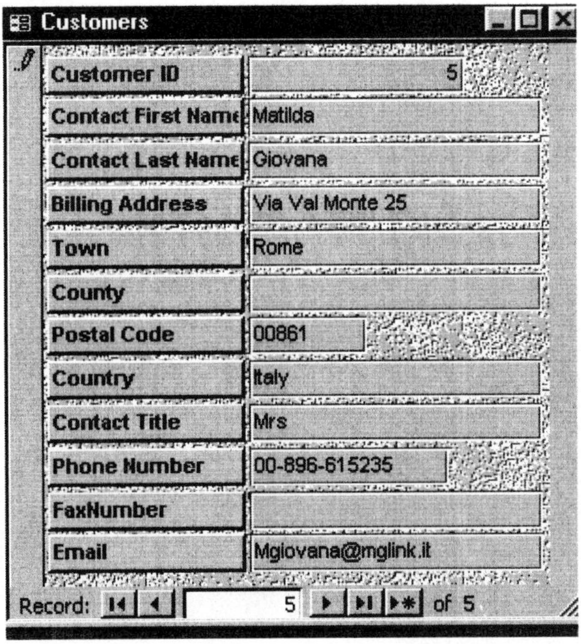

Figure 10.13 New Customer added using Customer AutoForm

10.7 Create a Form using the Form Wizard

Although the AutoForm tool is fast for setting up forms where all the fields from a table are displayed or entered on the one screen, there are limitations. It is not possible, for example, to select which fields should be displayed on the screen, nor is it possible to select more than one related table. The Form Wizard will allow you to do this. Create the **Customer Bookings** form using the Form Wizard as follows (refer to Figure 10.5 earlier in the chapter).

1. Click the **New** box. The same dialogue box as in Figure 10.11 will be displayed. This time, click **Form Wizard** and select the table **Customers** before clicking **OK**. The first Form Wizard dialogue box will be displayed. Refer to Figure 10.14.

2. In the same way as with the Query Wizard, you must select the fields you wish to see on the form. Since you want all the fields from the **Customers** table, click the double-right arrow to add all the fields to the **Selected Fields** box.

3. Click the down scroll arrow on the right of the tables/queries box to display a list of tables and queries. Select **Table: Booking**. A list of fields in that table will be displayed.

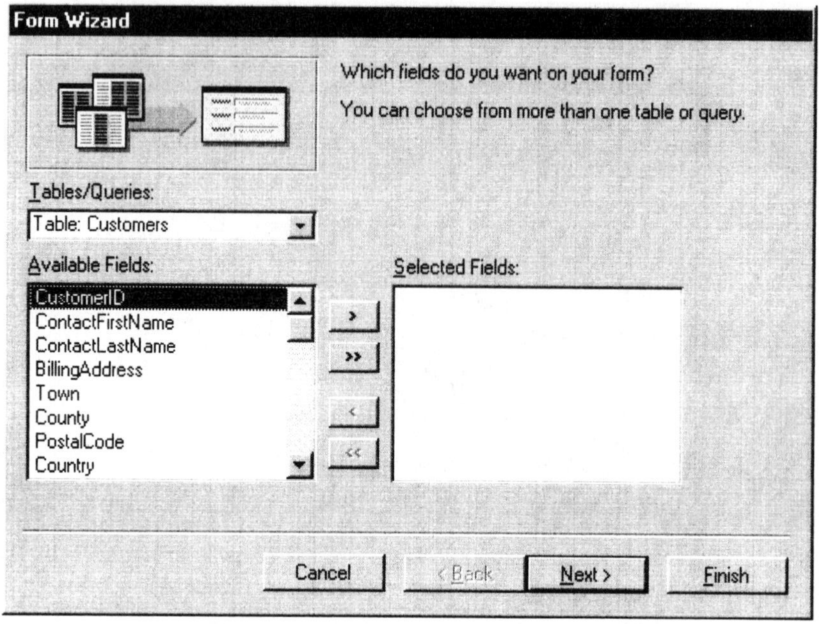

Figure 10.14 Form Wizard dialogue box

4. Click the double right arrow to select all the **Booking** fields. Click the **Next>** box.

5. The next dialogue box will ask you how you wish to view the data. Refer to Figure 10.15. When two related tables are included on the same form, in our example, the **Customers** and **Booking** tables, there are two ways to display the fields:

- **by Customers** – in this case, the table at the *one* end of the relationships (in our case, Customers) is displayed at the top of the screen, with every occurrence of the table at the *many* side of the relationship (Booking) listed below

- **by Booking** – in this case, each record from the table at the *many* end of the relationship is displayed on the screen, along with the details of the table at the *one* end of the relationship: in this way, you would see the Customer Details displayed on the screen with every Booking, one screen per Booking.

Click on each of the two types of view to see the difference. Finally, select the **by Customers** view.

6. When a view is selected where more than one occurrence of a record is displayed at the bottom of the screen, you can select to display the multiple records in a table/worksheet layout, called a **Subform**, or you can select to click a box on the screen and view the multiple records on a separate screen, called a **Linked Form**. Click each circle to see the difference. Finally, select the **Linked Forms** option and click **Next>**.

How do you want to view your data?

by Customers
by Booking

Customers.CustomerID, ContactFirstName, ContactLastName, BillingAddress, Town, County, PostalCode, Country, ContactTitle,

Booking Code, Start Date, End Date, Room Number, Booking.CustomerID, Total Price

● Form with subform(s)   ○ Linked forms

| Cancel | < Back | Next > | Finish |

Figure 10.15 Form Wizard dialogue box – view options

7. The next dialogue box will ask you to select a background. Leave the selection on Stone. Click Next>.

8. The final dialogue box will ask you to enter the name of your forms. Type the first form name: Customer Bookings, and the second form name: Bookings. Then click Finish. The first Customer record should be displayed, with a **Bookings** button at the top of the screen. Refer to Figure 10.16.

9. If the **Customer Bookings** form does not fill the screen, click the Maximise icon on the top right corner of the Customer Bookings window.

10. Click the Bookings button on the screen to view the Bookings for the current Customer. Click the Close icon on the Bookings window to close the form and return to the Customer Details again. Click the right scroll arrow at the bottom of the window to view the next Customer. Click the Bookings button to view the Booking details again. Click the Close icon on the Bookings again to return to the Customer Details screen.

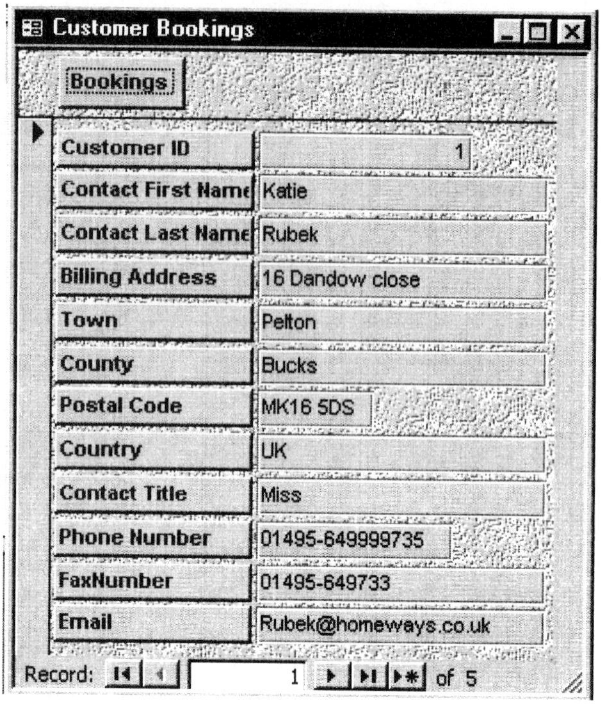

Figure 10.16 First Customer Record displayed in the Customer Bookings form

10.8 Enter Data into a Form and Linked Form

Entering data into this type of form is similar to entering data into a simple form with only the one table of data in it. The only difference is that instead of simply typing the data into the screen, you must also type data into one or more occurrences of the associated record on the linked form. Create a booking for the new Customer as follows:

1. Click the Display Last Record scroll arrow at the bottom of the screen. ▶️ 
   The Customer Details for Customer ID 5 should be displayed. Click the Bookings button at the top of the screen.

2. A blank Booking record should be displayed at the top of the screen.

3. Type the following into the Booking record:

   Start Date: 20/1/1997
   End Date: 21/1/1997
   Room Number: 2
   Customer ID: 5
   Total price: 146   (The currency format is added after by Access)

Note that the Booking Code created automatically by Access for this Booking is 7.

4. Click the Close icon on the top right of the Bookings window to return to the Customer Bookings window. Then Close that screen in the same way.

5. Click the Tables tab. To complete the Booking data on the database, and since the Booking Log form has not yet been created, enter the following two rows to the Booking Log table (open view):

```
20/1/1997   2  7
21/1/1997   2  7
```

Close the Booking Log table.

10.9 Finding Records in a Form

As well as using a form to display and enter data in a database, a form can help you find data quickly, given some initial search criteria. You may, for example, need to answer a Customer enquiry and find and update the Customer Details for a Customer without knowing their Customer ID. To do this, you could search through the Customer records displayed on the Customers form, using the Customer name as the search criterion. Do this using the Find tool, as follows:

1. Click the Forms tab. Click on the Customers form and click Open.

2. Click on the Contact Last Name field and click either Edit on the menu bar, then Find, or click the Find icon on the toolbar. Refer to Figure 10.17.

3. Type the text Giovana into the Find What box. It is possible to state whether you wish the search to be applied to records above or below the current one, or to all. Leave the Search set to All. It is also possible to state whether you wish to search for the whole field to match the entered text, or for some of the text to match the entered text. Leave the Match set to Whole Field. Click Find First.

Find in field: 'Contact Last Name'		? X
Find What:		Find First
Search:	All ▼	☐ Match Case	Find Next
		☐ Search Fields As Formatted	
Match:	Whole Field ▼	☑ Search Only Current Field	Close

Figure 10.17 Find tool

4. Customer ID 5 will be displayed on the **Customers** form. Since this is the one you want, click **Close** to remove the **Find** dialogue box. If it had not been the Customer you wanted, you would have clicked **Find Next** to see the next record matching the search criteria.

5. Click the **Close** icon in the top right corner of the **Customers** window to get back to the database window.

10.10 Create a Form that includes User-Entered Search Criteria

So far we have only created forms that enable the user to look through the whole table of information and perform a search on a particular field on the form. If you look at back at the first form defined in Section 10.3, *Find Available Room,* this form expects the user to be able to type in the *Room Occupancy* and *Start* and *End Dates* based on a Customer's enquiry, and have displayed on the screen a list of suitable rooms that are not booked for that period.

Since this form is going to request that the user enters some data, called **parameters**, to be used as search criteria, it must therefore be based upon a query, not on tables. A query will use the entered parameters to search for matching data. Create a query and then a form for the **Find Available Room** screen as follows:

1. Click the **Queries** tab, then click **New**. Select the **Design View** option, then click **OK**.

2. The query Design View will appear, with the **Show Table** dialogue box. Select and **Add** the **Room Price, Room** and **Booking Log** tables (in that order) to the Design View, and then **Close** the dialogue box.

3. Click and drag the following fields from the appropriate tables to the **Field** box in each column of the query design at the bottom of the screen:

   From **Room** table: **Room Number, Room Occupancy, EnSuite**
   From **Room Price** table: **Price per Night**
   From **Booking Log** table: **Booking Date, Booking Code**

4. Click on the **Criteria** box under the **Booking Code** column, and type:

   = 0

   This will extract only those entries where the Booking Code is zero (or empty).

5. There is no point seeing the Booking Code since it will always be empty, therefore, click on the **Show** tick box under the **Booking Code** column to remove the tick.

6. Click on the **Criteria** box under the **Room Occupancy** column. To instruct Access to ask the user for a Room Occupancy value, you must type the requesting instruction for the user in square brackets, with an equals sign before it so that Access will search for entries with a Room Occupancy equal to that entered. Type the following:

```
=[Enter Room Occupancy]
```

Note that the text in the brackets must not be the same as any field name in the query, otherwise that field will be used, and the user will not be requested to type in anything.

7. The user-entered criteria for the Booking Date are slightly different. In this case, you want the user to enter both a Start Date and an End Date, so the criteria will need to use an *And* statement to place the Booking Date within a range of user-entered dates. Type the following into the Criteria box in the Booking Date column:

```
>=[Enter Start Date] And <=[Enter End Date]
```

8. Click the Save icon and enter the name Find Available Room. Click OK.

9. Click the Run icon on the toolbar.

10. Enter the Room Occupancy criteria of 4, a Start Date of 17/3/1996 and an End Date of 17/3/1996. Only one entry will be displayed. Refer to Figure 10.18.

11. Close the query by clicking the Close icon on the top right of the Query window.

12. Now that the query has been created, you must create the form to display that query information. Click the Forms tab and click New.

Find Available Room : Select Query				
Room Number	**Room Occupancy**	**EnSuite**	**Price per Night**	**Booking Date**
2	4	☑	£73.00	17/3/1996

Figure 10.18

13. Select the Form Wizard option, click on the Select Tables/Queries box and select the query Find Available Room, then click OK.

14. Click the double right arrows to load all of the displayed query field into the Selected Fields box. Click Next>.

15. Select a layout of Tabular and click Next>.

16. Select the background Standard and click Next>.

17. Leave the title as Find Available Room (taken from the query) and click Finish. You will be asked for Room Occupancy as Start and End Dates, as you were before. Enter the same values as before and see that only one entry is displayed on the form.

18. Close the form using the Close icon on the top right of the Form window.

10.11 Create a Simple Listing Report using the Report Wizard

Creating a report using the Report Wizard is very similar to creating a form with the Form Wizard. You tell the Wizard which fields from which tables or queries you require, and how to organise the layout. There are two basic types of report that are used most often:

- *Simple listing report* – this lists specified data from the database in a particular order or grouping. For example, a report could list all Customers' details, including their bookings, from the database, one customer after the next, in Customer Last Name, then Booking Start Date order.

- *Report based on user-entered selection criteria* – this lists specified fields of data from the database for given selection criteria. For example, the Booking Confirmation Report lists Booking Details for one specified Customer only.

Both types of report are constructed in exactly the same way. In this section, you are going to use the Report Wizard to build them. The only difference between the two types of report is that the second type must be based upon a query that requests user-entered selection criteria, as in the Find Available Room form.

In this section, you are going to create the simple listing report for a requirement to list the Customer Details, with their Bookings for all Customers on the database.

1. Click the Reports tab and click New.

2. Select Report Wizard, select the Customers table and click OK.

3. Select all fields by clicking the double right arrow.

4. Select the Table: Booking entry in the Tables/Queries option list and move all fields into the Selected List, except Customer ID, by clicking the double right arrow top select all the fields, then click on CustomerID and click the single left arrow to de-select it. Click Next>.

5. Leave the view by Customers and click Next>.

6. Click Next> on the next window.

7. The booking details should be sorted by Start Date, so click the down scroll arrow in the first sort box and select Start Date. Then click Next>.

8. Select Align Left 1 layout, Landscape orientation and click Next>.

9. Select Soft Gray background and click Next>.

10. Enter the title Customers and Bookings and click Finish.

11. A preview of the report will be displayed on the screen. Click the Print icon to print the report, then click the Close icon on the top right corner of the Report window.

10.12 Create a Report based on User-Entered Selection Criteria

In this section, we are going to create the Booking Confirmation report, which will request the Booking Code from the user, so that only data about that particular booking will be printed. Refer to Figure 10.7 in Section 10.3 of this chapter.

In the same way as the Find Available Room form was based upon a query that requested user-entered data to be used as selection criteria, a report that requires user-entered selection criteria must also be based on such a query. The first task therefore when creating the Booking Confirmation report is to create a query that will display the required data and request the selection criteria.

1. Click the Queries tab and click New.

2. Select the Simple Query Wizard option, then click OK.

3. Select the Table: Customers option in the Tables/Queries box.

4. Since we need to select all fields except Customer ID, the quickest way to do this is to click the double right arrow to load all fields into the Selected Fields box. Click on the CustomerID field and click the single left arrow to de-select it.

5. Click on the field at the bottom of the list of selected fields (Email) to ensure that the Booking fields will be displayed after the Customer fields in the query.

6. Select Table: Booking in the Tables/Queries box and add the fields to the Selected Fields list in the same way as before, selecting all fields except Customer ID.

7. Click on the Room Number field name in the Selected list, then select the Room table in the Tables/Queries box. Select the Room Occupancy field, and click the single right arrow to add it to the selected box. This will position the Room Occupancy field next to the Room Number field in the query. Click Next>.

8. Click Next> again, then type the name `Booking Confirmation` into the Query Name box. Select Modify Query Design and click Finish.

9. Enter the following text into the Criteria box in the Booking Code column:

   `=[Enter Booking Code]`

10. Click the Save icon to save the changed query, then click the Run icon to try it out. Enter a Booking Code of 3. Only the details for Booking Code 3 will be displayed.

11. Click the Close icon on the top right of the Query window.

Now that the query has been created to allow a user-entered selection criterion, we can build the report that will be based upon this query.

12. Click the Reports tab and click New. Select Report Wizard and select the Booking Confirmation query and click OK.

13. Load all the fields into the **Selected Fields** list by clicking the double right arrow icon and click **Next>**.
14. Since there is only one booking that is selected, select the **By Booking** display option of the next window. Click **Next>**.
15. Click **Next>** on the next two windows.
16. Select **Columnar** layout on the next window (orientation should be **Portrait**) and click **Next>**.
17. Select **Soft Gray** on the next window, and click **Next>**.
18. Change the title to `Booking Confirmation` on the next window and click **Finish**.
19. When asked for a Booking Code, enter `3` and click **OK**. A preview of the report will be displayed. Refer to Figure 10.19.
20. Click the **Print** icon to print the report.
21. Close the **report** window by clicking the **Close** icon on the top right corner.

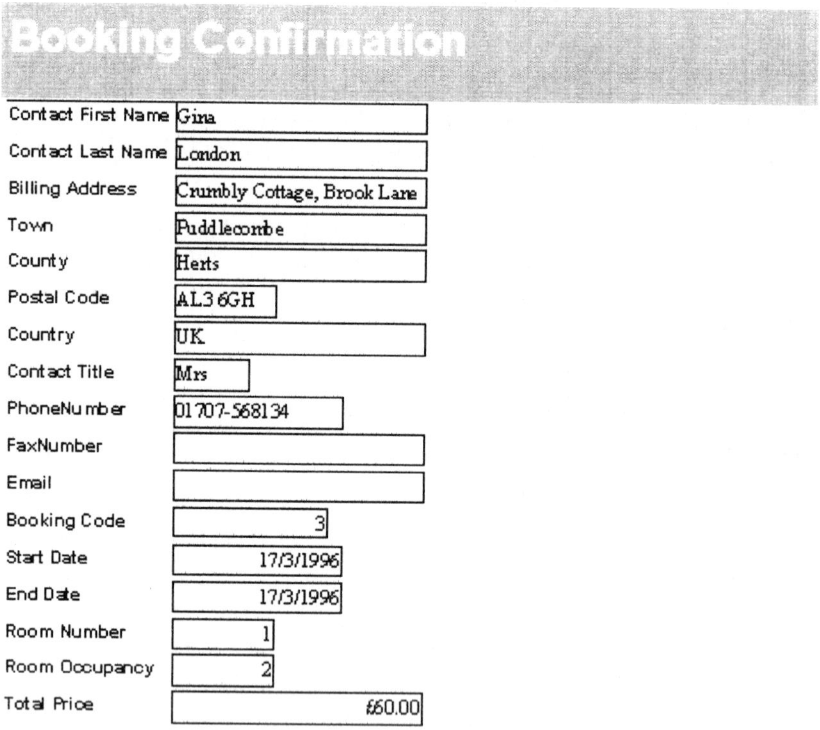

Booking Confirmation

Contact First Name	Gina
Contact Last Name	London
Billing Address	Crumbly Cottage, Brook Lane
Town	Puddlecombe
County	Herts
Postal Code	AL3 6GH
Country	UK
Contact Title	Mrs
PhoneNumber	01707-568134
FaxNumber	
Email	
Booking Code	3
Start Date	17/3/1996
End Date	17/3/1996
Room Number	1
Room Occupancy	2
Total Price	£60.00

Figure 10.19 Booking Confirmation report

10.13 Modifying Forms and Reports

In the same way that Design View can be used to modify tables and queries as well as to create them, the Design View can be used to modify and create forms and reports. Although you have only used AutoForm and Form and Report Wizards to create the forms and reports, the Design View will enable you to modify the design, if you want something slightly different to the automated format.

Modify the Booking Confirmation report using the Report Design view, to group the Customer and Booking Details more clearly.

1. If you are not already in the **Reports** tab, click on it.

2. Click on **Booking Confirmation** report and click **Design**. The Report Design window will be displayed. Refer to Figure 10.20.

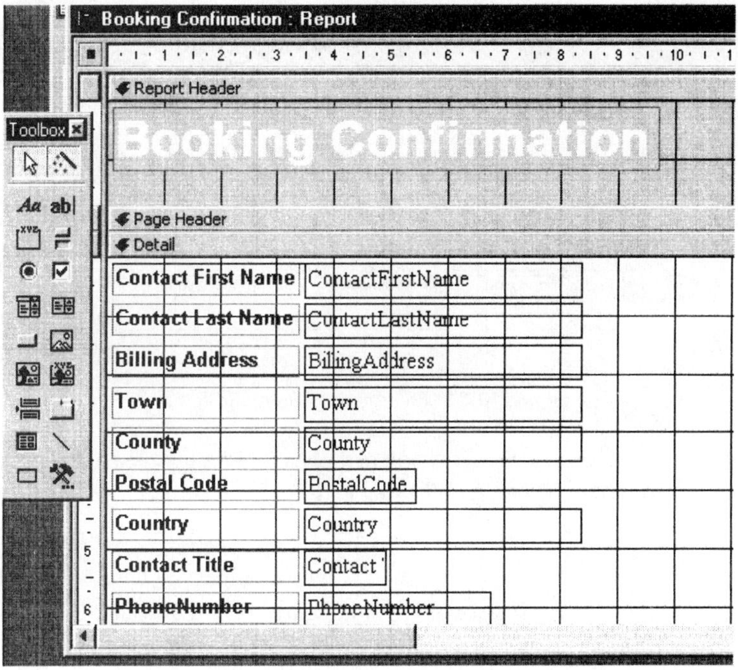

Figure 10.20 Booking Confirmation Report Design window

As you scroll down the window, you will see the whole report layout. There are five sections on this report:

*   **Report Header** - appears once at the top of the report.
*   **Page Header** – appear at the top of each page.
*   **Detail** – displays the main body of the report.

- **Page Footer** – appears at the bottom of each page.
- **Report Footer** – appears at the bottom of the report.

In this section, you will amend the layout of the detail of the report.

3. Click and drag the Contact Last Name text box so that it is placed to the right of the Contact First Name data box. As you do so, notice that black boxes appear around the text to show that it is selected and a little black hand appears to show you that you are dragging it. Notice that both the text and data boxes will move together.

4. Move the other Customer text boxes in the same way to rearrange the fields as shown in Figure 10.21.

Booking Confirmation							
◆ Page Header							
◆ Detail							
Contact First Name	ContactFirstName			Contact Last Name	ContactLastName		
Contact Title	Contact T						
Billing Address	BillingAddress			Town		Town	
County	County			Country		Country	
Postal Code	PostalCode						
PhoneNumber	PhoneNumber		FaxNumber		FaxNumber		
Email	Email						

Figure 10.21 Rearranged Customer fields

5. Click the Label icon on the Toolbox and click and drag a rectangle above the Booking Code. Type the following text:

   ```
   We have great pleasure in confirming the following
   reservation:
   ```

6. Click and drag the End Date along side Start Date. Click and drag the Report Footer down to elongate the details section. Click and drag the Total Price down to leave a gap between it and Room Occupancy. Refer to Figure 10.22.

7. Click the Save icon on the toolbar to save the changes. Then click the View icon to view the changes. Enter a Booking Code of 3 again. Click Close then click the Close icon on the top right corner to close the Booking Confirmation window.

8. Close the Hotel Reception: Database window.

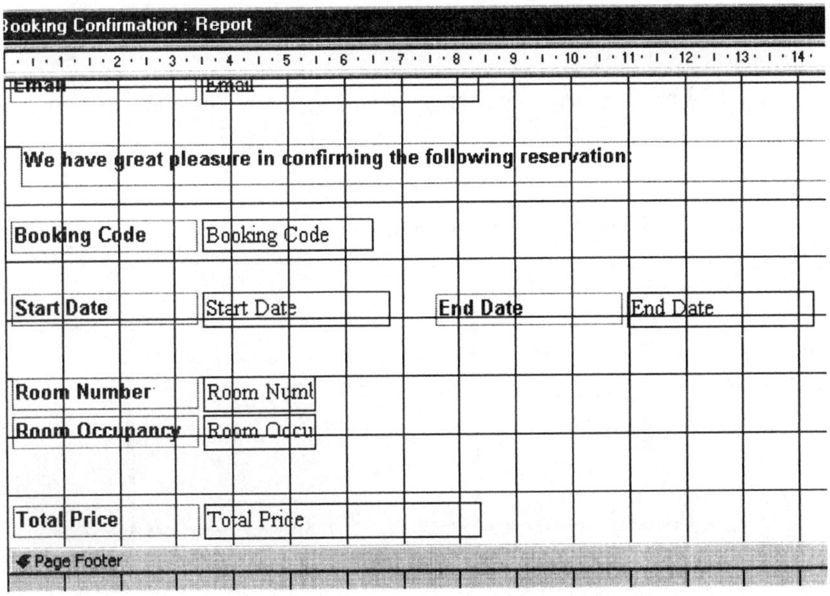

```
· · I · 1 · I · 2 · I · 3 · I · 4 · I · 5 · I · 6 · I · 7 · I · 8 · I · 9 · I · 10 · I · 11 · I · 12 · I · 13 · I · 14 ·
```

Email   Email

We have great pleasure in confirming the following reservation:

Booking Code   Booking Code

Start Date   Start Date   End Date   End Date

Room Number   Room Numl

Room Occupancy   Room Occu

Total Price   Total Price

◆ Page Footer

Figure 10.22 Rearranged booking details

10.14 Summary

This chapter has covered the following material:

Part I: Database Design Theory

- How to decide which screens and reports are required.
- Defining each screen and report.
- Adding further screens to allow data entry – usually for system data.

Part II: Access Practical

- Create a form using AutoForm.
- Enter data into a one-table form.
- Create a form using Form Wizard.
- Enter data into a form and sub-form.
- Finding records in a form.
- Create a form that includes user-entered search criteria.
- Create a simple listing report using the Report Wizard.
- Create a report based on user-entered selection criteria.
- Modifying forms and reports.

10.15.1 Describe the three main areas you must refer to when determining the screens and reports that will use your database system.

10.15.2 Refer to Figure 10.23. Create screen and report definition tables (refer to section 10.3) the following screens and reports:

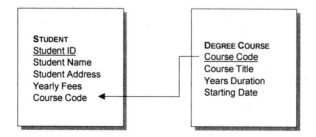

Figure 10.23 Degree database

(a) The admissions clerk needs to be able to enter student details, one after the other, on one screen.

(b) The course leaders need to be able to view and enter details about each course on one screen – showing one course per row on the screen.

(c) The admissions clerk needs to have a printed list showing each Course Title and Starting Year, with a list of all students registered on that course. The report should be sorted, first by Course Title (ascending), then by Course Year (descending), then by Student Name (ascending). All student details should be shown, except Course Code.

(d) The course leaders also need to be able to enter a specific Course Code, and see all the details for that degree course, with a list of Student IDs and Student Names of all the students registered to it.

(e) Design a report to print out the Course Details of all courses with a Starting Date between a range of user-entered dates.

10.15.3 (a) Refer to the following documentation for the **Painting and Decorating Company** described earlier on in the book, and create screen and report definition tables (refer to section 10.3) for the **Painting** database system:

- System Description in Section 3.6.3.
- Feasibility Report drawn up in Section 3.6.3.
- System Description in Section 4.9.3.

- Data flow diagram created in Section 4.9.3.

(b) Refer to the database design for the **Painting and Decorating Company** database in Section 9.15.3 and design any additional screens (using screen definition tables) to enter any data not already on a screen in part (a) into the tables.

10.16 Practical Exercises

10.16.1 Update the Hotel Reception database system to create the four forms listed below to enter the remaining data into the database (refer to Figures 10.6, 10.8, 10.9 and 10.10 in Section 10.4):

Booking Log   Room Pricing
Room Details   Booking Log Set Up

Note that the first form, Booking Log (refer to Figure 10.6) will need to be based upon a query that requires two parameters to be entered: Room Number and Booking Date.

10.16.2 Use the Degrees database created in Section 9.16.1 to create the forms and reports described in Section 10.15.2, using AutoForm Form Wizard and the Report Wizard where appropriate.

10.16.3 Using the Degrees database and the screens and reports created in the previous question, do the following:

(a) Enter some new course and student data into the database.

(b) Request each of the reports.

(c) Use the Find tool on the screen displaying the student details to find the student called John Colder.

(d) Use the screen described in part (d) of Section 10.15.2 and enter the course code 215 to view the course information and students registered on that course.

10.16.4 Use the **Painting and Decorating Company** database and create the screens and reports defined Section 10.15.3.

11 Testing

11.1 Introduction

One of the most important areas of systems development, apart from analysis and design, is **testing**. If a system is not tested correctly, when it is used in a **live environment** any number of errors could occur, from minor inconveniences to major system failure or data corruption.

Even if the system is relatively small, comprising only a few screens and database tables, it is important to test it thoroughly.

Although there are several names given to different types of testing in different system environments, they can be grouped together under the following general headings:

- *unit testing*
- *system testing*
- *integration testing*
- *interface testing*
- *performance testing*
- *user testing.*

Although it would be possible to write volumes of text about testing, this chapter will only go into brief detail about each type, and provide a few example layouts for testing plans and documents. The importance of test data is also introduced, as well as some suggestions about test execution.

11.2 Unit Testing

Unit testing checks that each unit of the system is working correctly, according to the original design. A unit could be a screen-based program, a report-based program or a program that updates the database without a screen interface, called a **batch program.** In large systems, batch programs are often run overnight when the rest of the system is not being used. In a banking system, for example, several batch programs will run overnight to incorporate all the monetary transactions carried out during the day into the appropriate accounts.

In a system developed using a database management tool such as Access, the units are the screens and reports.

When designing a test for a unit, you must refer to the original design since you are testing that the developed unit does what the original design wanted it to do. You must also refer to the data dictionary, which will define the range of values that will be accepted for each field. Testing a screen is different from testing a report, since in a screen you need to consider the actions that need to be taken if the user enters an incorrect piece of data or an incorrect combination of data, whereas a report will usually select its own data from the database using pre-defined rules. In general, testing a screen requires more tests than a report.

Using the **Hotel Reception** Find Available Room screen as an example:

1. Refer to the design for the screen, Figure 11.1. Also refer to the data dictionary in Figure 8.1 in Chapter 8.

Screen/Report Title: Screen - Find Available Room

Table	Field	Selection Criteria	Display/ Enter	Sort Order
Room	Room Number		Display	
Room	Room Occupancy	= User Entered Room Occupancy	Enter	
Room	EnSuite		Display	
Room Price	Price per Night		Display	
Booking Log	Booking Date	>= User Entered Start Date And	Enter	
		<= User Entered End Date		
Booking Log	Booking Code	= zero	Neither	

Figure 11.1 Find Available Room screen/report definition table

2. Identify a list of tests that will check each field on the table depending on whether it is a data entry field or a data display field. The test you may have to do could come under the following headings:

Data entry (only if your screen accepts data entry)

E1 each field can accept correct data
E2 appropriate action is carried out (error message or not) when a field is left empty
E3 each field displays the correct error message for incorrect data
E4 all data entry fields can accept correct combinations of data
E5 correct error message is displayed for each incorrect combination of data.

<u>Data display</u> (only if your screen displays data – it may just receive data to use when printing a report, for example)

D1   correct data is displayed from the data entered
D2   there is no data to display from the data entered
D3   there is only one record of data to display
D4   there is more than one record of data to display
D5   there is more than a screen full of records to display.

Note that each of the test types has been given a category, E for Entry and D for Display. It is useful to categorise the tests in this way, so that when you list your actual tests you can number then appropriately, and be able to tell at a glance what type of test it is.

For example, when you design the tests for the Find Available Room screen, since there are three data entry fields there would be at least three tests to check that those fields accept correct data. This type of test comes under the E1 test heading. The first three tests, therefore, would be labelled E1.1, E1.2 and E1.3.

In the case of the Find Available Room screen, a sample list of tests could be:

E1.1   Room Occupancy is a number > 0
E1.2   Start Date is a valid date
E1.3   End Date is a valid date

E2.1   Room Occupancy is left blank
E2.2   Start Date is left blank
E2.3   End Date is left blank

E3.1   Room Occupancy is 0
E3.2   Room Occupancy is a negative number
E3.3   Room Occupancy is a letter
E3.4   Start Date is an invalid date
E3.5   Start Date is not a date
E3.6   End Date is an invalid date
E3.7   End Date is not a date

E4.1   Valid Room Occupancy and Start Date < End Date
E4.2   Valid Room Occupancy and Start Date = End Date

E5.1   Invalid Room Occupancy and valid Start and End Dates
E5.2   Valid Room Occupancy and End Date, and invalid Start Date
E5.3   Valid Room Occupancy and Start Date, but invalid End Date
E5.4   Valid Room Occupancy and Start Date > End Date

D1.1   Correct available Room details are displayed for given Occupancy and Dates
D2.1   There are no available Rooms for the required Occupancy and Dates
D3.1   There is only one available Room for the required Occupancy and Date
D4.1   There are two available Rooms for the required Occupancy and Dates

D5.1   There are more available Rooms to display than fit on one screen

It is often unnecessary to list every possible numerical combination of correct and incorrect data, so a judgement must be made on how many combinations are acceptable to consider that the system is working correctly. If there is a screen that is very complex or that will have a high usage rate in the new system, that screen may have a larger number of combinations tested than other less used or simpler screens.

3.   When a test plan is originally drawn up, it is anticipated that every test will be carried out. However, during the development of a system, the analysis, design and system building phases can sometimes take longer than expected, and if the deadline is immovable, the testing phase can come under pressure to be condensed or split in to two or more phases. When this happens, the scripts that test areas of the system that, if there were to be an error, would have minimal impact on the rest of the system, could be omitted or deferred. These tests would be defined as **low priority**.

Since the test scripts are usually designed by staff who have a good knowledge of the system and its design, script creation would be the ideal stage to define the priority of each test.

In our example, each test listed is given a priority level, ranging from 1 to 5. 1 is the lowest, 5 the highest.

Tests D1.1, D2.1, D3.1 and D4.1 would probably be priority level 5, whereas tests E3.5 and E3.7 would probably be priority level 1.

4.   For each of the tests identified so far, draw up a testing table, called a **test script**, listing all possible fields that can have data entered into them and all those that have data displayed. Fill in the data entry columns to show the combinations of data you would need to enter into the screen to carry out that particular test. For each combination of entered data, write down the correct result that you would expect to see, either in terms of the data displayed, or in terms of an error message. Refer to Figure 11.2, which displays a test script for test D4.1.

Script Number: D4.1							Priority: 5		
Test Description: There are two available rooms for the required occupancy and dates									
Data Entry			Data Display					Action	
Room Occupancy	Start Date	End Date	Room Number	EnSuite	Price per Night	Booking Date	Error Message No.	Correct	Comment
4	16/3/1996	18/3/1996	2	✓	£73	17/3/1996			
			2	✓	£73	18/3/1996			
Error Message No.			Message						

Figure 11.2 Unit test script

11.3 System Testing

System testing checks that the individual units or programs (screens and reports), already tested during unit testing, work together to perform the overall functions required of the system.

The two main types of functions you would test for are that:

- data stored on the database by one unit can be read, amended or printed by another unit
- data required by one unit has been set up previously by another unit.

To carry out a system test you must test how each unit functions in relation to the others, using test data set up specifically to reflect the most common and extreme types of data combinations created by the system. You are not only testing how the units work together, but you are also checking that the flow of data around the system is transferred and modified correctly according to the systems design.

You do not need to test every combination of correct and incorrect field values on the screens or reports, since unit testing has already done this. You must assume that the units all work correctly.

To create system test scripts, you must design a series of 'story boards' or 'scenarios' for a range of test data, that will describe which units are used in a particular sequence, and what data is to be entered, modified, displayed or deleted by each.

In the **Hotel Reception** system, for example, refer to Figure 11.3 for one system test 'scenario'.

Depending on the complexity of the system or the system development procedures, you may create test scripts for each of the units referred to in the system test scenario to detail which values are entered and what is expected to happen. These test scripts will look similar to unit test scripts, except that you are not testing every field this time, you are just using them to define exactly what information needs to be entered into which screen in the test scenario. It is important to number the test scripts so that they correspond to the numbers in the system test scenario document.

System Test No: 15			
Test Description: New Customer requires two consecutive nights in room for occupancy 4 over the year end 1996/7.			
Initial Data Set Up: Room 5 has occupancy 4, is en-suite and is available on 25/12/1996 - 3/1/1997. Room 6 has occupancy of 4, is not en-suite and is also available for same dates. Room 3 has occupancy of 2 and is available on both 31/12/1996 and 1/1/1997, and Room 2 has an occupancy of 4, is en-suite and is available on 31/12/1996, but not 1/1/1997.			
Unit		**Action**	**Outcome**
15.1	Find Available Room (Screen)	Enter Room Occ. 4, Start Date 31/12/1996, End Date 1/1/1997	Room 2 available for 31/12/1996 only, Room 5 is en-suite and available for both 31/12/1996 and 1/1/1997, Room 6 is not en-suite and is available for both 31/12/1996 and 1/1/1997
15.2	Customer Bookings (Screen)	Enter new customer's details	New Customer added to Customers table. Customer ID displayed.
15.3	Bookings (Linked Screen from Customer Bookings screen)	Enter new booking for Room 6, Start Date 31/12/1996, End Date 1/1/1997	Booking added to Booking table. New Booking Code displayed.
15.4	Booking Log (Screen)	1. Enter Room 6, and Start Date 31/12/1996. 2. Enter Booking Code from 15.3 against the two Dates 31/12/1996 and 1/1/1997	1. Booking Log entries displayed for Room 6 for 31/12/1996 and 1/1/1997. 2. Booking Log entries amended for 31/12/1996 and 1/1/1997.
15.5	Booking Confirmation	Request Booking Confirmation for new Booking Code	Booking Confirmation for new Booking Code printed

Figure 11.3 System test scenario

11.4 Integration Testing

So far in this book, we have only looked at the development of one system. In many instances in large organisations, several computer systems will be developed at the same time. Systems development is often easier if a huge system is broken down into smaller interacting **sub-systems**. When this is the case, each of the sub-systems will have been unit and system tested independently, and then tested together to ensure that the data being created and used by one sub-system can be used where required by other sub-systems.

Integration test scripts will look like system test scenarios, listing which units should be used with which data. The only difference is that the units will be selected from two or more different sub-systems.

11.5 Interface Testing

Once the unit, system and integration tests have been carried out successfully, it would be safe to say that the newly developed system(s) work correctly according to the systems designs. The only area of testing that has not been carried out is to test that data being entered into the system from an external system, or data being delivered to an external system from the system(s), is being supplied correctly. An external system is any system that is not part of the sub-system group tested during integration testing.

For example, in the **Hotel Reception** system, an external system could be as simple as a program that imports BOOKING LOG records to the database from a file created in Excel. Another example, could be if the new system were to create a file listing all the Bookings made by a particular company over the past year to send to that company.

Interface testing is usually file-based and therefore the scripts will be one of two types:

- *Input from external source* – This script will list a range of file contents for different sizes of files (for example, an empty file, an average file and a large file), and the corresponding changes to the database expected as a result of receiving and processing the file. Different combinations of data for each file would be listed to test how the database will be modified in each case.

- *Output to external source* – Details about existing data on the database will be listed, with corresponding files created from that data. Again, different sizes of expected file will be included, especially empty files, average files and large files.

The next section will address the issue of testing large amounts of data, whether they are in files or on the database.

11.6 Performance Testing

One of the final areas of testing that is carried out is **performance testing**. This type of testing tests the length of time taken for units in the system to perform their functions, using realistic amounts of data, rather than the small amounts of data used in testing so far.

You can imagine the headaches caused on one project where it was discovered, after the system went live, that the overnight batch programs took collectively 16 hours to process the huge amounts of data on the database. Unfortunately, there were not 16 hours available between when the on-line part of the system was switched off at 1800 hours and switched on again at 0700 the next day!

This story illustrates how important it is that the system can carry out its work in an appropriate time. Imagine a screen used continually by a member of staff answering telephone enquiries. It would be unacceptable to expect the member of staff to wait a minute or more for the screen to search through the database to find the required information. It would not matter, however, if the report to print the required information to post to the customer took several minutes, since that information will not be required *instantly*.

The ideal way to test the performance of the system is to use **live data**. This is real data that will be used when the system is running in a **live environment**. There are two advantages to using live data:

- If available data can be used, this saves time creating large amounts of test data.
- There is a chance that the *live* data may highlight any errors in the system not picked up by the previous test data – since live data sometimes contains all sorts of weird and unforeseen combinations of data not strictly permitted by the new system or identified by the analysts.

Note that *live* data can only be used it if is compatible with the new system.

Performance testing scripts vary depending on the areas of the system being tested. The test scripts should include reference to the names and sizes of the database table(s) or file(s) being used and the name of the unit(s) being actioned upon that data. An estimate of the expected duration of the unit is also provided, along with a maximum acceptable time for that action.

11.7 User Testing

So far, all the testing being carried out has been to check that the system performs correctly according to the system design. The designer will have drawn up scripts based on the design, the data dictionary and his/her perception of the required system, ideally based on numerous meetings with the users, watching the existing system in action, and sifting through large amounts of system documentation.

But what if the systems design is not completely correct? How could this happen?

- Insufficient analysis.
- Inappropriate design based on the analysed data.
- Inaccurate design.
- Inadequate range of staff consulted during analysis e.g. only senior/supervisory staff consulted who did not give an accurate or up-to-date picture of the current system.
- System requirements change.
- Appropriate staff were consulted, but they found it hard to describe how the current system works.
- Inadequate handover communication with new development staff.
- New user staff with different working practices/requirements.

In any system, a mixture of some or all of these events may occur. The reason for this is that most of these problems occur as a result of the users and development staff being human and having different perceptions of their environment and different ways of explaining and interpreting actions and events.

To ensure that the final system not only does what the designs say, but does what the users actually wanted in the first place, the users *themselves* must test the system. They will produce test scripts rather like the system test scenarios and unit test scripts. Hopefully, if the users have been consulted and involved in the development throughout, there should be few errors or discrepancies discovered at this stage.

The following example illustrates a case where user testing, had it been carried out, could have identified an analysis blunder.

A small system enhancement was carried out for a broadcasting company. The enhancement was required because a Tape ID number was rapidly reaching its maximum size. This was overcome by extending the ID into a spare two-digit field that had originally been intended to contain another tape code, but was no longer used for that purpose. The manager assured the analyst that any data in that two-digit field related to the old unused code and could be deleted and the new extended Tape ID fields placed there instead. The problem was therefore solved without requiring any major changes to the system and the manager was delighted. Without wasting any time, since the Tape ID number was about to hit its limit, the changes were put live. However, there was soon uproar as the staff using the system wanted to know what had happened to the two-digit field they had been carefully entering their initials into over the past several years!

11.8 Test Data

When specifying the tests that must be carried out on the system, the designer must specify the data that is to be used. Ideally each test phase should use its own test data, so as not to replicate any omissions in the type of data being used or introduce data corrupted by an earlier erroneous test. If the data is incorrect, it is difficult to tell whether the unit is in error or not.

Refer back to the system test scenario in Figure 11.3 where specific Room Numbers are referred to with pre-defined Ensuite flags and Occupancies. It would be no good if this test script requires Room 5 to be en-suite with a room Occupancy of 4, if the next test script requires that Room 5 is *not* en-suite and has an Occupancy of 2. To enable the scripts to be written using compatible data in each test phase, a **test database** must be used. This is a list of all the data that will be used during each test phase. The idea is that if there is some data that fits the requirement of the script you are writing you would use it, otherwise you would create new data and add it to the test database. It is important however to show on the test database how the data will change as the test scripts are executed. It would be no good, for example, if script 17 requires Room 5 to be en-suite, if an earlier script changes the flag from Yes to No.

The test database should be documented by creating a test data booklet for each table in the database, each booklet containing one or more sheets for each record, showing when the data is modified. Refer to Figure 11.4 for an example of a test data document for the ROOM PRICE table. Note that the *initial* script refers to how the database should be set up before the other test scripts are carried out. During system testing, however, scripts should be used to set up all the data – since this will be part of the test.

Table: **Room Price**

Record 1

Script	Room Occupancy	EnSuite	Price per Night
Initial	4	No	£73
12	4	No	£55
16	4	No	£65
67	4	No	£69

Record 2

Script	Room Occupancy	EnSuite	Price per Night
Initial	4	Yes	£73
28	4	Yes	£86

Record 3

Script	Room Occupancy	EnSuite	Price per Night
5	2	Yes	£100
19	2	Yes	£110

Figure 11.4 Test database sheets for the ROOM PRICE table

11.9 Test Execution and Error Reporting

It is easy to see why testing is so important, but another important area that is often overlooked in the rush to test the system is how the errors are being reported and re-tested.

Brilliant test scripts can be rendered ineffective if the errors identified are not being documented correctly and being passed on quickly for correction.

When a test script is created, in whatever phase of testing, the script should also include information to tell you what is the expected outcome of the test. If the actual outcome differs from that on the script, this is obviously a discrepancy that must be investigated. The discrepancy must be marked as such on the test script, and screen prints and other printed evidence of the database before and after the action must be attached to the script to be passed on to whoever is investigating the errors.

An error can usually be classified as coming from one of five main sources:

- *Script error* – the expected result on the script is incorrect and the actual result was correct.
- *Execution error* – the person executing the script made a mistake and did not carry out the instructions provided on the script.
- *Data error* – the data being used to carry out the test was not set up on the database as required by the script.
- *Unit error* – the unit being actioned processed the supplied data in a way that was different to the unit design.
- *Design error* – the unit being actioned processed the supplied data according to the unit design, but the design itself contains an error (for example, a calculation of VAT may have been written incorrectly in the design and built incorrectly in the unit, but picked up when executing the script).

When the error has been investigated, it is useful if it is annotated with a code to show what type of error it is (from the above error source list perhaps). The test scripts that contained script errors may not need to be repeated since the system was acting correctly. The scripts, however, must be updated to show the correction. Any execution or data errors can be corrected when the script is repeated. Unit errors will require that the unit is corrected, and any scripts that refer to that unit carried out prior to the erroneous test must be repeated, since the change could have introduced new errors. Design errors will require that the design is re-analysed and possibly changed. The unit may need to be changed and any scripts referring to that unit will need to be re-tested.

It is important to note that when a test script is repeated, it will probably be carried out of the original sequence of tests. The test database must be reset to contain the data specified in the test database sheets for that test script number. For example, if you were to re-test script 16 on the ROOM PRICE record number 1, you would need to set the Price per Night back to £55 so that the script 16 could change it to £65.

11.10 Summary

This chapter has covered the following material:

- unit testing
- system testing
- integration testing
- interface testing
- performance testing
- user testing
- test data
- test execution and error reporting.

11.11 Written Exercises

11.11.1 Describe the different levels of testing carried out during systems development.

11.11.2 Refer to the screen and report definition tables for the **Degrees** database, constructed in Section 10.15.2.

    (a) Draw up a list of unit tests for all screen and reports to check that the data can be added and amended with appropriate results. The tests should be numbered using the *data entry* and *data display* numbering schemes shown in Section 11.2.

    (b) Design a unit test script for each test. Refer to Figure 11.2 for the layout of the script.

    (c) Design a system test script to carry out the following test scenario (Refer to Figure 11.3):

    a new course is set up
    the report that prints out courses and their students is requested
    five new students are added to the database, and registered on that course
    the course title is changed
    the report that prints out courses and their students

    (d) Design the test data you will need to carry out the above system, using test database sheets. Refer to Figure 11.4 for layout.

11.11.3 Draw up the following test documentation for the **Painting** database screens and reports designed in Chapter 10:

    (a) Draw up a list of unit tests using the *data entry* and *data display* numbering schemes shown in Section 11.2.

(b) Design a unit test script for each test. Refer to Figure 11.2 for the layout of the script.

(c) Draw up some suitable system tests scripts to test the whole of the system, rather than the individual screens and report. Refer to Figure 11.3.

(d) Design the test data you will need to carry out the above system tests, using test database sheets. Refer to Figure 11.4 for layout.

11.12 Practical Exercises

11.12.1   Using the **Degrees** database:

(a) Execute the unit and system test scripts designed in Section 11.11.2. Refer to the test database sheets to set up any data required for the tests.

(b) Ask someone else to execute some of the tests and record any difficulties they had understanding and carrying out the instructions.

(c) Document any results that do not match the expected results. Investigate each error, and classify the source of the error. Refer to Section 11.9 for the five main sources of error.

11.12.2   Using the **Painting** database:

(a) Execute the unit and system test scripts designed in Section 11.11.3. Refer to the test database sheets to set up any data required for the tests.

(b) Ask someone else to execute some of the tests and record any difficulties they had understanding and carrying out the instructions.

(c) Document any results that do not match the expected results. Investigate each error, and classify the source of the error. Refer to Section 11.9 for the five main sources of error.

12 Documentation

12.1 Introduction

Imagine the scenario: a new employee joins the Sales department in a company, and after the first week is asked to update the database system to include a Customer Credit Limit for each customer. This change will require not only a field being added to the Customer table, but also a change to the screens that display and accept Customer details. A change will then be required to check the Customer's Credit Limit whenever a Sale is being made. Several reports may also need to be changed to include the Customer Credit Limit.

How is that new member of staff going to know which specific areas of the system need to be changed, and how to carry out the changes? There are three approaches that can taken:

- talk to other members of staff with some knowledge about the system
- explore the system itself, looking at completed table designs and screen layouts, etc
- refer to the dust-covered folder on the shelf that contains information about how the system has been built and how it should be used.

The first option, talking to other staff, could be very useful. If another member of staff has prior experience of building or amending the system, they could provide useful information about the areas of the system that require changing. It is unlikely, however, they will know the exact names of the screens and queries upon which the system will have been built, although they may be able to point the employee in the right direction regarding the areas of the system that should be examined.

The second option, explore the system itself, could also be useful, and indeed will need to be carried out at some point, since it is this system that the employee will be amending. It is quite easy to see how a table or query has been designed and built by looking directly at that table or query in Access. The query, for example, will display which tables and fields the information is being extracted from and which criteria are being used to do that. Screens and reports are often not so easy to examine. In Access, for example, although it is easy to build a form (screen) using a query to provide the data, once the form has been built, it is not so easy to find the source of the displayed data.

The third option, therefore, could be the ideal option. If the appropriate information is collected about the system, it should enable whoever needs to do the amendment to design and carry out the changes to the database (tables and relationships), queries, screens and reports. It is important to recognise, however, that as with any information, it must be up to date and must be complete. If the information is out of date, or some areas of system are not included, any changes made to the system could be incorrect and cause problems to the rest of the system. Obviously, the documentation should be updated to reflect any changes made to the system.

This chapter will concentrate briefly on which areas of a database should be documented and what that documentation should include.

12.2 Which areas of the System should be Documented?

The answer to this question is "all of them". However, what *are* the areas of the system that require documentation? Three main areas come under this banner in order to provide a useful and accurate record of the system as a whole:

- *the system itself*
- *procedures for using the system*
- *development documents.*

Each of these areas is described next.

12.2.1 The System Itself

If Access were used to develop the database system, for example, then the tables, relationships, queries, forms and reports would all need to be documented. Each part of the database system should be documented as it is built, thereby providing useful information when building later parts of the system.

When the tables are designed, for example, a printout of each table should be obtained, showing the names, data types, descriptions, and specific properties for each field. Printouts of all tables will provide valuable information when creating the relationships between them. Although the database design should already have been completed by this time, the field names are not always the same as those in the design and it helps to be able to refer to the actual table structures. In our **Hotel Reception** database, the en-suite flag in the ROOM table is actually called **EnSuite** in the database, although the design documentation refers to it as the **EnSuite Flag.**

Some parts of the system, such as the tables, relationships and queries are fairly self-explanatory. They show the fields and table names they contain and they relate to each other. In these cases, print outs of the table designs, relationships and query designs would probably be adequate documentation.

However, other areas of the system, such as the screens and reports, are not easy to dissect. Although it will depend on the database management system used to build the system, a printout that simply shows the layout of a screen will not provide clear information about the queries or tables upon which the screen is based. In this case, you will need to add your own documentation for each screen/report to explain where each field has come from, either a table or a query, and other relevant information about the properties of the fields on the screen/report or any user-entered data that is required.

The main contradiction encountered when creating documentation about a system is that in order to document a system, the author of the documentation must have detailed knowledge about that system. However, when someone *has* such detailed knowledge, he/she can inadvertently assume that the reader will have more knowledge about the system than they will have. There are two recommended ways to check the readability of the documentation:

- Ask a third party, with no knowledge of the system, to review the documentation.
- Ask the author to design a small change to the system some several weeks after the documentation has been written, so that the system is not fresh in his/her mind.

Either of these approaches may highlight gaps in the information provided where the author made assumptions about the knowledge of the reader.

12.2.2 Procedures for using the System

A document called a **Procedures Manual** or **User Manual** should be produced to accompany each system. This document will provide clear instructions about how the system should be used. This document is often used as the basis for training staff to use the new system.

Ideally, these instructions should be written as if the reader is not computer literate. The document should include step-by-step instructions about how to use each screen and each report; which data should be entered; what the data that is displayed represents; etc. It is also important to include information about the sequence in which the screens should be used, and the frequency required for requesting the reports. Some reports, for example, might be produced on an ad-hoc basis, others might be produced at the end of each week.

In the **Hotel Reception** system, a procedure should be written for handling a Customer Booking Enquiry as follows (the actual document should include example screens and reports too):

1. Open Find Available Room screen, and enter Room Occupancy and Start Date and End Date. A list of available rooms, available dates, price per night and the en-suite flag will be displayed.

2. If the Customer requests one of those rooms, open the Customer Bookings screen. If the Customer tells you he/she is new, click the Display New Records box and add their details to the screen. These will include Customer Name, Customer Address, Customer Telephone Number, Fax Number and EMail Address. A Customer Code will be displayed automatically.

3. If the Customer has made a booking before, find the Customer by clicking on the Contact Last Name field and click the Find icon on the toolbar. Type their name

into the Find What box and click Find First. If the details displayed are not theirs, click Find Next. If they are not there, add their details as a new Customer as above.

4. Click the Bookings button on the screen to open the Bookings screen and click the Display New Records box. Enter the following details for the requested booking. Note that a Booking Code will be automatically created: Room Number, Customer Code, Start Date, End Date, Total Price.

5. Open the Booking Log screen and enter the Room Number and the Start Date of the booking. The Booking Log entries for that room from the Start Date onwards will be listed on the screen. Enter the Booking Code against each of the Dates of the Booking.

6. Request a Booking Confirmation report. You will need to enter the Booking Code.

12.2.3 Development Documents

These documents should be the final versions of all reports, charts and diagrams used to design the system. These documents would include the following:

- feasibility report (including the terms of reference)
- data flow diagram
- entity-relationship model
- normalised table designs
- data dictionary.

It may not be necessary to store all of these documents along-side the *User Manual* and System Documentation, since these development documents will probably only be referred to if a significant change is made to the system. The data dictionary, however, is a very useful tool since it provides information about the data that is used in the system and what the permitted ranges are for each field. This document should be stored with the *System Documentation* and be updated whenever a new field is added to a table, or a change is made to an existing field property in the database.

12.3 When should the Documentation be Produced?

The three types of documentation can be produced at three different points in the development project.

12.3.1 Documentation about the System Itself

Some of the earlier documentation will be produced as part of the development. For example, it is useful to print out the tables and relationships, so that the actual field names can be referred to in the query designs, etc. Although it is useful to be able to build up the 'pile' of documentation as the system is being built, it is important to remember that if any of the system already printed out is changed during later development or as a result of testing and subsequent error corrections, it must be reprinted. An effective way to relate each recent edition of any document to the changes made to the system, is to use **Version Numbers**. Refer to Section 7.5 in Chapter 7 on change control.

12.3.2 Procedures for using the System

These documents cannot really be written until the screens and reports have been completed, since they must reflect *exactly* the function of the system. Although the screens and reports will have been designed, so some documentation can be written from the designs, so much would probably change as a result of the developed screen/reports differing from the designs that it is probably worth waiting until the development is competed.

Likewise, the documentation could be written before or in parallel to the testing but, again, the testing may highlight errors or omissions and the documentation would need to be changed in line with the system changes. It will depend on the resources and timescale available when building the system. If there are only a few people designing, developing and testing the system, the documentation will probably be written once the testing is complete. If however, there is a short timescale, and many people, it might be quicker for one or more people to write the documentation during the testing phase and then change it after testing corrections have been made.

12.3.3 Development Documents

These documents will be written and updated as part of the system development itself. Documents such as the data dictionary will be used and updated continually throughout the development, and after during system maintenance.

12.4 Summary

This chapter has covered the following material:

- introduction explaining the need for documentation
- which areas of the system should be documented
- documentation about the system itself
- procedure documentation
- development documents
- when documentation should be produced.

12.5.1   Describe the three main types of documentation, explaining when each type should be produced and how each is used.

12.5.2   Create a full set of documentation for the **Hotel Reception** system described throughout this book.

12.5.3   Create a full set of documentation for the **Degrees** database designed and built in earlier chapters' written and practical exercises.

12.5.4   Create a full set of documentation for the **Painting** database designed and built in earlier chapters' written and practical exercises.

13 Setting up the Data

13.1 Introduction

So far, we have looked at how the data in the system will be stored in terms of the database tables, and have added some data to the database to test out the queries, screens and reports. You may even have added larger amounts of data to the database to carry out the system testing.

It is very unusual for a system to be ready to be used in its live environment with a completely empty database. The minimum data usually required is the system data to enable the rest of the system to function. However, as well as setting up system data, careful consideration must be given to how much existing working data, already collected in the current working system, needs to be loaded onto the database of the new system. This will depend on the type of implementation that is being carried out. When a new system is ready to **go live**, it can be implemented using one of four main approaches:

- **Parallel implementation** – The new system will go live with little or no working data. All new transactions will be carried out on the system, but all transactions referring to existing working data will still be carried out on the current working system. This procedure will continue either for a specified period of time, or until all the previously existing working data on the current system becomes out-of-date, and can be archived or discarded.

- **Big Bang implementation** – The new system will go live with all the data relating to current and recent transactions from the current working system loaded onto its database. The current working system will no longer be used.

- **Phased implementation** – If the system is made up of smaller sub-systems, one sub-system will go live, and then the next, etc. With this approach, some degree of parallel running is required, until the last sub-system is in place.

- **Pilot implementation** – If the system is going to be used in more than one site, only one of the sites will be given the new system (in a Big Bang implementation for that one site). Once any teething troubles have been ironed out with that first site's implementation, more and more sites will have the new system implemented, until all the sites are running the new system.

Most of these implementation approaches require system data and at least some working data to be loaded onto the database. This can be done in one of two ways, either manually, via screens and tables, or directly, using an imported file.

This chapter will identify the issues that must be considered when deciding how much working data must be set up on the database before a system goes live and will go on to describe the two main methods of entering data onto the database.

13.2 How much Working Data should be loaded onto the database before the System is used live?

When deciding how much working data to load onto the new system's database before going live, the current working data must be examined carefully and compared with the fields on the database tables to decide which piece of data will relate to which field. There may be some data on the current system that you no longer require and will not load into the database. Alternatively, there may be some data that the new system requires and the current data does not contain. You may need to find out this information, or you may simply leave the fields for the current data empty, and request that data when you carry out new transactions on the system.

As well as considering which parts of the data should be used, another important consideration when loading data onto the database of a new system is how *much* current working data should be loaded. How far back in time should your data go? This decision will be based mainly upon two factors:

- *working practice*
- *database performance.*

The first factor, w*orking practice*, refers to ways in which the system is used. If one of the procedures on which the new system is based uses data that is three months old, it will therefore be necessary to keep at least three months of old data. For example, in a new system for a Kitchen Installation business, a quote may be effective for three months after the quote date. Every quote on the system must therefore be kept for at least three months.

The second factor, *database performance*, refers to how quickly the new system will display and print out information whilst being used in the live environment with the live amount of data on the database. The performance of the system will depend on how the tables, relationships, queries, screens and reports have been designed, as well as the speed of the processor. Some database management systems have a tool that examines the database and offers suggestions for enhancing its performance. In Access it is called the **Performance Analyzer** (click **Tools** on the menu bar, click on **Analyze**, click **Performance**). You may find that the system becomes slow to use when it is holding over six months of data, so you may need to load up only four or five months of data, depending on your working requirements, and plan to archive every month. Refer to the next chapter on archiving.

Once you have decided how much and which parts of the working data are to be loaded onto the database, both the system data and working data can be entered onto the database. This can be carried out in one of three ways:

- using screens
- into the tables
- directly via an import from another source.

When a large amount of system and working data is going to be loaded onto the database via screens or tables, this becomes a significant task in its own right and is called **take-on**. If the rules regarding selection of data are clear, this can often be carried out by staff unfamiliar with the system, and in a large system, this can be one of the major tasks in the implementation phase of the system development.

13.3 Enter Data onto the Database via the System's Screens or Tables

As referred to previously, there are two types of data: *system data* and *working data*. Working data is the data that is entered during the everyday running of the system, and will probably be on the system for specified period of time before being archived (see the next chapter) to make room for more new working data.

The system data is not data that is changed very often. It is nearly constant data that other screens and reports refer to. In the **Hotel Reception** system example, the Room Occupancy field in the ROOM table would be system data, whereas the Customer Fax Number in the CUSTOMERS table would be working data.

Generally, screens will have been designed to allow the entry of most of the working data in a system. In some systems, working data can also be entered onto the database directly. See the next section.

Since system data is not entered onto the system or amended very often, the development budget for a system may not always allow for screens to be developed for the system data. If this is the case, the system data will need to be entered into the database via the tables. Once the system data is set up, it is often useful to print it out for reference.

13.4 Enter Data directly onto the Database via an External Source

It is possible to set up data on the database directly from an external source to a particular table. A Sales department system may send a tape containing Customer Sales information to be transferred into the Marketing department system. Instead of a user typing in all the data stored on the tape, the data from the tape will be transferred electronically directly onto the database. There are two main advantages to this type of data entry:

- it saves time
- it removes the chance of an error being made as the data is typed in.

In the **Hotel Reception** system, for example, the BOOKING LOG table needs to be set up like a diary, with one entry for each day, for each room. This data will probably be added to the database at the end of each month, containing BOOKING LOG entries two or three months in advance. The data will be set up on Excel and loaded into the BOOKING LOG table directly.

In this case, the Excel Worksheet will be set up with the same column contents as the fields in the BOOKING LOG table. Once the Booking Date and Room Number fields have been filled in the worksheet and saved, the worksheet can be imported into the database.

To do this, open the Access **Hotel Reception** database, then click the File menu option. Click Get External data, then click Import. You will need to select the folder containing the Worksheet, and change the Files of type setting to Microsoft Excel. Once you click Import, the Input Spreadsheet Wizard will help you to input the data into the specified Access table.

13.5 Summary

This chapter has covered the following material:

- why data needs to be set up on the database before the system goes live
- how much working data should be loaded onto the database
- entering data onto the database via screens and tables
- entering data directly onto the database via an external source.

13.6 Written Exercises

13.6.1   Describe the four main approaches for implementing a new system.

13.6.2   Describe the main issues that must be addressed when deciding how much working data to load into the database before the system goes live.

13.6.3   Consider the **Hotel Reception** system. If the current date is 3/3/2000, provide guidelines to identify the data, both system and working, that must be entered into the system before the system goes live in two days' time. Refer to the following information:

- The manager regularly needs to refer to information about recent customer bookings, at the most two months in the past.
- The receptionist can make bookings for customers up to three months ahead.
- There are ten rooms in the hotel, with occupancies of 2, 3 and 4.
- Each type of room can be with or without en-suite facilities.

13.7 Practical Exercises

13.7.1 (a) Design some data to enter into the **Hotel Reception** system according to the initial data set-up guidelines drawn up in Section 13.6.3. You should design data for the following tables:

Room Price   Room
Booking Log   Customers
Booking

(b) Add the relevant data to the **Room Price** and **Room** tables using the appropriate form.

(c) Create an Excel worksheet containing two columns:

Column A   Booking Date
Column B   Room Number

Enter the Booking Log data into the rows of the worksheet, and save the Excel workbook as BookingLog.xls.

(d) Import the Excel file BookingLog.xls into the Hotel Reception database using the instructions provided in Section 13.4 of this chapter.

(e) Enter the Customers and Booking data into the database, as well as updating the Booking Log records, using the appropriate forms.

14 Housekeeping

14.1 Introduction

Housekeeping is the title given to a set of tasks that are needed to maintain the performance and reliability of any computer system. Housekeeping includes the following tasks, which are described briefly in this chapter:

- making regular *back-ups* of the system
- archiving 'old' data from the database
- maintaining security.

14.2 Making regular back-ups of the System

Everything stored on the computer is stored as a file. Most small computer systems will be stored as a series of files on the hard disk of the computer or server providing the system. A **back-up** of any one of those files is simply a copy of the file, placed on a floppy disk, magnetic tape or another hard disk, and stored in a separate location from the original. A back-up will not be used unless the original file becomes corrupted or lost.

In many offices where the computers are networked and the staff store their work on the server, the hard disk of the server will have a back-up copy of it taken once or twice a day onto a tape cartridge (or CD-ROM). Since the back-ups are not used unless the server becomes corrupted, the back-ups are often stored on a set of fourteen tape cartridges, two for each day. Once the fourteenth tape is used, the next day's back-up will overwrite the first back-up taken a week ago. In the same way, security video cameras record on seven videotapes, always overwriting last week's video.

If your system is not located in such an environment, you will have to make your own back-up procedures, considering the following issues carefully.

Any system comprises both the data stored on the database and the programs (table structures, queries, screen and reports) that make up the database system itself. When the database system was being developed, regular back-ups of the programs that make up the system should have been taken and stored in a separate location. Once a system has gone live, as long as back-ups of the system programs were taken at the end of development, no further back-ups will be needed unless the system changes in any

214

way. If any amendments are made to the table designs, relationships, queries, screens or reports, then a new back-up of the programs should be taken.

The data on the database, however, will change frequently once the system is live. It will be necessary therefore to take back-ups of the database contents regularly. How often the back-ups should be taken depends on how often the data changes on the system. If the system is being used daily, and new data is added throughout the day, it would probably be sensible to take a back-up at the end of each day. If you use the system mainly as a reference medium, and only change the data on it a few times in a week, you may be able to do a back-up once per week.

The way to decide is to ask the question:

"If the database were to become unusable and the most recent back-up loaded in its place, how much inconvenience/danger would be caused without the missing data and how much effort would it take to replace the data not included in the back-up?"

As well as considering the consequences of losing data, you should also consider the other side of the equation.

"How much time will be taken carrying out the back-ups and how much storage space will be required to hold the back-ups?"

Note that in some database systems such as Access, the back-up taken of the database includes the system description itself, such as the tables and queries, as well as the data on the database.

14.3 Archiving 'Old' Data from the Database

This subject was discussed briefly in the previous chapter. Most databases will contain both system data, which is used by the everyday functions in the system, and working data, which is created and amended as part of the everyday transactions carried out on the system. System data does not often change, and as such, will usually remain on the database indefinitely. Working data, however, often becomes historical data, since the transaction it was documenting, such as a sale or a stay in a hotel, has long since passed and been completed.

Since the performance of the database may degrade significantly if the database becomes too large, it must be recognised that it is not possible to keep adding data to the database without ever removing some of the historical or 'old' data.

How much data should be archived? That will depend on how well the system performs and how much information the system needs to carry out its functions. If, for example, you need to keep a Sales Quote for at least three months, then the minimum number of Sales Quotes kept on the system should include the last three months. If the system performance begins to slow down when there is about four and a half months' worth of historical data on the database, then the best time to archive would be once per month, and to remove all Sales Quotes over three months old.

Although all archiving methods remove data from the current database, there are several different ways to remove that data and to display and store it once it has been removed. The method you use will depend on the tools available to you, how often you may need to refer to that archived data once it has been archived, and in what way you would need to retrieve that data. Some archiving methods include:

- Use special query tools available on the database management system to select the data to be archived and then print it and delete it, or remove it and place it into a new table in a different database. In Access, you would need to specify a query to extract the required records, then select one of two types of *archiving* query. The Make Table Query places the extracted records into a new table on a different *archived* database (this can then be referred to easily via Access). The Delete Query just deletes the extracted records, although it is important to print them out first to provide a **hard copy** of the archived material.

- Use a suitable programming language to remove the relevant records from the database and store them in another medium, such as magnetic tape, a writeable optical disk, a DAT tape, another hard disk or a floppy disk. A file of archived material can be used to produce microfiche.

14.4 Maintaining Security

As described previously, the database system is made up of two distinct areas:

- the system itself – i.e. the tables, queries, screens and reports
- the data on the database.

Once the system is live, it is unwise to allow all users to have unlimited access to the database system. Although it is unlikely that anyone would willingly meddle with the system, inexperienced staff may unwittingly change a table design or a report layout by mistake.

Likewise, the data on the system, whether it is working data or more importantly system data, can also be amended incorrectly by inexperienced or unauthorised hands. System data is especially sensitive to change, since it is used by many other areas of the system, and an incorrect change would cause many errors and invalid information.

There are several ways of stopping unauthorised personnel from accessing all or some of the database system. These methods can all be described as providing varying levels of system **security**:

- **Database system password** – One person sets up a password on the system, so that whenever a member of staff tries to open the database, they must type in the password. This password can be changed as frequently as required. In Access, this is applied using the Tools menu option and the Security, Set Database Password function.

- **User-Related Access Permissions** – Each user must type in a user name and personal ID or password to use the system. Once in the system, the user will be part of a group of users who share a common set of access permissions to the database. For example, the **Hotel Reception** database system may have two sets of access permissions set up: one for the reception staff who are only given permission to read, modify and insert data in the Booking and Customers tables and to modify the Booking Log table. The Hotel Manager would belong to another set giving him/her complete access to the system. In Access, these permissions are set up using the Tools menu options and the Security, User and Group Account functions.

- **Encrypting the Data** – the previous two methods can stop an unauthorised person opening the database. However, that same person could use Word to read the data files. Although the files contain some complex symbols as well as text, some of the data can be detected. A way around this potential problem for databases that contain sensitive information is to store the data on the database in an **encrypted** (coded) style. It must obviously be **decrypted** when the database is opened. The main disadvantage of this approach is the time it takes to carry out the decrypting. In Access this is carried out using the Tool option in the menu bar and the Security, Encrypt/Decrypt function.

14.5 Summary

This chapter has covered the following material:

- an explanation of what housekeeping tasks are
- when and why you should take regular back-ups of the system
- when and how you should archive data from the database
- methods for maintaining system security.

14.6 Written Exercises

14.6.1   Explain the issues that must be addressed when deciding how often to take back-ups of the system files.

14.6.2   Explain the main issues that must be addressed when deciding how much data to archive from the database, and how often.

14.6.3   (a) Describe the two main areas of the system that must be considered for protection from unauthorised viewing and amendment. Describe three ways in which security can be applied to a system.

(b) Suggest suitable security mechanism(s) for the **Hotel Reception** system, explaining which staff can access which areas of the system.

14.7 Practical Exercises

14.7.1   (a) Enter some Booking Log data onto the database for January 1995 for Rooms 1 and 2 (with no Booking Code).

(b) Create some new Customers.

(c) Enter some Bookings and corresponding Booking Log data into the system for the new customers, for rooms 1 and 2, for January 1995.

(d) Use the Delete Query function (as described in Section 14.3) to archive the Customers, Bookings and Booking Log entries for Room 1 only for January 1995 from the database. Make sure you print them before deleting them.

(e) Check the remaining Customers, Booking and Booking Log data to ensure you have deleted the correct data. Make sure the Booking data for Room 2 for January 1995 is still there.

14.7.2   Use the Help facility to find out how to set up a User Group on the **Hotel Reception** database system, and create two User Groups as described in the *User-Related Access Permissions* paragraph in Section 14.4.

A | Reference

A.1 Operators

A.1.1 Arithmetic

Operator	Description
^	Raises a number to the power of an exponent.
*	Multiplies two numbers.
/	Divides two numbers and returns a floating-point result.
\	Divides two numbers and returns an integer result.
Mod	Divide two numbers and returns only the remainder.
+	Sums two numbers.
−	Subtracts two values (or used to indicate a negative value).

A.1.2 Comparison operators

Operator	True if	False if	Null if
< (Less than)	expression1 < expression2	expression1 >= expression2	expression1 or expression2 = Null
<= (Less than or equal to)	expression1 <= expression2	expression1 > expression2	expression1 or expression2 = Null
> (Greater than)	expression1 > expression2	expression1 <= expression2	expression1 or expression2 = Null
>= (Greater than or equal to)	expression1 >= expression2	expression1 < expression2	expression1 or expression2 = Null
= (Equal to)	expression1 = expression2	expression1 <> expression2	expression1 or expression2 = Null
<> (Not equal to)	expression1 <> expression2	expression1 = expression2	expression1 or expression2 = Null

A.1.3 Logical operators

AND, XOR, OR, EQV and IMP

The logical result of the AND, OR, XOR, EQV and IMP operators on the operation for *Expression1 operand Expression2* is:

Expression1	Expression2	AND	OR	XOR	EQV	IMP
True	True	True	True	False	True	True
True	False	False	True	True	False	False
True	Null	Null	True			Null
False	True	False	True	True	False	True
False	False	False	False	False	True	True
False	Null	False	Null			True
Null	True	Null	True			True
Null	False	False	Null			Null
Null	Null	Null	Null			Null

The bitwise result of the AND, OR, XOR, EQV and IMP operators on the operation for *Bit1 operand Bit2* is:

Bit1	Bit2	AND	OR	XOR	EQV	IMP
0	0	0	0	0	1	1
0	1	0	1	1	0	1
1	0	0	1	1	0	0
1	1	1	1	0	1	1

NOT

The logical result of the NOT operator on the operation for NOT *Expression* is:

Expression	Result
True	False
False	True
Null	Null

The bitwise result of the NOT operator on the operation for NOT *Expression* is:

Expression	Result
0	1
1	0

A.1.4 Concatenation Operators

Operator	Description
&	Forces string concatenation of two expressions
+	Sums two numbers

A.2 Operator Precedence

Operator precedence determines the order in which the operators are used. The order is:

1. Parentheses. These have the highest precedence and are evaluated first.

2. Arithmetic operators. These are operated on after the parenthesis. The order is:

   - Exponentiation (^).
   - Negation (-).
   - Multiplication and division (*, /). Precedence is from left-to-right.
   - Integer division (\).
   - Modulus arithmetic (Mod).
   - Addition and subtraction (+, -). Precedence is from left-to-right.
   - String concatenation (&).

3. Comparison operators. These are operated on after the arithmetic operators. All comparison operators have the same precedence and are operated on in a left-to-right order. They include: Equality (=), Inequality (<>), Less than (<), Greater than (>), Less than or equal to (<=) and Greater than or equal to (>=).

4. Logical operators. These have the least precedence. The precedence is:

   - Not.
   - And.
   - Or.
   - Xor.
   - Eqv.
   - Imp.

Index